JUDAISM ON THE WEB

JUDAISM ON THE WEB

Irving Green

A Subsidiary of
Henry Holt and Co., Inc.

MIS:Press
A Subsidiary of Henry Holt and Company, Inc.
115 West 18th Street
New York, New York 10011
http://www.mispress.com

MIS:Press and M&T Books are available at special discounts for bulk purchases for sales promotions, premiums, and fundraising. Special editions or book excerpts can also be created to specification.

For details contact: Special Sales Director
                         MIS:Press and M&T Books
                         Subsidiaries of Henry Holt and Company, Inc.
                         115 West 18th Street
                         New York, New York 10011

10 9 8 7 6 5 4 3 2 1

Associate Publisher: *Paul Farrell*

Managing Editor: *Shari Chappell*	**Production Editor:** *Gay Nichols*
Editor: *Andy Neusner*	**Copy Editor:** *Melissa Burns*
Technical Editors: *Eric Simon*	**Copy Edit Manager:** *Karen Tongish*
Johanna Ginsberg	

...We are a people of memory and prayer. We are a people of words and hope. We have neither established empires nor built castles and palaces. We have only placed words on top of each other. We have fashioned ideas; we have built memorials. We have dreamed towers of yearnings—of Jerusalem rebuilt, of Jerusalem united, of a peace that will be swiftly and speedily established in our days. Amen.

FROM AN ADDRESS BY ISRAELI PRESIDENT EZER WEIZMAN TO THE BUNDESTAG AND BUNDESRAT OF THE FEDERAL REPUBLIC OF GERMANY

January 16, 1996

[http://www.israel-mfa.gov.il/mfa/speeches/presbund.html]

Dedication

To Dagmar, my wife and friend

Acknowledgments

This has been a labor of love.

My editor Paul Farrell of MIS:Press has allowed me a great deal of freedom and shown much sensitivity to the topic of this book. That is duly noted and appreciated. Andrew Neusner of MIS:Press has had the task of turning my manuscript into a final product. I hesitate to say a finished product because we both know that finishing a book is an almost impossible task. I am grateful for his suggestions and wise counsel. Professor Chaim I. Waxman has been my friend since childhood. I've bounced many an idea off his head. We don't always agree. But he always tries to steer me in the right direction. His experience and the resources of his library been most welcome. Allison Kaplan Sommer of the Jerusalem Post pointed me to the right places on the Israeli web. For this I am extremely grateful. The reference librarians of the Peninsula Public Library in Lawrence, N.Y. have fielded many a question and supplied me with a steady stream of books and articles. I appreciate their efforts.

My dear friend Rabbi Aaron Gelman would have enjoyed the idea of this book and I would have welcomed his counsel. Very often during the course of the writing of this volume, I could almost here his voice and feel him poking at my ribs. "Isser", he would say. "Call it the way it is. Don't care what they would say. Be yourself". Aaron, I tried!

When you undertake a project such as the writing of a book, time seems to have little meaning. you ignore the people you love and the things that you like to do. My wife, Dagmar, is one of the most courageous people I know. She puts up with me and doesn't allow me to forget that there is a world away from the word processor. I've ruined many a day off with my forays at the computer and she's said nary a word. This book is merely one excuse in a long street of self involvements which have left her wringing her hands in despair. Yet there is always the gentle smile and the cheery and upbeat countenance that marks her very being. For this I am eternally grateful.

My son Michael always knew I could do it. He even found a publisher that agreed with him. I am thankful. My daughter Andrea married a talented writer, Robert, and he made me realize that I have to measure my words because he'd change what he didn't like. I've enjoyed every minute of it.Of all the members of my family, my daughter Atara will probably be the one to actually look up the most sites in this book. I hope that she will enjoy it and remember me favorably for it.

I would have liked to have shown this book to my mother, Rose, but it was not to be. But just as this manuscript was finished, we welcomed the arrival of our first grandchild, her namesake, Shoshana Menucha (Madison Arianna Schechter). This is the world in which she will live and hopefully her education will be complete with the tools that are required in today's time.

Finally, I have been blessed with wonderful friends. They have given me every encouragement. For this I am deeply grateful.

I.G

CONTENTS

Part I: The Jewish World 1

Part II The Jewish Year

Part III Jewish Culture

Chapter 13: Museums and Archives 209

Part V: Current Issues in Judaism

EASY ACCESS

Live links to all the Web sites mentioned in this book can be accessed at the following page from the MIS:Press Web site:

http://www.mispress.com/judaism

Add this address to the 'favorite addresses/bookmarks' section of your Web browser, then use these links to jump to any sites that sound enticing.

At our site, the author and publisher invite readers to make suggestions about future editions of *Judaism on the Web*. The Internet is ever-changing and expanding, and your suggestions will help us make later editions even more comprehensive.

Introduction

Welcome to the world of the Jewish Internet!

This book was not written because I am a computer person, though I enjoy using a computer. Rather, it was written because I enjoy Judaica and I believe that there are many people out there in cyberspace who, given the opportunity, would like to learn more about Judaism.

When I was growing up, there was a very limited amount of English-language Judaica available. There was the venerable Soncino Press, The Jewish Publication Society, and several niche market publishers as well as a lot of academic materials that never made it into mainstream publishing. Many very fine vessels of Jewish knowledge never saw the light of day. You could access them through microfilm, if you were really interested. But it was like hunting for a needle in a haystack. You had to have a librarian who was willing and able to help you along. Then it still took an interminable amount of time before you actually could read anything substantial. By and large, Judaica was a very closed field—almost non-existent.

The growth of Jewish publishing in the 80s was really a natural development. The baby boom, the development of an indigenous American Jewry, and the rebirth of Jewish consciousness (brought about in large measure by the growth of the State of Israel) made people aware of their Jewishness. It also made them painfully aware of their lack of knowledge of basic information about Judaism. The publication of *The Jewish Catalog* in 1972 created a great sensation and proved that there was a mass market for this product. Here was a resource guide that almost everyone could use. Its major problems were that it simply couldn't cover everything or be updated fast enough to take into account all the changes taking place on the Jewish scene. In fact the original catalog, though woefully outdated, is still in publication.

Even today, with the advent of Jewish press in America, there is not much material available. Part of this problem has been the major expense involved in preparing them for publication. Because of their rather short press runs, books on Judaica simply can't be produced cheaply. Another and much more important problem is the difficulty of reaching people in small communities in the United States and far-flung communities throughout the world.

Just about two years ago I published *The First Electronic Jewish Bookshelf*, a CD-ROM containing a dozen different popular volumes on Judaica. The project was really started as a hobby, albeit an expensive one. But I was soon very quickly rewarded by what I call *Der Pintele Yid*. (An English translation of that Yiddish term might be something like *the marginal Jew*.) What I was trying to do was create a CD-ROM that would appeal to a broad spectrum of people—Jews and non-Jews alike—and contain a great deal of information. What people did with that information, or moved on from the starting point of that CD-ROM, was really up to them. From almost the moment it appeared, *The First Electronic Jewish Bookshelf* struck a responsive chord in many people. Orders came in on a daily basis, and interestingly enough, they came from estranged Jews as well as from devout individuals. They came from grandparents who were worried that their children were growing up without knowing anything about their faith. There were plaintive cries from parents and grandparents whose children were living in some of the most Jewishly remote regions of the world. I understood that no one effort, no matter how sincere or well intended, could do the job. Then, almost by accident, I began to look at the Internet as another way of reaching people.

I have been on Compuserve and America On-Line for several years now. My experience with the actual Internet has been much more limited. I've simply joined the legion of people who have become part of this information revolution. I've watch the Internet grow and grow. There are those who question the value of the Internet. Certainly, it has problems which need to be addressed. There will be people who use the Internet for illicit purposes, and those who run to bring pornography into the Internet home. There are those who spout anti-Semitism. Indeed, you can search the Internet and learn about revisionists who deny that the Holocaust ever took place! It's a shame. But it is also a fact of life.

But the Internet can be a positive place. It can create meaningful experiences. It can open up new worlds for Jews who are far removed from their roots. It addresses almost any aspect of Judaism you could possibly imagine. There are limitations. Some of the Web home pages that you will read about in this book are devoid of any real content. But, you will also come across other *sites*—that's what these places are called in the Internet lingo—that show you what a good Web page should look like and what the power of the Internet is all about. The existence of these sites on the Internet and their proliferation in such a short period of time are very positive indicators. They show that the Internet can become an important source for reaching out to Jews wherever they might live.

Most importantly, the Internet delivers a poignant message to the viewer. It says that no matter where you are, and where your interests lay, there is a Jewish connection. Whether it be language or religion, lifestyle or hobby, history or folklore—even just a good Jewish recipe—as a Jew there is someplace out there for you. All you have to do is look and you'll find it.

One of the great criticisms of the computer world in general, and home computer use and the Internet in particular, is the loneliness that it is thought to create. People become anonymous. They are connected by a fragile phone wire. They don't even know who is really on the other side of the connection. That is certainly true. There is no substitute for personal contact. No computer program or book for that matter can substitute for interaction between people.

We also live in a very lonely society. There are large distances between family members. We spend an inordinate amount of time away from our homes and families. We spend long hours trying to make ends meet. With the fascination about technology of our age comes the concomitant difficulties in dealing with the challenges it poses to our lifestyles.

We view this book as an attempt to reach out to people. Its purpose is to make the individual within Jewish society aware that he is connected to a much larger world and that he has just to look and he can become a part of it. Hopefully, he can use this resource to emerge from the confinement of being the lonely believer or non-believer and find comfort with his co-religionists.

At the same time, however, there are great challenges ahead of us. For the Jewish population technology poses a great opportunity. We are a nation of immigrants. Our parents and grandparents came to this country from every part of the globe and they settled in every nook and cranny of America. In the past, this cut them off from their contact with Judaism. The Internet gives Jews, no matter how far away they are from any form of community, the opportunity to join as one. You can dial into the Internet and learn about Judaism by touching the keyboard.

To the non-Jews who buy this book and use the resources of the Jewish Internet, there is also a very clear message. Judaism is a very open religion. It is what it says it is and you are invited to search the World Wide Web to see for yourself. Learn about Judaism and what makes Jews believe and act as they do, and hopefully you will understand and become a better person for it.

There is no easy way to go through the labyrinth that is the Internet. But certainly there are guideposts and hints. Enjoy our survey of Web sites, lists, gophers, FTPs and all that jazz. We hope you won't have to go through the whole book to find out what you are looking for. But if you do, we hope that it will be worth it.

For your ease, this volume contains some general information on using the Internet, not just the Jewish sites. It also contains information that will help making using the Internet an enjoyable and productive experience.

My own flirtation with the mixture of computers and Judaism began more than 20 years ago. I was very young at the time and was employed by the American Committee for Bar-Ilan University in Israel. The university had just purchased an IBM 360/50, a mainframe computer. It had also just opened its law school. Several faculty members of the university had put together a proposal to the National Endowment for the Humanities to computerize the Responsa Literature. Responsa are questions posed to Rabbis on issues pertaining to Jewish law and the Rabbis "response" to the queries. They are the equivalent of "Case Law". It was a groundbreaking project that would have far-reaching implications in Jewish law.

One day we received notification that the project had been approved and that the first part of the grant money was available, but there was a catch. The money would be made available as a matching-funds grant. I picked up the phone and called Ludwig Jesselson, one of the most outstanding Jewish philanthropists of our day, and I told him the situation. He didn't hesitate for a moment. "I'll send you a check right away," he responded. Within the hour, his driver appeared at our door with a check for the matching funds and the Responsa Project was born.

20 years ago, the idea was to create a database of information that would be available to scholars and judges. Little did anyone dream this database would, by virtue of changes in technology, be available to anyone who had access to a personal computer. The past two decades have also witnessed a vast change in the way we collect, analyze and transmit information to people. When I was in college, the computer scientists were "geeks." They poured over punch cards and other monstrous-looking materials. If you weren't one of them, you couldn't possibly understand what they were doing. Today, even very young children can sit down and use a computer.

This book started out as a lark. Last summer I started to explore the Internet. I found a great deal of material on Judaism and Israel on the Web. But I was overwhelmed by the helter-skelter arrangement of the information. Data is only usable if you can see order in it or make order out of it.

In writing this book, I have come up against myriad problems involving what to include and exclude. The decisions were not easy. The more I uncovered, the more I was aware of my inability to do justice to the topics. The more topics I selected, the more topics I wanted to include.

This volume should include more material on Jewish communities outside the United States, Canada and Israel. However, much of this material is not in English, and I felt that would be too limiting. The same is true of many Israeli sites that are in Hebrew. I felt that they would not be useful to our readership. For this reason, I have also included very little about the Hebrew language. I also limited the number of synagogue sites in this book. I didn't want to overload the book with repetitive information that would serve a very limited purpose. I have included very little information about libraries and library collections. This material has been collected and made available in other publications.

On the other hand, I would like to see more information on games and projects for children. There is a need for Jewish educational tools for youngsters. Judaism is often presented as a religion which obligates people to live a certain way. It is also presented as a religion with a frightful past. There are many fun things about Judaism. I would have liked to present some more of the light side.

I would also have liked to include additional chapters on lifestyles, Kabbalah, major issues in Judaism, conversion, and a host of other subjects. Some of them are extremely important, but have a limited presence on the Web. Others are very complex and present great difficulties in presentation. Perhaps I can tackle them in our next edition.

I have attempted to give this volume a sense of balance. Wherever possible, I have made use of the Web site's own words to describe the site itself. I have editorialized only where necessary. I have tried to liven up the concept of a directory by giving you the benefit of some of my own life experiences and thoughts. If I have succeeded, I am pleased. Where I have failed, I apologize and hope to do better next time.

I have included my e-mail address (scanrom@ix.net-com.com) for your comments and suggestions for the next edition. I trust that you will make use of it.

If you were to ask me my outstanding reaction to the task of writing this book, I would have to say that I never thought it would be so all consuming.

As I pen these words just days before Yom Kippur, the Day of Atonement, the responsibility for my efforts lays heavily on my being. I am reminded of these words from the High Holiday Prayer Service:

> I firmly hope in God and plead with him.
>
> I ask him to grant me the gift of speech,
>
> That I may sing his praise among people,
>
> And utter chants concerning his actions.
>
> A man may prepare the thoughts in his mind,
>
> But the power of speech comes from the Lord.
>
> Lord, open my lips that I tell thy praise.
>
> May my words and my heart's meditation
>
> Please thee, O Lord, my Stronghold, my Savior.

Irving (Yisroel Isser ben Moshe) Green
Erev Yom Kippur, 5757
September, 1996

The Jewish World

CHAPTER 1

Jewish History

The Web gives a very disjointed, even distorted view of
Jewish history. The bulk of the materials on the Web are
"about" Jewish history rather than historical documents or
complete studies of particular events or eras. And the documents offered are mere glimpses of the historical times in
which they were written.

Unfortunately, at the present time the Internet does not
play a major role in conveying the depth and breadth of Jewish
history. There is simply a paucity of Jewish historical materials
available on-line, but the Internet can act as a catalyst. It can
show certain guideposts and provide bibliographies that provide
links to important source materials. Hopefully, this will change
rapidly and in a few years, one may be able to search the Web
and find materials on Judaism and Jewish history previously
available only to dedicated researchers.

There is one Web site that is, perhaps, a glimpse of
what the future might hold in the area of history on the
Web—the Facts About Israel site produced by the Israel
Ministry of Foreign Affairs, reviewed in this chapter. The
potential of the Web can also be seen in the availability of
substantial detail about obscure or still-developing topics,
as on the Khazar page, the Turkish Jews page, or the page
focusing on polygamy in Jewish history.

Jewish Culture and History

http://www.igc.apc.org/ddickerson/judaica.html

A fine collection of links to other sites, along with solid descriptions of where these links lead—something that is too rare among self-professed "resource" pages. This is an excellent jumping-off point for Web exploration of this subject. A Polish synagogue link (see below) is also part of this site.

The University of Colorado Jewish History Page

http://ucsu.colorado.edu/~jsu/history.html

This is actually one page of the Ultimate Jewish/Israel Link Launcher—a large compilation of Jewish-related links anywhere on the Net. The history section is an eclectic mix and a veritable treasury of history links. Under the subheading of ancient Israel, you can find a wealth of documents on archaeology in Israel. These include links to a number of important archaeological sites. There are a tremendous number of links classified as "Diaspora History," and "Israel History." In my numerous visits here, I've found some unbelievable links (including a few literally unbelievable), as well as some dead links. As long as you have a sense of adventure, and are not too prone to frustration, this page can be rewarding and lots of fun.

The American Jewish Historical Society

http://www.ajhs.org/

The AJHS, housed at Brandeis University is "often referred to as the 'national archives' of American Jewry, its holdings are the preeminent resource for scholars, museums, film makers and publishers who want to document American Jewish life from the 1590s to the present."

While there is very little reference material at this site, there is a tremendous amount of material here to help you find some, including a list of other Jewish historical societies. Links to other institutions offer: information on American Jewish historical sources; a list of American Jewish history departments in schools around the United States; a directory of their archival holdings; and a top-notch bibliography of suggested readings.

The Canadian Jewish Historical Society

http://www.oise.on.ca/webstuff/otherprj/cjhs1.html

The Canadian Jewish experience has been an interesting one. Jews first settled in Canada at the same time that they came to the United States, and developed communities in the far-flung outposts of Canada. Jewish traders and merchants could be found in small towns in Saskatchewan and Quebec, and in Vancouver and Alberta. In this century, most of Canada's Jews have opted for the two major population centers of Toronto and Montreal.

Often Canadian Jewry is likened to its American cousin. While it has many similarities, it also has many differences. Canadian Jewry deserves its own presence on the Web. Unfortunately, this site contains little useful information other than the names of contacts within the organization and a gateway to its reading-list archives. The Society does publish an excellent journal, portions of which should be put on the Internet. Canadian Jewry maintains excellent materials on its history. It is very proud of its contributions to the building of Canada and of the pioneer spirit of its early Jewish settlers.

The Jewish War Veterans

http://www.penfed.org/jwv/home.htm

The Jewish War Veterans Museum contains much information about the contributions of American Jews to the war efforts since colonial days. Chapter 13 on museums has more information about this group and Web site.

The Khazaria Information Center
http://acad.bryant.edu/~kbrook/khazaria.html

"A thousand years ago, the far east of Europe was ruled by Jewish kings who presided over numerous tribes, including their own tribe: the Khazars." Does this sound like it's out of a science-fiction novel? It's not.

The story of the Khazars is one of the most romantic chapters of Jewish history. What was the Khazar Kingdom? How did it come about? When did it fall apart? What happened to it? This site doesn't provide all the answers. But it raises some very interesting questions. It will tell you where to go for information on the Khazars, and give you a feel for their history and the times in which they lived. Those who quibble with some of the details on the site can either enjoy it as a bit of allegorical history or choose to accept whatever parts of it they want.

> "You will find the communities of Israel spread abroad... as far as Dailam and the river Itil where live Khazar peoples who became proselytes. The Khazar king Joseph sent a letter to Hisdai ibn-Shaprut and informed him that he and all his people followed the rabbinical faith. We have seen descendants of the Khazars in Toledo, Pupils of the Wise, and they have told us that the remnant of them is of the rabbinical belief."
>
> *Abraham ibn Daud of Toledo, Spain, The Book of Tradition,*
> *1161*

Ethiopian Jewish History
http://www.cais.com/nacoej/

This site contains a great deal of material about Ethiopian Jewry—it's an absolutely fascinating story. That there is a long history of Jews in the Ethiopian area is unquestioned, possibly going back to before the fifth century B.C.E. Where did they come from? How did they get there? How were they rediscovered by modern society?

There was little contact between the Jews of Ethiopia and mainstream Jewish communities until the late 1860s, when the Alliance Israelite made contact with them. Since that time, various attempts have been made to keep in touch with this community. Its problems were seriously heightened with the fall of the Emperor Haile Selassi. It is to the credit of the State of Israel and many friends of the Ethiopian Jewish community in the United States that these Jews were not abandoned. Israel made a Herculean effort to rescue this community in the 1980s and continues to do so today. This has not been an effort without problems. There were questions of the religious affiliation of some of the members, and problems with their integration into and acceptance by Israeli society. But, once again, Israel has shown itself to be selfless in its attempts to unite Jews of the Diaspora.

Kulanu ("All of Us")
http://ube.ubalt.edu/www/kulanu/

Ethiopia isn't the only place where outsiders have discovered Jews in the midst of a strange land. Are they descended from the Ten Lost Tribes? Jewish communities have been discovered in India, Burma, Pakistan, and China.

Some of the groups were Jews that were lost to forced conversions. "Many of these so-called "Marranos" continued to practice Judaism in secret. Their descendants can be found today in Brazil, Mexico, the southwestern United States, and Majorca, as well as mainland Spain and Portugal."

And there are still other pockets of Jewish communities that are descendants of other groups that have adopted Judaism. One of the better known groups is the *Abayudaya*, a group of native Ugandans who have been practicing Judaism since 1919, when their leader adopted the observance of all Moses' commandments, after studying a Bible left by missionaries.

Kulanu's goal is to find these lost and dispersed remnants of Jewish migrations and to help those who wish to rejoin the Jewish people—their motto is "Helping Lost Jewish Communities."

Their newsletters appear here, which often contain absolutely compelling firsthand accounts of meetings between mainstream Jews, and the Jews in these far-flung communities, as well as a tremendous number of essays documenting the incredibly varied stories of these communities. If you think you know Jewish history, check this site out.

The Works of Manfred Davidmann on Judaism

http://www.solbaram.org/indexes/judais.html

History is a series of interpretations of events. In this case the interpreter is Manfred Davidmann, whose presence is often felt at Jewish sites on the Web. He has some provocative essays here—one is called "History Speaks: Monarchy, Exile, and the Maccabees." It takes a different view of the reign of King Solomon, moves on to the prophets, the Exile, and the Maccabees. His interpretation of the events which led to the fall of an independent Jewish state give one a great deal to think about. What were the Maccabees all about? Why did they come into being? Why were their efforts crowned in a defeat so bitter that many centuries later Judaism would still be reeling from it? Davidmann looks at history and explains it in terms of the people, the events and the times in which they lived. It makes for interesting reading.

Raoul Wallenberg

http://www.hera.algonet.se/~hatikva/wallenberg/

The name Raoul Wallenberg often strikes reverence and awe among those who are aware of him—he was, indeed, the personification of "The Righteous Gentile."

Raoul was born into a family that might be called the Rockefellers of Sweden, except that, to Sweden, the Wallenbergs were more like the Rockefellers, Carnegies, and Fords all rolled into one.

Raoul, still a young man, landed a diplomatic job in Hungary—his job was to save Jews—as Sweden had already negotiated with Hitler that those holding Swedish passes were not to be rounded up. He hired Jews, printed phony passes, stopped trainloads full of Jews already on their way to Germany, made some well-placed bribes, built safe houses—there seemed to be no limit to his creativity.

There are different figures regarding the number of Jews Raoul Wallenberg eventually saved in Budapest, Hungary. Some say he saved 30,000 people. Others estimate the number of persons saved directly, or indirectly, by Wallenberg to be 100,000. No matter what, Raoul Wallenberg must be one of the greatest heroes during World War II.

As Russia marched into Hungary, just ahead of the fleeing Germans, Wallenberg set up a meeting with some Soviet officials. He was never heard from again. His fate? This site tells his story. It is an exciting one and deserves retelling.

When the Holocaust Museum opened in Washington, D.C., an adjacent street, 15th St., was renamed Raoul Wallenberg Place.

This is part of the Hatikva Project, a collection of Swedish Jewish resources (*http://www.algonet.se/ ~hatikva/english.html*).

NOTE

The History of the Jews of Turkey

http://pulex.med.virginia.edu/turkish_jews/ahist.htm

One of the many scatterings of Jews occurred in 1492, when the huge Jewish population of Spain was expelled. But Jews flourished in other places around the Mediterranean before that fateful year. This site contains a brief history of Turkish Jewry from ancient times until the present. The "modern" Turkish Jewish community is celebrating its 500th anniversary. The site is interesting but not very complete. It gives you some highlights of history and a bibliography to learn more about it.

Images of Polish Synagogues

http://www.igc.apc.org/ddickerson/polish-synagogues.html

This is but one section of the Jewish culture and history page mentioned earlier. The history of Jews in Poland goes back to at least the 14th century, when there was significant Jewish immigration (many fleeing from other areas of Europe). Over time Polish Jewry became a vibrant part of the Polish landscape, in some cases measuring more than 30% of the population of major cities. In 1931 Pinsk was 63% Jewish, and at the start of World War II over three million Jews lived in Poland, some 10% of the population. But the destruction of Jewry during the Holocaust was nowhere as great as in Poland—home to some of the most notorious death camps, such as Auschwitz. Today Polish Jewry measures in the thousands.

Here you can see images of several Polish synagogues, each accompanied by a brief description. The site also has a small but good bibliography and links to a number of related sites. A good attempt is made to convey an understanding to Poland's Jewish past. Sadly, it is a nearly impossible assignment.

Jewish Heritage Society

http://mail.glas.apc.org/~heritage/

The JHS, a Russian-based organization, asks: "What makes up a people's identity?—Its History. What makes up its History?—Sources: documents, books, artifacts, and so on—the speechless heritage of the past." Jewish history commissions have existed in Russia before, but the last one was closed by authorities in 1948. A new group, the JHS, was formed in Moscow in 1989, to pick up where former Russian-Jewish historians had left off: "to collect, to preserve and to share among scholars the remnants of the remnants—the documentary heritage of the Jewish past in Eastern Europe."

Tradition has it that the Russian Jews are descendants of the "Ten Lost Tribes". They settled in Armenia and Georgia and other regions beyond the Caucasus Mountains a very long time ago. Russian Jews have been a significant part of the population for centuries—indeed, most Jews in America have Russian ancestors that came to these shores during the massive wave of immigration from 1881 to 1920. The history of Russian Jewry is a lifework by itself.

But where to start documenting what's left in Russia? Jews were severely oppressed, towns were evacuated, cemeteries destroyed—and that was before the Russian revolution in 1917! Afterwards, Judaism itself (along with other religions) was effectively banned, and a new, higher level of destruction and devastation was employed by the rolling armies of Hitler's Germany. The answer: Start by making a determination of what already exists. Pour through existing archives, ascertain which records pertain to Jewish history, produce publications describing findings, compile bibliographies, and so on. A monumental task, to be sure—the task of the JHS.

This site describes the enormity of the task that lies ahead, but also documents what has been done so far. Over 1,000 archives have been found, and lists of all of them are available here, as are e-mail addresses to local genealogists. Some of the publications themselves are available here, too, but many are in Russian, and most are only available for downloading, as opposed to viewing.

A great deal of work has gone on thus far, and we can only expect the site, and the information in it, to grow. In the meantime, however, the publications that are available can be ordered at no cost. Read all about them here.

Rav Kook
http://www.ort.org/anjy/hadracha/kook/orot_en.htm

Rabbi Avraham Isaac HaKohen Kook was a unique personality. While he was known as a brilliant Torah scholar, he also had unique leadership qualities that wew recognized by individuals of all religous persuations, and played an active role in the national revival and rebuilding of then–Palestine. He is the spiritual founder of modern Religious Zionism. He was a much beloved figure, and was the first Chief Rabbi of what was then known as Palestine. This site is a tribute to the man and an invitation to learn more about him and his works.

The site contains a short biography and full bibliography of Rav Kook, with e-mail links making it easy to join a number of lists that are devoted to understanding and propagating his works and philosophy. This site was created in France. It is a sign of the respect accorded Rav Kook by Jews all over the world.

The Ancient Ghetto of Venice
http://www.doge.it/ghetto/indexi.htm

Not many are aware of the origin of the word *ghetto*. It was first applied by the Italians to an area of a city where Jews had permission to live. While Jewish settlements existed in the area 1,000 years before the great expulsion from Spain and Portugal, many of the expelled Jews came to Italy and created or joined in many thriving communities. "The Governor of the Republic, then, decided that the Jews had to live in only one area of the city and on 29 March 1516 a law decreed that that area was to be in the S. Girolamo parish and would be called 'Ghetto Novo.' Thus the first ghetto of Europe came into existence. Today it is a lively and thriving quarter, with its religious and administrative institutions, particularly two Synagogues, still open to service."

Unfortunately, it is very difficult to convey the beauty of Venice or to adequately relate the stateliness of its restored synagogues. You have to do that for yourself. But this site is a must for anyone actually planning to visit the city itself. This relatively small site gives an inkling as to the rich history and tradition of the Jews of Venice. It not only includes historical information, but also a tour of the library and museum, and current information, including hours of operation for various sites to visit, and current phone numbers and addresses of some officials of the Jewish community.

Jews in Cape Verde
http://www.umassd.edu/specialprograms/caboverde/
ewswerlin.html

"The names Lopes, Mendes, Pereira, Cardozo and Levy sound like the ship's manifest of the 'St. Charles,' the ship that brought the first known Jews to New Amsterdam and began American Jewish history. But they are also the names of many people in the Cape Verde Islands, off the west coast of Africa." There are virtually no practicing Jews there now, but since their independence from Portugal some 20 years ago, there has been considerable interest on the part of the Cape Verdians to discover their past.

The whole site is just a page or so in length, but is most interesting.

Guidelines on Religious Relations With the Jews
http://www.christusrex.org/www1/CDHN/v9.html

In 1965, the Second Vatican Council broke new ground in terms of relations with Judaism, and was an important milestone in the history of Jewish-Christian relations. This document, issued in 1974, attempts to elaborate on some of those declarations by setting some specific guidelines in Jewish-Christian relations and is the basis for the present-day relationship between Judaism and the Catholic Church. From a historical perspective, it is viewed as an important document denoting the relationship between Catholicism and Jews. Note that this is not a Catholic-Jewish presentation, but an official document of the Catholic Church.

The Goldwaters: An Arizona Story And a Jewish History As Well

http://dizzy.library.arizona.edu/images/swja/v13gold.html

Barry Goldwater was one of the most colorful figures of American politics in this century. Was Barry Goldwater Jewish? The answer:

> "When Senator Barry M. Goldwater ran for the presidency in 1964 there were nationally-syndicated columnists who wrote that the Arizona Republican was hiding the fact that he was Jewish. In *Goldwater*, an autobiography written in 1988, the senator wrote: 'Neither my father nor any of our family ever took any part in the Jewish community. We never felt or talked about being half Jewish since my mother took us to the Episcopal church. It was only on entering the power circles of Washington that I was reminded I was a Jew. I never got used to being singled out in that way. My answer was always the same. I'm proud of my ancestors and heritage. I've simply never practiced the Jewish faith or seen myself or our family primarily of the Jewish culture. In the jargon of today's sociologist, we've been assimilated. We're American.'"

Don't get the impression that this is an investigation into the Jewishness of the Goldwaters; rather, it's a fascinating tale of two immigrant brothers, and their families, as they make their way from Poland to England to New York, and then to California to join the gold rush, and eventually to Arizona. This is the tale of many Jews whose families settled in the southwestern part of this country and in many other parts as well. It is a compelling story. Don't miss it.

Cemeteries

http://home.intranet.org/~polygon/cemeteries.html

Cemeteries are the repositories of information that often can't be found elsewhere. At times, they silently tell the story of entire communities. Several cemeteries—besides those normally referred to in relationship to the Holocaust—can be found on the Web.

At this particular site you'll find three of them. The story of the Jewish Cemetery on infamous Boot Hill in Arizona makes for good reading. The second one is the Marysville Cemetery in California. The first Jewish burial in Marysville took place in 1850, a year after the Gold Rush began. Among the cemetery's more dramatic headstone inscriptions: "Simon Glucksman. Aged 24 years. A native of Kempen, Prussia. Was murdered Friday, August 26, 1859, on the high-way between La Porte and St. Louis." The third is the Congregation Mikvah Israel Cemetery, in Philadelphia Pennsylvania.

> "In 1738, a son of Nathan Levy, the man whose ship brought the Liberty Bell to America, passed away. No Jewish cemeteries existed in Philadelphia at that time. Levy approached Governor Thomas Penn, William Penn's son to buy land in which to perform a burial. Penn sold him property on the wooded north side of Walnut Street between 8th and 9th."

Bob Dylan: Tangled Up In Jews

http://www.well.com/user/yudel/Dylan.html

This Web page is devoted to studying and collecting trivia relating to the Jewish religious/cultural odyssey of Shabtai Zisel ben Avraham, a.k.a Bob Dylan.

There is nothing wrong with your eyes! Journalist Larry Yudelson is the expert on Bob Dylan and the Jews. Among the entries here is a reprint of an article that appeared on the subject in the *Washington Jewish Week*. You'll also find all kinds of Dylan-Jewish-related trivia, reports of sightings of Dylan at Chabad houses, the Hebrew translations to some of his songs, and, of course, numerous other links to Dylan sites. Check out this gem:

"Our synagogue's Rebbetzin (the Rabbi's wife) hails from Minneapolis, and her mother once attended a wedding of some distant cousin along with Bob. Three of the women attending had a tradition of singing a medley at all family simchas. Bob seemed apprehensive and muttered something about how 'they better not ask me.'

One of the women, overhearing this, then exclaimed 'Oh take it easy! Nobody's here to hear you!'

A little shot of humility, along with the hor d'oeuvres!"

Facts about Israel: History

http://www.israel-mfa.gov.il/facts/hist/fhist1.html

This site, produced by the Israel Ministry of Foreign Affairs, is an excellent summary of the history of Israel, from the time of the Patriarchs right up through the Knesset elections of 1996.

This is not the history of a Jewish people, but rather a history of the land of Israel and its Jewish inhabitants. What makes this site stand out among all others in this chapter is its thoughtful use of Web technology—that is, smartly placed links, as opposed to the more common simple narratives that are often found in the area of history.

The home page is a complete time line, a quick overview/summary of the entire history, with links to various other pages such as biblical times, Roman rule, the Crusaders, and the State of Israel. This use of links seems obvious enough, but on each of the pages there are further supplementary links—to maps, to other documents, museums, bibliographies of notable characters, and other resources. See a map of the original 1948 Partition Plan, a copy of Theodore Herzl's diary (in Hebrew), pictures of Masada, and more.

What will the presentation of history on the Web look like in the years to come? Take a glimpse of that future at this site.

The Virtual Shtetl

http://sunsite.unc.edu/yiddish/shtetl.html

There is a full description of this Web page in the Yiddish chapter later in the book.

Center for Jewish History

http://www.cjh.org/

The Center for Jewish History is a consortium of four outstanding Jewish historical institutions: The American Jewish Historical Society, the Leo Baeck Institute, Yeshiva University Museum, and YIVO Institute for Jewish Research. Plans are to create a "campus complex devoted to the furtherance of Jewish scholarship in the heart of New York City: The Center for Jewish History" comprising all four institutions. Descriptions of and links to all four organization are here, as well as an exciting description of their future plans.

The center is not scheduled for completion until late 1997. It is hoped that a major Web presence will be included in their plans, although that is unclear. Watch this site for developments and future exhibits.

The YIVO Institute for Jewish Research

http://spanky.osc.cuny.edu/~rich/yivo/

YIVO, dedicated to the study and preservation of the Eastern European Jewish heritage, is an international Jewish treasure; its value to researchers and to Jewish cultural history is unsurpassed. The library contains more than 350,000 books and periodicals, and their archival holdings exceed 22 million and include the world's most extensive collections of East European Jewish sound recordings and Yiddish children's literature, and more than 200,000 photographs.

Information from YIVO News is here, in addition to a description of the of holdings and a short history of YIVO, but there's not a whole lot more at this site. As noted in the Center for Jewish History entry, the institute expects to move in 1997. It is hoped that it will, eventually, make extensive use of Web technology.

C H A P T E R   2

The World Wide Web in Israel

Israel is the focus of the modern-day Jewish world, and the primary historic wellspring of Jewish observances and culture. Israel is also the focus of a burgeoning high-tech industry and the source of thousands of Web sites. The sites in this chapter are merely the tip of the iceberg, but they will give you an idea of the rich Internet culture growing in Israel that serves the world's Jewish population.

Israeli Sites Sorted by Name
http://199.203.130.102/israel/sites/sites.htm

There are close to 2,000 Israeli Web sites here, sorted by name, that is, by the name of the URL. While its less-than-optimal means of organization might not make this your first choice when looking for an Israeli site, its thoroughness will make it a great backup if you can't find the site you're looking for another way.

The (almost) Complete Guide to WWW in Israel
http://www.math.technion.ac.il/~nyh/israel/

This guide has more then 1,200 links to Israeli Web sites, divided into hierarchical categories, In fact, it's a bit reminiscent of the earlier days of Yahoo, but without a search engine. This is a valuable site if you plan to cruise the Israeli Web.

Walla On-Line

http://www.walla.co.il/new/p_wie.cgi

This is yet another Web site directory. They are primarily, though not exclusively, Israeli. Walla has a search engine with some nice options, and the site can be accessed in English (at the above URL) or in Hebrew at *http://www.walla.co.il/*.

Israel Xpress

http://www.ix.co.il/

This site contains a great many links to commercial sites in Israel. Quite a few export companies and several directories are found on this server. If you are interested in the commercial aspects of Israel, this could be a helpful resource. The Products and Services Guide is the best part of this site.

SABRAnet

http://sabranet.com/

This easy-to-use award-winning site is very attractive (due in part to the large number of graphics, which makes the home page a bit slow to load), and it has some pleasant surprises. In addition to finding links to various Israeli sites, you can also download free software (freeware, demos, and shareware) from Israeli authors and companies. More surprisingly, you can listen to snippets of top Israeli songs from the last few years via **.wav** files.

The World Wide Web Server for Israel

http://www.il/

This Web server attempts to be the central point to list most of the Internet servers (WWW/gopher/ftp) located in Israel. Interestingly, the site has an Israeli map that lets you search servers with a click of your mouse. If you have even the most cursory knowledge of Israel's geography, you will be able to use this feature. It also has links to other Israeli Web servers.

Netvision

http://www.netvision.net.il/

Netvision is a joint venture of some of the biggest Israeli software developers, and they've put together this nice-looking page with a good compendium of links as well as information on the companies themselves. As you might expect, the links are particularly strong in the area of technology, but recently they have begun adding other areas as well. And, of course, what's a good technology Web site without some advertisements of job opportunities? If you're a computer techie who might be interested in working in Israel, this page is a must.

Jewishnet Global Jewish Information Network

http://jewishnet.net/

This is one of those supersites that contains a tons of links to Web sites, as well as mailing lists, newsgroups, ftp, and gopher sites. If you don't understand all of that, then you have an idea why this book is focused on Web sites (the other reason, of course, is that more and more of these sites are being converted to Web sites). If you *are* comfortable with gophers and the like, then this site has a lot to offer—hundreds of Israel- and Jewish-related mailing lists, and more. There are also a number of links to Jewish libraries (from Brandeis to Bar-Ilan), and a few of them telnet right to their on-line catalogs. Some of the information here, however, is a bit outdated.

The Knesset

http://www.knesset.gov.il

This graphically stunning site is one of the newest and best of the Israeli government sites. It includes a guided tour of the Knesset, gives a history of the institution and shows you how it works. It has links to a great many other institutions. A visit to this site is a valuable educational experience.

The Jewish Agency for Israel
http://www.ja-wzo.org.il/

The Jewish Agency for Israel was the de facto government of the Jews in Palestine prior to the establishment of the Jewish state. When the state was established many of the activities of the Agency were transferred over to the new government. However, the Agency still retains jurisdiction in myriad areas, particularly those pertaining to education in the Diaspora, the settlement of new immigrants in Israel and in conducting educational programs in Israel. This site tells you all about their activities and programs.

The Israel Foreign Ministry Home Page
http://www.israel.org/

This site, produced by the Israel Ministry of Foreign Affairs, is probably the closest thing to the English version of "the official Israel page." There is a ton of information here, with well-placed hyperlinks to official documents and other original sources. Additionally, a nice section, called "Israel Update," has links to recent news and press releases and this is a really nice feature links to that day's news from various independent publications (such as the *Jerusalem Post* and *Ha'aretz*). This is an excellent jumping-off point into the Israeli Web—or at least "official Israel" Web sites. The next four sites are also part of this site, but they are worthy of their own entries.

Ministry of Foreign Affairs
http://www.israel-mfa.gov.il/mfa/

It's like this: the Ministry of Foreign Affairs, as part of its duties, maintains a general Israel Web site (the preceding entry). *This* page is about the Ministry itself, and the information here is surprising, both in terms of its great volume and its varied content. You can find texts of treaties, speeches (see the next entry below), links to Israeli embassies abroad, and so on—things you might expect to see, albeit extremely well put together. But the site also offers a few things you might not expect to see: the Ministry also maintains more than 10 photographic Internet exhibits, each full of photographs and explantory text. In fact, it has more images than you can see in most of the sites in the Museum chapter! This site also includes the full text (and pictures and archives) of *PANIM: Faces of Art and Culture in Israel,* a publication produced by the Ministry, and three Arabic-language publications also published by them.

Israel Government Information
http://www.israel-mfa.gov.il/gov/

This is basic, and some detailed, information about Israel and its form of government. While Israel has no constitution, it is guided by what they call *Basic Laws,* and the text to them all are here as well as the text to the famous Law of Return, which grants every Jew the right to immigrate to Israel. There is a fine description of how the entire election process works, (including party lists, public financing information, and links to the major political parties themselves). Addresses, phones, and fax information (but not e-mail addresses or Web sites) of all the branches and ministries of Israel are here, as well as details of the present Israeli government and its ministers.

Government Position Papers and Speeches
http://www.israel-mfa.gov.il/mfa/speeches/speeches.html

This site has the official word from the Israeli government. Here you can find the text to many of the important speeches made since 1995, including ones made to various bodies both in Israel and in the United States by Prime Ministers Netanyahu, Rabin, and Peres. In addition to the political speeches that this site contains, you will also find a speech that President Ezer Weizmann made to the German Bundestag upon his visit to that country, the first made by any Israeli head of state. You can also read the speech Prime Minister Rabin made moments before he was assassinated.

Facts about Israel

http://www.israel-mfa.gov.il/facts/

This site is like having an abbreviated encyclopedia about Israel right at your fingertips. The title, "Facts about Israel," just doesn't do it justice—there is information here about all aspects of Israel: education, foreign trade, social services, technology, and so on. The history section is extremely well done, and it is covered in the History chapter. There's not a whole lot of depth here, but there is an incredible amount of breadth and some well placed links to places that can give you good detail for some of the subjects.

MATIMOP

http://www.matimop.org.il/

MATIMOP, a public, nonprofit organization, focuses on "promoting the development of advanced technologies in Israel and on creating fruitful partnerships through industrial cooperation, joint ventures, and contract R&D." To that end, they have developed a great resource here. This site will allow you to search various databases (by company and by project) for R&D opportunities. This is not for the casual user but for someone genuinely interested in sophisticated business transactions. When I last visited the site, there was information about the business opportunities fair on Israeli lasers, and electro-optics. Serious stuff.

The BIRD Foundation

http://www.birdf.com/

The BIRD Foundation (Israel-U.S. Binational Industrial and Development Foundation) is similar to MATIMOP. It is set up to "stimulate mutually beneficial cooperation between the private sectors of U.S. and Israeli high tech industry." But there's a real potential for money here, as they note that they support some 40 projects annually with a total investment of around $15 million per year. The site contains information about contacting the Foundation, a summary of its activities, a listing of its projects, and how it operates.

Israeli Politics

Political Parties

http://www.israel-mfa.gov.il/gov/platform.html.

Many political parties have their own Web sites which are described in this chapter. For others, particularly such important ones as Israel Ba-aliya and the National Religious Party, you can read their platforms at the address listed here.

Israeli politics revolves almost exclusively around three issues: the peace process; the place of religion in Israel; and the economic structure of Israel.

The first issue, the question of peace, is the overriding one—after all, Israel was attacked by its neighbors within hours of securing independence in 1948, and it has been in four other major wars since then. How do you deal with an enemy that has attacked in the past and who has engaged in terrorism? What combination of force, strength, and concessions should be made? How much territory should be given—noting that the 1967 borders of Israel leave the state, at one geographic point, only 9 miles wide.

Here are the Israeli political parties that are on the web, as well as a sampling of the various movements and organizations in Israel that are positioned across the spectrum on these issues.

Israel Labor Party

http://www.inter.net.il/~avoda/

The Labor Party, based upon the values of the Jewish labor movement, and descendants of the old socialist movement (the Mapai party), dominated Israeli politics from Israel's birth until shortly after the Yom Kippur War in 1973, a war that, some thought, caught Israel unprepared. Until then its leaders (technically, Mapai's leaders) included David Ben-Gurion (Israel's first Prime Minister), and noted historical figures such as Golda Meir and Moshe Dayan.

Since the mid-1970s, however, the electorate has veered between the left-wing Labor, most recently under the leadership of Shimon Peres and Yitzhak Rabin, and the right-wing Likud parties. It was the Labor party that negotiated the first Oslo agreement and, of course, remains fully behind it. There are some good "talking points" of their point of view on the peace process, but there's not really a whole lot of other information here.

Likud
http://usa.likud.org.il/

Their page puts it clearly: "The right of the Jewish people to the Land of Israel is an eternal right, not subject to dispute, and includes the right to security and peace." Of course, like everything else in Israel, even this clear statement has hidden ambiguities: what, precisely, are the borders of the "Land of Israel", and what constitutes security in a land surrounded by past and present enemies? While some of Likud's past leaders, such as Yitzhak Shamir, have been accused of stalling the peace process, others have implemented the biggest peace agreements in Israeli history. Begin signed the Camp David accords with Egyptian president Sadat; and while Labor entered into the Oslo accords, it has been left to Netanyahu to implement them.

This site is among the best of the political parties, with good text and graphics to justify their point of view. (The full text of the Palestinian National Charter it here—it is quite sobering and a must read for anyone who wonders why it's an issue).

Meimad—The Movement for Religious Zionist Renewal
http://www.barak.co.il/meimad/

Meimad is a good example of the complexity of Israeli politics. While on one hand, they are to the right on religious matters (i.e., they are Orthodox), they are somewhat to the left on political matters (i.e., "land for peace"). In fact, their view is that "the majority of the religious Zionist community is entrenched on the extreme right, so far from the center of Zionism that it seems marginal, at best, to the majority of Israelis."

Their platforms and press releases, available here, are deeply thought-provoking and provide another face for the Orthodox Israeli—one that is different from the monolithic entity often portrayed by the media. Two of the essays here, "The Jewish Character of Israel Culture" and "Halacha and Democracy," raise fundamental questions about the relationship between Judaism and Jewish Law and Israel.

Meretz

http://www.meretz.israel.net/ENGLISH/INDEX.HTM

As the National Religious Party is further to the right than Likud in terms of religious and political issues, Meretz is further to the left than Labor. They have strong stances, both in the area of the peace process (they believe that a Palestianian state is inevitable and the only arrangement possible for long-term peace), and in the area of religion (they oppose the Orthodox monopoly on many Israeli Jewish affairs; for example, they want Yeshiva students to be eligible for the draft, non-Orthodox Jewish denominations to be fully recognized, public services to be open on the Sabbath, and an insitution of civil marriages and divorces). The full platform is here (but not much else), and makes for interesting reading. Sometimes you just have to wonder how Israel can be home to so many strong Jewish factions that are so diametrically opposed on so many issues.

The Third Way

http://www.aquanet.co.il/the_third_way/

The Third Way is a new party that attempts to position itself between Labor and Likud. While they would retain a great deal of strategic land (including the Golan Heights, the settlements, and a strip of land along all along the West Bank), they are also in favor of political autonomy for the Palestinians. This site is entirely in Hebrew, making it less accessible to most American Jews.

Chadash—The Israel Communist Party
http://www.gezernet.co.il/chadash.html

This is the site of the Israeli Communist Party, and it is mostly in Hebrew. The only English page in this site, and, in one respect, the best part of this site, is a page full of links to other Communist and Socialist sites throughout the world. You can find links to "Another View of Stalin," "The Che Guevera Page," and works on Fidel Castro, Marx and Engels, Tito, and to the Communist and Socialist parties of other countries. Looking at this page made me feel like I was opening a time capsule.

The following sites prove, again and again, that many groups advocating particular policies do a much better job, at least on the Web, of informing the public about the issues than the political parties themselves do. It is quite remarkable how sensible so many of the conflicting positions seem to be. Reading two different sites with opposing views can make you wonder how *any* agreements have been able to be worked out. Every detail has a political angle, including the wording itself. Simply giving the land just west of the Jordan River a name implies a point of view: should it be called Judea and Samaria or the Occupied Territories?

Foundation for Middle East Peace
http://www2.ari.net/fmep/

The Foundation, a U.S. non-profit independant organization, has a clear agenda: it supports the peace process and it does so by providing a huge amount of information and news reports in a fairly unbiased manner. They publish the bimonthly (and free) *Report on Israeli Settlement in the Occupied Territories*, and provide speakers, award grants, and take out ads in U.S. papers. They call the *Report* "the authoritative English-language source for information about settlements and the settler community."

A great deal of information is here, including the full text to all their reports going back to 1993, special reports, and quite a number of maps and pictures. Even if you don't agree with them, you can learn a great deal about what is going on in "the territories" from this site.

The Yesha Council of Jewish Communities in Judea, Samaria and Gaza

http://www.yesha.virtual.co.il/

This group describes iteself as "an umbrella organization for local and regional councils in Yesha (*Yesha* is the acronym, in Hebrew, for Judea, Samaria, and Gaza), coordinating the various regional and local authorities, and was established in order to concentrate broader representative power in dealings with governement ministries and other government authorities."

In other words, Yesha represents the settlers of the Jewish settlements in Judea, Samaria, and Gaza. The movement was a major thorn in the side of the Labor government, which overrode its objections to the Oslo Peace Accord, and it is proving to be more than an annoyance for the Natanyahu-led Likud government, which it strongly backed in the 1996 election. Plainly put: Yesha is just as vociferous in arguing against giving land back to the Palestinians as the Peace Now Movement is in advocating the return of land in exchange for peace. This site is put together very well and has a great deal of information about who the Yesha Council is, what it stands for, and why. There is contact information on all the settler sites, and a list of upcoming events (including information on whether there is full army protection for the event or not).

Peace Now

http://www.peace-now.org/

Peace Now, among the largest grassroots movement in Israel, was founded by 348 former Israeli Army officers in 1978. One of their mottos is "real security can be achieved only when we achieve peace." Needless to say, Peace Now has been an active advocate of the peace process, and it has been extremely critical of the Likud government. The site carries press releases, monthly reports on activities (with archives), links to other like-minded organizations, and other materials about the movement.

The Golan Heights Information Server

http://www.golan.org.il/

This site carries a great deal of information about the Golan Heights—land captured and later annexed from Syria that literally overlooks Israel and was often a staging area for mortar and rocket attacks on Israel. Not only is the area militarily significant, it also is the source, according to this site, of 30% of Israel's water supply. Needless to say, the idea of giving back the Golan Heights to a country that is hostile (to put it mildly) is unsettling to many. There are some press releases and other information here, most put out by an associated group called Peace with the Golan, which actively presents the belief that a lasting peace for Israel can not occur with a Golan Heights surrender. Although the site is a bit out of date, one area is of particular interest: it is often said that you have to see the Golan Heights in relation to the former border of Israel to fully appreciate the strategic significance of it. This site features a photographic slide show of just these kinds of views.

Dor Shalom

http://www.dorshalom.org.il/

Dor Shalom, ("the Peace Generation" in Hebrew), was created in the aftermath of the Rabin assassination. As they write: "We support the Peace Process initiated by Yitzhak

Rabin. We view the Peace Process as a mandatory factor in the establishment of the State of Israel as the leading economic and cultural power in the Middle East."

In addition to its own materials that are on this site (which include an audio file of Rabin's last speech), it also contains links to other peace related sites on the net.

B'Tselem—The Israeli Information Center for Human Rights in the Occupied Territories
http://www.btselem.org/

Tradition has it that mankind was made *b'tselem elohim*, in "the image of God." Therefore, logic dictates that even enemies must be treated with respect. B'Tselem was founded in 1989 to monitor and document human rights abuses in the West Bank and Gaza Strip. While often thought of as a group that existed to criticized Israel, B'Tselem gained newfound respect when, after the Oslo accords granted some autonomy for the Palestinians, they started releasing reports sharply critical of the human rights abuses carried on by the Palestinian Authority against other Palestinians. This site contains a number of their past press releases. War and its aftermath isn't pretty.

BibiWatch
http://www.ariga.com/bibiwatch/

"BibiWatch is an independent weekly newsletter produced in Israel; its first issue appeared less than two weeks after the 1996 elections. Its goal is to keep an eye on Israel's Prime Minister, Binyamin Netanyahu."

It would be wrong to call BibiWatch nonpartisan—it doesn't like the Likud and what it stands for, and it takes every opportunity to poke fun at Netanyahu and his associates. There's humor here, but it bites. Anyone who follows Israeli politics knows that there's plenty of material to skewer all the big players. Ouch!

Americans for a Safe Israel
http://www.covesoft.com/afsi/

Like many other organizations, there's no doubt where this organization, founded in 1971, stands: "Israel must retain possession and control of Judea, Samaria, Gaza and the Golan" as is the only way to insure a lasting peace. Strong supporters of Likud in the 1996 elections, this group pulls no punches. Instead of BibiWatch, this site offers Shimon Says, quotations from Shimon Peres, the former Prime Minister of Israel and chief architect of the Oslo agreement. They like Peres as much as Peace Now likes Netanyahu.

Basic Laws of the State of Israel
http://www.israel-mfa.gov.il/gov/laws/basiclaw.html

As Israel has no Constitution, it is guided by what are called Basic Laws, and the text to all of them is at the Ministry of Foreign Affairs site. The text to two other important laws are here as well (not technically classified as "basic") the famous Law of Return, which grants every Jew the right to immigrate to Israel, and the Protection of Holy Places law, which guarantees that protection and freedom of access to the myriad places sacred to the many religions in Israel.

Haim Ravia Law Offices
http://www2.netvision.net.il/~ravia/

The law offices of Haim Ravia have produced an incredible resource here. It has a great many links to Israeli legal pages, the English translation of Israel's Declaration of Independence, selected documents on the Peace Process, the Basic Laws, various peace treaties, information on Israeli Law Faculties and a listing of a number of Israeli law firms with an Internet presence. What's more, while special attention was given to Israeli lawyers, it is of use for lawyers around the world, and there are a number of excellent links, divided nicely by subject, to American legal documents, policies, and explanations. There are links here to the burgeoning field of cyber law, the "ten myths of copyright," and links to on-line legal dictionaries, law journals, and even how to find an attorney, for Israelis, Americans, and other citizens.

TravelNet Israel
http://www.insite.co.il/tour/index.html

This on-line guide is based on the famous *Bazak Guide to Israel*. It has many interesting features, not the least of which are several columns on Israeli food and wine by Daniel Rogov. His tour of Israel's wineries is superb. One thing to keep in mind is that most of the restaurants listed by Rogov are not kosher.

Infotour—The Israel Tourist Guide
http://www.infotour.co.il/

This site contains information about hotels, hostels, guest houses, and bed and boards throughout Israel. You will have a hard time finding some of this information else-where in the travel sites that are listed in this book and those that are on the Web in general. Also on this site you'll find information about museums, tourist attractions, events, and many other tidbits that you simply won't find elsewhere. If you've been in Israel before or are interested in seeing a "different" Israel than the one you've already seen, this site is a must. You can probably spend hours just going through the various travel-related links from this site. You're best off studying it with a notebook and a map at your side.

EL Al Israel Airlines—U.S. Information
http://www.elal.co.il/

El Al's Web site has a great deal of information for American tourists preparing to visit Israel. The site contains El Al special offers, vacation packages, the El Al route map and time table, the details of the El Al Frequent Traveler Matmid club, and the locations of El Al sales offices in the United States and car rentals in Israel. To find listings of El Al offices throughout the world, go to *http://www.hospitalitynet.nl/iha/congress/airline.htm.*

Arkia Airlines

http://arkia.co.il/

Arkia is a primarily domestic Israeli airline, connecting Tel Aviv, Eilat, Jerusalem, the Dead Sea, Haifa, and the Galilee. Arkia also has a "flying ambulance" that can be used to provide medical transportation around the world. Arkia's services described on its official Web site include international flights to Israel, domestic flights around the country, tours, vacation packages, accommodations throughout Israel (hotels, kibbutz guest houses, and rustic B and Bs), sightseeing trips, car rental services, cruises, skiing, climbing, diving (including diving courses), and even deep-sea fishing.

NOTE Many other airlines offer air travel to Israel. Please contact your favorite airline for information. This address will take you to most of the airlines of the world; it is arranged by country: *http://www.travelpage.com/air/airlines.htm.*

Israel National Parks Authority
National Parks and Archaeological Sites

http://www.webscope.com/inpa/

The National Parks Authority was established in 1963 by a special act of the Knesset. Its purpose was to protect the country's natural beauty from rapidly encroaching urbanization and to restore and maintain antiquities that were sitting lost or neglected amid centuries of rubble and dust. The National Parks Authority, often in cooperation with local councils, set to work and today operates forty-three national parks that criss-cross the country and cater to more than seven million visitors every year. Some of these poular parks are highlighted on this Web site, including Ashkelon, Bar'am, Belvoir, Caesarea, Masada, Tel Megiddo, Nimrod's Fortress, Bet She'arim, Yehiam Fortress, and Zippori.

Israel Interactive Tourism Guide
http://www.insite.co.il/tour/index.html

The on-line Insite Tourism Center provides information on various Israeli cities. The information is presented in a very organized and well-presented style. You will find vital, tourist-oriented information about each of Israel's major cities, including special events, hotels, dining, transportation, museums, sports activities, and other useful facts that you will not find at other Israeli city sites.

Jerusalem One
http://www.jer1.co.il/

Go to this site and you see a live shot of The Western Wall on your screen. KoTelCam and the rest of this site bring Jerusalem to you. Although you can find a wide variety of materials about Jerusalem and Judaism on this site, it is not a site that you can simply click on and expect to find what you are looking for right away. You might be pleasantly surprised—or a bit frustrated—by material on this site that really doesn't belong there. On the other hand, the listings of Jewish communities are really quite interesting. You may want to spend some time wandering around this site, which is graphically one of the most pleasing of all the Israeli pages on the Internet. Every time you click on to this site you will find some new feature.

Focus On Israel
http://focusmm.com.au/israel/is_anamn.htm

This Australian site was created primarily for tourists. It is a generalized site, don't expect a lot of details. But you can expect to find some very interesting information about Israel and its tourist sites, activities, etc. We expect that this site will be expanded to carry more details.

The Virtual Tour of Israel

http://dapsas.weizmann.ac.il/bcd/bcd_parent/tour/tour.html

This on-line tour provides you with interactive maps of many of Israel's cities and tourist sites. It shows pictures of the locations, describes their history and lists the reasons they might be of interest to you. We suggest that you go on this tour accompanied by a printed travel guide.

N O T E

Before you buy a specific travel guide, we suggest you browse through several. Every guide book addresses a different audience, and what may interest one person may not interest another. If you're traveling to Israel with your family, it might be a good idea to get several different guide books so that you can get different perspectives on the country.

Events in Israel

gopher://israel-info.gov.il:70/00/cul/960100.trm

This list is provided by the Israel Foreign Ministry. It describes major events that are taking place in Israel during the calendar year. This gopher site is not particularly interesting to look at because it is entirely text. However, if you're planning to visit Israel, this is an excellent place to research events that will take place around Israel while you will be there. It might provide you with some interesting things to do during your visit.

The Israel Hotel Association

http://www.jer1.co.il/travel/travel/hotelassoc/

This is the official site of the Israel Hotel Association. It's primary resource is a listing of most of the hotels in Israel.

The prices it lists are only estimates—very often these prices do not reflect what you are really charged if you are part of a travel package or if you travel at off-peak times. However, the listings will give you an accurate reflection of the comparative costs of hotels, their ratings, and facilities that they offer. The Web site also lists kibbutz guest houses which are often quite pleasant and not very expensive. We've stayed at a number of them.

Israel Kibbutz Hotels

http://www.kibbutz.co.il

The kibbutz movement first began in 1909 with the establishment of Kibbutz Degania. At present, 269 kibbutzim exist throughout Israel. The original aim of these communities was to settle the land, create a society based on equality, and to nurture a spirit of sharing and mutual collaboration. Although still committed to farming, many kibbutzim have branched out into numerous other industries, including tourism.

The Kibbutz Hotels Chain (KHC) is Israel's largest network of hotels, holiday villages, and country lodgings. Many KHC hotels are located near national parks and recreational facilities. Others are near important historic, archeological, and geographical sites.

You can research prices, contact names, rates, and regional attractions at this KHC Web site.

IsraelVisit

http://www.israelvisit.co.il/

This very interesting site is good for experienced Israel tourists. It contains information about many facets of living in Israel and about quite a few of its cities and tourist spots, including some that are a bit off the beaten track.

Each of the tourist-oriented sites listed in this chapter has blind spots as well as strengths. For example: most of the Israeli Web sites we have listed dwell only on the major tourist attractions. IsraelVisit, however, will help you find out about places that you might not ordinarily visit.

Another Web site to visit if you want to find out more about Israel's cities is City.Net.Israel at *http://www.city.net/ countries/israel/*.

The Jerusalem Mosaic

http://www1.cc.huji.ac.il/jeru/jerusalem.html

"Travel the city through the different periods, meet the people, taste the food, enjoy the special costumes and visit the sites."

This site, created by Hebrew University in Jerusalem, takes you through Jerusalem from its earliest days to the present time. It is interesting but not overwhelming. Perhaps it is a bit too academic in style. Other sites on the Internet do the job in a more graphically interesting fashion, but the content of this site is excellent. Another part of the Hebrew University site, at *http://ftp.cc.huji.ac.il/md/ vjt/*, offers the Virtual Jerusalem Tour, which introduces you to Jerusalem by proceeding through your choice of one of the eight gates that make up the entrances to the Old City. The text that accompanies the pictures is all too brief, but the pictures make up for it.

You can also view the major religious sites of Jerusalem from this page.

Neot Kadumim—The Biblical Landscape Reserve In Israel

http://www.neot-kedumim.org.il/

In Hebrew 'neot' means places of beauty; 'kedumim' means ancient. At Neot Kedumim you can tour landscapes of beauty, all planted within the last twenty-five years, to learn the connection between the Land of Israel and the Judeo-Christian tradition. The Bible speaks in the language of nature and once you become familiar with this idiom, the Bible gains amazing dimensions of depth and color. At Neot Kedumim, hundreds of varieties of plants flourish alongside ancient and reconstructed agricultural installations, conjuring up the everyday life of the Biblical farmer and shepherd.

Neot Kedumim has ... created a microcosm of the Land itself, featuring flora of the Sharon Plain, Carmel Range, Arava, Negev desert, natural Mediterranean forest areas and the Jordan River Valley. In addition, Biblical animals, many now extinct in the wild, roam special areas of Neot Kedumim. All these allow visitors to see and feel the environmental context of the Scriptures.

This well-organized but not very detailed site is the official Web presence for Neot Kedumim, a unique nature park with a Biblical bent. The site offers details about tours, a guide to Israeli plants, handicapped- access information, events at the park, the park's quarterly newsletter, contact and reservation numbers, and details about the biblical meals served at the park.

Red Sea Experience
http://www.redsea.co.il/

This site, sponsored by *Red Sea Magazine,* is chock-full of information about all sorts of sports activities on the Red Sea. It's a handy document, and its writing can be pretty evocative and inviting:

The Red Sea appeared as a crack on the earth's surface 75 million years ago, part of the rift separating Asia and Africa. It is accessed by the narrow straights of Bab El Mandab: "The Gate of Tears." Very little water flows through these shallow straights, making this one of the saltiest seas on the planet. Climatic conditions around the Red Sea are very dry, and the surrounding desert deposits no vegetable sediment into its waters. The result: a perfect laboratory for coral growth. The luxuriant coral gardens of the Red Sea attract divers from all over the world. With such specialized conditions, it is no surprise that a quarter of the marine life found here is exclusive to the Red Sea alone. Divers pronounce the experience captivating. But you don't have to know how to dive to enjoy the Red Sea. Snorkeling is a popular alternative, and introductory diving courses are freely available. SO GET WET.

Get Red! Coral Sea Diving

http://www.coralsea.co.il/

This Web page displays the tours, courses, and facilities offered by the Coral Sea Divers group. This is a particularly useful site if you are considering going diving for the first time and need instruction

> Coral Sea Divers would like to present you with the various diving opportunities in Eilat, Sinai and beyond..... Our dive center is dedicated to the highest standards in dive education from beginner level to the experienced diver and specializes in dive travel services.

Another diving club Web site worth checking out is the Siam Divers Club, which you can find at *http://www.siam.co.il/*. They descibe themselves as "the newest and most advanced [club] in Eilat."

Dolphin Reef-Eilat

http://www.dolphinreef.co.il/

This is the colorful Web site for Dolphin Reef, a unique open-sea facility in Eilat, where visitors can observe, swim, and dive with dolphins in their natural habitat. At the Dolphin Reef site, you can read about and check rates for the dive center, the diving with dolphins program, family packages, and diving safaris to the Sinai and Jordan.

One Shekel Equals

http://bin.gnn.com/cgi-bin/gnn/currency?Israel

The handy Koblas Currency Converter on the GNN pages gives you a frequently updated converter that allows you to check the price of the Israeli Shekel in relation to the various currencies of the world. This can keep you from trading in your foreign currency at a bad exchange rate, a mistake sometimes made by first-time tourists.

Other sites that tell you how to finance purchases on your trip to Israel are the Israel Welcomes Visa site at *http://www.visa.co.il/welcome/home.htm*, which has information about using your Visa card in Israel, and the Israel Postal Bank site at *http://www.postalbank.co.il/*, which has information on transferring money to and from Israel, Western Union money transfers, Mastercard, and Israel Postal Authority Banking Services.

FEMI

http://www.femi.com/Foreign.html

If you intend to come to Israel for work or for travel, you should have medical insurance:

> FEMI administrates a very large medical insurance plan for foreign nationals in Israel and as a medical services company. FEMI provided its insured with private medical care based upon a designed medical services "basket" to accommodate the medical insurance policy.

The company's Web site lists a schedule of benefits. It also lists the names of many of its corporate and institutional clients. If your youngster is planning to attend school in Israel, chances are FEMI may already cover the institution. Check here to see if that is the case.

Israel Flowers

http://www.flowers.co.il/

You can send flowers anywhere in Israel. You look at the offerings on the site, choose the flowers you want, and e-mail your order directly to Israel Flowers. It's as simple as that.

Click-It Corp.

http://www.order-click.co.il/

This site offers a number of items that you can buy on the Internet. For the most part they are not terribly exciting, Click-It does have one service that is really quite fascinating. You can e-mail them a Word or Word Perfect document and they will print it out and deliver it to your Israeli recipient the very same day.

JudaicaNet
http://www.realestate.co.il/

This site gives you a bird's eye view of the variety of Israeli crafts that are on sale via the Internet. It's a good site to look at before you go to Israel if you plan to do some serious Judaica shopping.

This site's efficient search engine allows you to look over more than 40 new Web sites of Israeli artists and order Judaica, collectables, ceramics, ethnic art, folk art, fabric, silk, hand-crafted wearable fine art, paintings, custom-made books, mezzuzot, challah covers, ties, kipot, sterling silver, gold, and Roman glass jewelry.

Jeff Seidel's Jewish Student Information Centers Homepage
http://www.geocities.com/Athens/7613/

This site summarizes many of the informational resources available for Americans, particularly students, considering a study program during their stay in Israel:

> Among the thousands of college students who flock to Israel each year for study or travel, many are looking for a reason to be Jewish. But it isn't easy to tap into Israel's vast world of Jewish learning....
>
> The Old City Center opened in 1986, functioning as a resource center, a guiding hand and a place offering heightened Jewish consciousness. The second Information Center opened in 1992 near the Hebrew University campus. The third Information Center opened in 1994 near the Tel-Aviv University campus. Included in its services that are made available, are educational tours around the Old City and other parts of the country, the Jewish Center and University lecture series and Holiday programs....

The Study of Jewish Folklore in Israel
http://www.tau.ac.il/%7Egila1/folklore/index.html

The authors of this site have managed to take a fascinating topic and infuse it with boredom. The site contains some very valuable information, but it is written very ponderously.

The essay contains an invaluable bibliography if you can manage to get through it. Hopefully, the site will be rewritten to make it more lively. Among the subjects detailed on this Tel Aviv University affiliated site are the study of Jewish folklore in Israel, the Israel Folktale Archives, contacting the relevant academic departments and scholars, conferences, periodicals, and the aforementioned bibliography. Here's a taste of the rather dry, academic style of the site's authors:

> Jewish folklore is one of the most ancient preserved folklores in world culture, but its study in Israel is one of the most recent. Although it can be considered as a continuation of the study of Jewish folklore in central Europe, as part of the wissenschaft des Judentum and the ethnographic studies of Jewish life in Eastern Europe in the 19th century, Israeli folkloristics as an academic discipline did not start before the 1960s.

Car Rentals

Tips on Renting a Car in Israel:

1. It's less expensive to rent a car before you get to Israel. Your travel agent can make the necessary arrangements for you.

2. Check with your automobile insurance carrier about the type of insurance you will need for your car in Israel. Chances are, you won't have to buy all the insurance that is offered by each rental agency. Insurance is very expensive, so don't order more than you need. Your insurance carrier and travel agent will be able to help you ascertain the types of insurance you will have to carry on the car you rent in Israel.

3. Check your credit card. Very often the use of a specific credit card will automatically confer a certain amount of insurance.

4. If you're not an experienced driver—or don't have nerves of steel—don't drive in Israel. Israel has one of the highest automobile accident rates in the world.

5. If you're driving in unfamiliar territory, get good instructions or take an Israeli navigator with you. You don't want to get lost, especially in a country on which not all of the signs are in English.

6. As long as you're renting a car, get a cellular phone to go with it. Cellular phone calls are very inexpensive in Israel and can be worth every penny. Even if you have no one in particular to call, you're buying peace of mind. If you get lost, someone can give you instructions on how to get to your destination. I've used it just for this type of occasion—and there have been quite a few of them.

The following Web sites represent the leading car rental agencies in Israel. Many Web sites offer special rates, and all give contact information and locations of offices:

Auto Rent

http://www.macom.co.il/Tourism/AutoRent/

Eldan Rent-A-Car

http://www.eldan.co.il/

Avis Israel

http://avis.co.il/

Budget Rent A Car

http://www.budget.co.il/

Kesher(Hertz) Rent A Car

http://www.visa.co.il/welcome/bs003.htm

National and Jewish Holidays

http://www.israelvisit.co.il/holidays.htm

If you're planning a trip to Israel, you might want to be there for a particular holiday or you might want to avoid holidays so that you will be able to get in more touring time without the accompanying holiday restrictions. This tourist-oriented site will tell you the dates of Israel's holidays for the 1997-1998 period.

Israel's Yellow Pages

http://www.yellowpages.co.il/cgi-bin/main.pl

The on-line Israel Yellow Pages is an interesting idea, but it doesn't deliver all it promises and is not easy to use. It takes some getting used to and is very incomplete. There are several other Israeli "Yellow Pages" on the Net, and they all suffer from the same malady. Hopefully, time will rectify this.

NOTE

Public telephones in Israel are no longer operated by tokens as they were in the past. They are now operated by a magnetic card called a *telecard*. These plastic cards, the same size and shape as a credit card, are available at post offices, some hotel reception-desks, street kiosks, and dispensing machines.

The charge for these cards vary. A 20-unit card costs about US $3.00, a 50-unit card costs about US $7.00, and a 120-unit card costs about US $16.00. A local call uses one unit for every five minutes of connect time. The cost of out-of-town calls varies with the distance and the time of the day. The maximum charge is one unit for each 24 seconds, which is charged between 8 a.m. and 1 p.m. on weekdays (Sunday to Friday) over a distance of about 30 miles. The cheapest period is from 10 p.m. and until 7 a.m. and on weekends (from 1 p.m. on Friday to 7 a.m. on the following Sunday). In addition, some public phones now take one-shekel coins. Calls to Directory Assistance (144) do not require the use of a telecard nor do the emergency numbers for Police (100) nor Fire (102).

Maccabi—Israeli Basketball Team

http://www.cs.bgu.ac.il/~herouth/maccabi/

Israel takes its basketball very seriously. You can get the history and schedule details for Israel's best-known hoopsters on this official team Web site:

Maccabi Elite Tel-Aviv is the most famous Israeli basketball team. Maccabi has won the Israeli championship for so many years, that nobody can imagine another champion. For the sake of accuracy, after 23 years of Maccabi championships, Hapoel

Galil Elyon took one championship in the 1992/93 season. Now Maccabi is the champion, leads the Israeli chart, and the fans are looking forward to another 23 years winning stretch.

First Israeli Internet User Survey

http://www.reshet.co.il/misc/survey/1/index.htm

> The First Israeli Internet Survey was conducted by DAPEY RESHET from JAN-1-96 till JULY-1-96. It was advertised on-line in various pages in the reshet.co.il domain and during the 6 months of the survey logged 556 valid responses from Internet users in and outside Israel.

You can tell from the low number of respondents that this is not an extensive survey. However, it does give some indications about Internet usage in Israel.

Butterflies of Israel

http://www.geocities.com/RainForest/1153/

This unusual Web page contains information about butterflies in Israel as well as links to related pages around the world. If you're into rain forests, this is also a good place to start your journey:

> Butterflies and moths belong to the order Lepidoptera which is part of the class Insecta. To date more than 160,000 species were identified by science, of which around 2300 are found in Israel. Out of this number, 150 are day flyers—butterflies.
>
> The reason for so many species of butterflies and moths, in such a small area, is the geographical place of Israel - the "junction" of three continents: Asia, Africa and Europe.

DryBones

http://drybones.org.il/

Dry Bones is Israel's preeminent political comic strip, and is syndicated internationally. *Dry Bones* has been a staple of leading Jewish newspapers and international publications for almost 25 years.

Dry Bones is an Israeli institution. It captures the spirit of the country and the issues that face it. It's cynical, humorous, and to the point. It can hit home with devastating accuracy. Take a look for yourself, you won't be disappointed. You can see the new strips that appear every Monday and Friday or just browse through the online archives of old strips.

Peace in Pictures Project
http://www.macom.co.il/peace/

The Internet can be an invaluable and creative tool. Here is a good example of how you can use the Web to get your ideas across.

> The "Peace in Pictures" project is a game, contest and collaboration involving children from all over the world. We launch this project to celebrate the peace process that we all hope is beginning to take root here in our region of the world. T he "Peace in Pictures" project invites children of all ages to draw their impressions of peace. We will place these pictures on the Internet for everyone around the world to view, enjoy, and be inspired. Very soon we will have here a tapestry of peace for all to enjoy and draw inspiration.

On this Web site from the MaCom network, you can see pictures of many of the submissions received by this project. Because of the graphically oriented nature of the site, skimming through this gallery can be a slow process.

Amos—Israel's New Communications Satellite
http://www.newsguide.com/news/1996/496/misc/amos1.htm

> The first Israeli commercial satellite was recently launched from Kourou, French Guyana... Amos is a commercial satellite... specifically suitable for developing countries.

This recent news bulletin summarizes a highlight of the impressive successes of the Israeli aerospace industry. The

Amos communications sattelites descibed on the site will be orbited over the Middle East and Eastern Europe. You can follow links on this page back to other articles about Israeli technological achievements.

The Israel Film Festival

http://www.bway.net/israel/

The Israel Film Festival is held in Israel, New York, and Los Angeles. This site provides information about the dates and locations of the next festivals. It also contains details about each of the films included in the festival, as well as a vido clip about the show. Israel's film industry is not terribly large, and its films have not made it big in the international marketplace, but that doesn't mean that there aren't some very good films being made. If you're into Israeli films or theatre you should look up this site. You can read abou the industry and find out about programs being held for Israeli filmmakers.

The Israel Jazz Festival

http://www.netvision.net.il/~peltrans/eilat.htm

> The International Red Sea Jazz Festival in Eilat is the major Jazz event in the Middle East, and has become a hit and a professional must for jazz fans. The Festival takes place in Eilat, the peaceful Southern tip of Israel and the renowned tourist site. Surrounded by a magnificent desert landscape, Eilat stands at the junction of three countries : Israel, Egypt an Jordan. The common recreation and the encounter with the music in this enchanted place, attract to Eilat thousands of tourists and jazz fans from all over the world, who plan their summer vacation by the Festival dates.

This show has become a big deal. Prominent American and international artists like Spyro Gyra and the Preservation Hall Jazz Band have been featured artists. Use this site to check out prices and travel packages, and get contact information on this year's show.

The Book
http://www.t-book.com/

> Welcome to Israel. You've decided to get married. It's not like
> in the States. You can't just go to city hall to get hitched. You
> can't even go to your local rabbi. You've got to go to the Chief
> Rabbinate. They want to know if you're really Jewish, if you've
> been married before and if you've been properly divorced; if
> you're a convert to Judaism, who performed the conversion; if
> you're a widow or widower, you have to prove the fact; if you
> haven't been married before you have to provide a Bachelor's
> Certificate. This site hasn't got all the answers. But it has the
> questions and it can make life a lot easier for you. Now that the
> technicalities have been taken care of you still have to make the
> arrangements for a hall, flowers, the photographer, the ring and
> even a honeymoon.

Come to this site and enjoy yourself. Apart from its focus
on weddings, it tells you about arranging a Brit Milah or a
bar/bat mitzvah. It also includes a listing of hotels, halls,
and gardens you can rent for events. So far, the site is centered on Tel Aviv and its environs. The listing of places in
this region to host an affair is quite extensive. The listings
for the other services is sketchy at best.

United States Government Information Services
http://www.usis-israel.org.il/

This nicely organized site, maintainted by the U.S.
Information Service of the U.S. State Department contains
information about cultural activities in Israel as well as links
to a variety of sites containing useful data about the United
States. It also contains a calendar of events and carries news
about current United States involvement in Middle Eastern
affairs.

You can find out how to reach the U.S. Embassy and
Consular offices, check out scholarship and fellowship programs, read the *Electronic Journal* (a compendium of articles

from government magazines), and check out the artist's corner, which lists American artists exhibiting in Israel and Israeli artists exhibiting in America. There are also a ton of links to other government agencies and American media Web sites.

Hatikvah

http://www.algonet.se/~hatikva/anthem.html

This Web site features Hatikvah, the national anthem of Israel. Learn the words, the history, and the music. You can print out the musical score directly from this site and see an amazing sight: music, words, and syllables that go from left to right, but Hebrew letters within the syllables that read right to left.

Communities

Throughout Jewish history, the traditional communal structure has been a major source of strength. Among European Jewry, these communal organizations set standards for education, Kashruth, religious observance, and the community's relationship to the non-Jewish world. In many instances, they were empowered to levy fees to maintain religious institutions and collect taxes for the government in whose domain the community resided. The Jewish community structure was often very powerful in determining the priorities of the community and representing it to all comers.

In the American (and Canadian) Jewish experience, this model has not been followed. With very few exceptions, there is no one communal organization within a Jewish community that regulates or sets the standards and practices of the community as a whole. On the contrary, the independence of each segment of the Jewish community within the whole has been the hallmark of Jewish communal life.

This has begun to change with the complex needs of the members of the community, the shrinking Jewish population in certain areas, and the increased demands being made on community institutions. The reality of 1990s economics demands that Jewish communities carefully manage their resources. Duplication of resources, with resulting dual expenses, is no longer acceptable. One benefit of this reality is the new cooperation found in groups that hitherto did not consider each other's needs.

Additionally, the religious requirements of American Jewry are vastly different than those of earlier Jewish communities. In many cases, religious practices have been changed or abandoned completely. The rigid orthodoxy of the *shtetl* was exchanged for the liberalism of the American Conservative and Reform movements and singularly American religious structures such as the Reconstructionist and Humanistic movements. In many communities, synagogues became temples, kashruth and Sabbath observance were neglected, and intermarriage became a fact of life.

The first Jewish settlers who came to this country traveled from Europe by ship, so the Eastern seaboard attracted the largest numbers of Jewish immigrants. They could land in Boston, New York City, Baltimore, or a range of other towns from Virginia to Maine—areas that were accessible to the sea. Once they arrived and settled in these communities, some ventured forth into Middle America and later the Far West. In the course of this movement, viable Jewish communities were created all over America. Some remain vigorous today.

Over time, many of these smaller cities suffered the blight of urban migrations, and their Jewish communities likewise declined. The Internet has the potential to remove some of the isolation of these communities by making it possible for them to contact each other and become more active participants in the American Jewish community. More importantly, it has also allowed small Jewish communities access to the resources of the major Jewish institutions, mostly located in big cities.

Dozens of Jewish communities have sites on the Web. It would take an entire book to go through each of them. The purpose of listings in this chapter is to convey the flavor of what is out there. Many of the sites can be used as models by other communities that will go on-line in the future.

I have visited dozens of Jewish communities in my travels. I have been struck by several facets of their being. First, there is the resiliency of Jewish life in America: Communities continue to exist where by all logic they should have long disappeared. Second is the great pathos of a community and its members when the patterns of modern life change all aspects of Jewish communal life, and third is the immense intellectual and cultural richness found in these different communities. If anyone wants to know and understand the Jewish contributions to American and Canadian life, one has merely to visit these communities, on-line or in person, and learn their strengths and weaknesses.

These listings can also point out the power of the Internet to serve as a uniting force for Jews and their communal activities. The Internet has the power to transcend distance and time. It can take resources from one spot on the globe and bring them to another as fast as a telephone link will allow. It offers richness and diversity that should not be underestimated.

While some major Jewish communities have an Internet presence—the best site of this type listed here is that of the Toronto Jewish community—others are not represented at all. Surprisingly enough, New York City, which has the largest Jewish population outside Israel, does not have its own Web site. Other communities are inadequately represented on the Web. Philadelphia's site leaves something to be desired. Miami and its environs have a large Jewish population but no Web site. The vast majority of American Jewry's major cultural, religious, and educational institutions are also not represented on the Web. Hopefully, this situation will change.

Atlanta Chai! (Atlanta, Georgia)

http://www.atlchai.org/

This is the central Web page for Atlanta Chai, a citywide network for the Jewish community. Because Atlanta's Jewish community has been growing so rapidly, Atlanta Chai was created to link the Web sites of Atlanta's Jewish schools and organizations.

Jews constitute approximately 3 percent of the Atlanta region, and it is estimated that by the year 2000, Atlanta will be home to roughly 83,000 Jews, nearly 11,000 more than in 1993. The growth of this Jewish community parallels that of Atlanta and the South in general. The Web site goes into greater detail on Atlanta's burgeoning Jewish population:

"Memberships in Atlanta's synagogues has also grown dramatically in the last 25 years. With the founding of 11 new synagogues since 1970, Atlanta's total synagogue memberships have increased from 4,735 in 1970 to 9,250 in 1993, an increase of over 4,500 members! In addition, it is projected that by the year 2000, the Atlanta region will have over 11,581 synagogue members."

This site clearly shows how the cooperation of various groups within a diverse community can work to strengthen the community. All of Atlanta's significant Jewish institutions are represented on this site. Additionally, many of the schools, communal institutions, and synagogues in Atlanta have their own links which radiate from Atlanta Chai.

Austin Virtual Jewish Community (Austin, Texas)

http://www.zilker.net/~austinjc/

In contrast to Atlanta, Austin has a small Jewish community. Its communal resources are more limited. This site, created by Alexander and Andrea Herrera, does a nice job of reflecting Jewish life in Austin and describing many aspects of it. The site also contains information about Jewish communities in Dallas, Houston, and San Antonio.

The contents of this site include:

- The Austin Kosher and Traditional Food Page
- Austin Jewish Heritage Foundation (Orthodox)
- Congregation Agudas Achim (Conservative)
- Congregation Beth Israel (Reform)
- Chabad House
- Chabad Jewish Student Organization (University of Texas at Austin)

Our Towns...Virtual Restoration of Small-town Synagogues in Texas
http://www.neosoft.com/~tjhs/VRsyn.html

This site, developed by Houston-based architect Robert P. Davis, illustrates a fascinating tale:

> "One hundred years ago Jewish communities flourished in many small towns throughout the State. Most are gone; a once-diffuse population contracted into the largest cities. What remains are a few flaking commercial signs, the cemeteries, and the synagogues. And those, if not sold for other uses or abandoned to decay, have nearly faded from the conscious memory of those who used them. Despite obvious historical and sometimes sentimental interest there is neither the will nor money to physically restore most of them. This project seeks to demonstrate an alternate means of preserving the memory and experience of these souvenirs of Jewish heritage.
>
> "Virtual restoration uses computer-aided design techniques to simulate the aural and visual experience of buildings that would otherwise be lost to decay.
>
> "By themselves the buildings don't say much; but they were once animated by people, some of whom are still around to tell their stories. Using the town itself as the "script" former (or current) residents will during a recorded walking tour guide us through time and place. In final presentation form the 3D model, photographs, and recordings will be combined to tell the stories of these places."

Even in its current, still evolving state, this is a rich slice of Jewish Americana. It's well worth a visit. It gives you some indication of the Jewish communities in Texas and elsewhere America that have come and gone over the past 200 years. There are photographs and artists' renderings of more than a dozen such synagogues on this site, some with RealAudio sound files and QuickTime VR (virtual reality) recreations of these synagogues that you can download and "walk" through using your mouse. These are large files, and take a while both to download and navigate. Also, when you do the QuickTime walkthroughs, don't be discouraged if all you see on starting up is a patch of green and a patch of blue. You just need to use your mouse to "turn around" and face the synagogue.

The Dallas Jewish Historical Society Home Page

http://dcwww.mediasvcs.smu.edu/dvjcc/DJHS.html

The Dallas Jewish Historical Society is an independent communal service organization dedicated to the preservation of Dallas Jewish history and to the cultivation of research and educational programming in Jewish history and culture. This site contains references to their resources and activities.

Ann Arbor (Michigan)

http://www.hvcn.org/info/jewish/jewish.htm?

The Jewish community of Washtenaw County and Ann Arbor, Michigan is anchored by the University of Michigan at Ann Arbor. The University of Michigan is a prominent academic institution, and has constantly attracted large numbers of Jewish students from throughout the United States and indeed from throughout the world. It is also quite close to Detroit's large Jewish community.

Taking advantage of its location, this Jewish community has grown and is now a vibrant entity. These pages, built from the *Washtenaw Jewish News Guide to Jewish Life in Washtenaw County,* reflect the diversity of the community and its members. The Jewish community of Ann Arbor coexists with a very strong Arab-American presence, which has made for an interesting relationship.

The site contains a thorough listing of all Jewish communal institutions in the Ann Arbor area, including synagogues, schools, women's groups, campus organizations and adult programs. It is very orderly and easy to use.

Jewish Resources in Boston

http://shamash.org/trb/jewish_boston.html

Solomon Franco tried to settle in Boston in 1649. He was paid to leave the area. Luckily, other pioneers were not dissuaded from moving here. Many Jews followed and they built all sorts of communal and educational institutions, ranging from Brandeis University, named after one of Boston's most famous sons, to the Hebrew Teachers College and dozens of synagogues and temples that have sprung up through the Boston area.

This page is essentially a yellow pages containing the names and addresses of every major Jewish resource in the Boston area. Inasmuch as Boston is the home of some preeminent educational and cultural institutions and attracts a very large Jewish population, this site is particularly important. It includes everything from kosher restaurants to Jewish schools and Jewish-sponsored radio stations and synagogues. There are also articles from the weekly *Jewish Advocate*. It's a very useful tool. It becomes even more meaningful, however, when used in conjunction with our next entry.

Jewish Boston On-Line

http://shamash.org/places/boston/

This site is more than a listing of institutions. It actually categorizes them and presents them in a user-friendly fashion. It bills itself as "a virtual community center." It doesn't really fill the bill—yet. But it has the potential to do so. If you look at both these sights, very little about Jewish Boston will fall between the cracks.

Jewish Resources in the Chicago Area

http://miso.wwa.com/~stevenc/chicago/chi_jewish.html

Jews first came to Chicago in the 1830s, and the earliest settlers were peddlers. This Jewish community today is one of the largest Jewish settlements in the United States, and is rich in communal activities institutions. As with other urban Jewish areas, the majority of Chicago's Jews have moved from the urban center to a string of surrounding communities. Now, the

Chicago Jewish community is centered in a dozen or so distinct neighborhoods and includes parts of northwestern Indiana. This site contains information about every aspect of Jewish life in the Chicago area. It covers Jewish community centers, children's services, schools, kosher food sites, organizations, libraries, book stores, religious requirements and more. It even offers a list of *Mohelim* and day camps. A very useful site, it is visually enhanced by a beautiful mosaic made by students at Skokie's Hillel Torah North Suburban Day School.

The Light of the North

http://www.mosquitonet.com/~hatzafon/

This Alaskan site provides a fascinating glimpse of Jewish frontier history:

> "Jews have played a prominent part in the history of Alaska since its purchase in 1867. Early Jewish fur merchants in San Francisco played a major role in getting the U.S. to make the purchase and in running the Alaska Commercial Company that took over for the Russian American Company.
>
> "Fairbanks began in 1902. By 1904, a Jewish community formed with the arrival of Robert Bloom, a Lithuanian Jew, who came from Ireland via the Klondike in 1898. Bloom ran a general store from 1906 to 1941 and was a mainstay and leader of the Fairbanks Jewish community for nearly half a century.
>
> "During the initial rush, 1904-1910, there were enough Fairbanks Jews to hold regular services on High Holy Days if not a *minyan* for Sabbath. The community had a Torah and formally organized as Congregation Bikkur Cholim in 1908. The Clay Street cemetery in downtown Fairbanks had a Jewish section where Jewish headstones can still be seen today."

The Fairbanks Jewish community has undergone various trials and tribulations since the early days. The congregation, Or HaTzafon, has been reorganized several times. While it is affiliated with the Reform movement, its members include adherents to all denominations within Judaism. The community does not have a full-time rabbi. The last time I viewed this site they were getting by with a summer intern, and were trying to raise money for a permanent rabbi by pitching "Support the Rabbi fund" and buy a "I sent a Rabbi to Alaska" T-shirt. I don't know how many T-shirts you need to hire a rabbi, but it's certainly an inventive approach. This site gives you an inkling about the fluctuation and change present in small, isolated Jewish communities throughout the United States.

Crown Heights Shmirah

http://www.inx.net:80/~mzr77chp/

Crown Heights, in Brooklyn, New York, is the home of the Lubavitch community. It was once the symbol of a well-heeled Jewish community. The homes along stately President Street were mansions. Today, the neighborhood is more mixed. The Chasidim, who now make up the majority of the Jewish inhabitants of Crown Heights, have an uneasy coexistence with the members of the black community with whom they share the neighborhood.

The area became famous (or infamous, whichever term you apply) after the death of Yankel Rosenbaum, a young Chasid from Australia. The resulting disturbances which rang through the neighborhood sent a chill throughout the entire Jewish community and were seen as one of the major reasons for the defeat of New York's first black mayor, David Dinkins. But Crown Heights Jewish and black residents have a history of conflict that goes back to the late 1950s.

The sponsors of this site, who run a neighborhood patrol called *Shmirah* (the act of watching), consider themselves responsible for watching out for the rights of the members of the Crown Heights Jewish community. Not all the community's threats come from outside, as demonstrated by this entry from the log of Shmirah located at this Web site:

"Monday 11:00 P.M.: Shmirah received a call from a lady in the woman's section of 770. (770 Eastern Parkway is the address of the central headquarters of the Lubavitch movement.) It seems that a "nice man" asked her for a donation and, after she responded by giving him a small amount, the "nice man" decided to take more for himself and mugged her. Shmirah was given a complete description and started canvassing the area looking for the thief. From the description, Shmirah felt that they knew who the thief was and one unit was sent to 770 to meet with the victim and to show her a picture of the suspect. The complainant identified the thief as a man who answers to the name "Eddy." Shmirah looked for the thief in all his usual hideouts, but was unable to find him. The next day, two Shmirah units saw "Eddy" in Williamsburg. The Shmirah units approached him and asked him what he was doing in Crown Heights the night before, since he had been kicked out of Crown Heights and warned never to return by Shmirah. "Eddy" then responded, "I did not touch the lady's purse!" The Shmirah units had never asked him about a purse. When the units started to question him further, he threatened them with a bloody drug-needle, claiming he had AIDS and would stick the units with the needle. The units were then forced into calming him down, which is only a fraction of what he will earn if he is seen in Crown Heights again. This "nice man"—"Eddy", is a Sephardic, dark male with black hair and a black beard. He wears an old black rain coat, dark pants, a white shirt and is always asking for money for a different reason. He is extremely dangerous and Shmirah should be called immediately if anyone fitting his description is seen asking for money.

For more information on Crown Heights Jewry, see our chapter on Chabad.

Jewish Life in the Bay Area

http://www.jewish.com/resource/toc.htm

Jewish federations were once known as the Welfare Fund. They're often thought of in conjunction with United Jewish Appeal, but the federations of today reach the Jewish community with a much broader stroke.

The three federations in this area are: the Jewish Community Federation of San Francisco, the Peninsula,

Marin and Sonoma Counties; the Jewish Federation of the Greater East Bay; and the Jewish Federation of Greater San Jose.

While the primary function of each is to sustain Jewish life and the Jewish people through encouraging the tradition of *tzedakah*—righteous giving—from Jewish individuals who live in the area, each federation is intimately involved with its entire community.

This page, presented by the *Jewish Bulletin* of Northern California, is rich in content. It includes information on:

- Lifecycle events
- Religious life & congregations
- Agencies & organizations
- Social services
- Children & youth
- Senior services
- College & adult education
- Socializing & schmoozing
- Israel connections
- Jewish media
- Culture, arts & judaica
- Simchas & celebrations
- Food & nosherei
- Business & services

What is unique about this site is the ability of a "local" Jewish newspaper to go way beyond normal print media to meet the needs of the community. This page represents a sizable investment in time, effort and funds to make a community newspaper go on-line. It is to be congratulated for its efforts.

This site is also the basis for the AOL Jewish Community Site. The AOL site is the most comprehensive Jewish site of any of the major on-line services.

Portland, Oregon

http://www.teleport.com/~jreview/frame2/frame2.html

The first Jews in this area arrived in the early 1850s, part of the westward movement that populated the then-remote Northwestern territories. Successive generations of Jewish settlers to the area mirrored the different Jewish migrations to the U.S. First they came from Germany and then from Russia and Poland. The community they built was diversified, but also quite cohesive and stronger than their small numbers would appear to indicate. Many other Jewish communities of this size have long since disappeared from existence. It is very difficult to ascertain why other communities with the same sociological profile disappeared while Portland hung on. Indeed, Portland has launched a fair number of important Jewish personalities.

This site offers a picture of a vital Jewish community and its institutions. The Institute for Judaic Studies was established in Portland in 1984, in response to increased interest in the role played by Jewish history, thought, and culture in the development of Western civilization. The site also has a list of kosher-food providers in the Portland area, and synagogues and temples in Oregon and Northern California. This is a useful and interesting site.

South Palm Beach, Florida

http://www.levisjcc.org/geninfo.htm

The Adolph and Rose Levis Jewish Community Center serves the entire South Palm Beach County community. It acts as a central meeting place, and a variety of JCC activities and programs enrich the area's Jewish identity, education, and community life.

Programs include an early childhood learning center; an elaborate sports, health and fitness center; children's programs; JCC camp; teen and tween events; cultural arts events and exhibits and adult programs and classes.

The site is very well organized and reflects the overall character of the Center and its policies.

Jewish People in Winona

http://wms.luminet.net/demographics/jewish/

As early as 1856, the Jews of St. Paul built Minnesota's first synagogue, Mount Zion Temple. Between 1881 and 1924, nearly 3,000,000 Jews emigrated from Europe to the United States. Although most, on arrival from Eastern Europe (primarily Poland, Russia, Rumania, and Lithuania), stayed in eastern cities like New York, approximately 8,000 Jews lived in Minneapolis by 1907.

By 1920, 4,000 Jews lived in small Minnesota towns. Many opened family-owned businesses. Frequently, peddlers or salesmen of small items, junk collectors and dealers were Jewish, since these businesses required little start-up money.

This site explains some of the hardships of rural Jewish life:

> "Maintaining Jewish culture and religion in small rural towns is difficult with no Jewish school, no synagogue or rabbi, and few families. But Winona's families are resourceful, creative, and enthusiastic about keeping the traditions and holidays of their faith.
>
> "The father of one family recites Jewish prayers each morning, wearing the traditional prayer scarf. Another family gathers every Friday night for the traditional Sabbath evening saying prayers, lighting candles, and enjoying a dinner together."

This site is maintained by the community of Winona as a way to display the diverse lifestyles available in Winona. It also shows the difficulties in maintaining a Jewish identity away from the main centers of Jewish life, especially when the community is not large enough to support its own schools, synagogues, and other religious institutions. It gives one a good perspective of life in a small town Jewish community. The site also has very interesting demographic information on Winona and its inhabitants.

The Winona Middle School received a Luminet Learningware grant to create this site. It was money well spent.

Jewish Toronto
http://www.feduja.org/

The Canadian Jewish experience has been an interesting one. Jews first settled in Canada at the same time that they came to the United States. Jewish communities developed in far-flung outposts of Canada. Jewish traders and merchants were in small towns in Saskatchewan and Quebec, and in Vancouver and Alberta and the Maritimes. However, in this century most of Canada's Jews have opted for two major population centers, Toronto and Montreal. Less than two decades ago, Montreal had the undisputed title as Canada's major Jewish population center.

Today, Toronto is Canada's largest and fastest-growing Jewish community. During the past decades, its population has increased significantly because of a large migration of Jews from Montreal caused by the political upheaveal the French Seperatists movement brought to the province. The community is well organized, and this organization is reflected in the Web site of the Toronto Jewish community, sponsored by the UJA Federation of Greater Toronto. You can find a great deal of information on this site. The community calendar tells you what's happening in Toronto on any given day. The community services listings are the most extensive of their type on the Web. The site includes every aspect of Jewish life in Toronto and provides links to other communities in North America as well. It is a model site for others to emulate.

There is no single major site for Montreal Jewry, perhaps due to the changes in Montreal's Jewish community during the past several decades.

The Maui Jewish Congregation
http://www.aloha.net/~bigrich/mjc.html

There is very little on this page from the Maui Jewish Congregation, as it is still under construction. There has been a Jewish presence in Hawaii for a very long time, but the resident community has always been small and has never been very organized. The limited information on this site might be of interest to Jewish travelers to Hawaii. By contacting one of the people linked to this site you can find out more about the community, its history, and its resources.

Detroit's Jewish Web

http://www.metroguide.com/jewishweb/index.html

Detroit has the largest Jewish community in Michigan. This site describes the many organizations and activities in the area. Unfortunately, the site itself has little pizzazz. Toronto, Portland, and Winona are good models to use to spruce this Web site up. The site does not accurately reflect the vitality of the community and its shopping directory is merely a link to Detroit's Internet Marketing Guide and does not reflect Jewish communal resources.

Jewish New Mexico

http://www.swcp.com/~thelink/

The Link is New Mexico's Jewish newspaper. It is distributed in print format and is regularly updated on this Web site. The Jewish community in New Mexico is not very large, but it is active and is fiercely proud of its heritage.

More of this heritage can be understood by visiting another Web site, that of the Bloom Southwest Jewish Archives. That site at http://dizzy.library.arizona.edu:80/images/swja/info.html. is one of my favorites. It has a great deal of information about Jewish settlement on the western frontier. Did you know that there was a Jewish cemetery in Boot Hill? See if you can find the information about it on the Southwest Jewish Archives site. You're in for a few surprises.

United States Southwestern history has traditionally focused on the contributions of Native American peoples, Hispanic peoples, and Western European peoples, but has not documented the histories and contributions of Jewish pioneers to the Southwest. These Jewish pioneers not only built Jewish communities, but also made significant contributions to the development of the Southwest.

This site lists synagogues, temples and other Jewish institutions in New Mexico.

Olam Katan

http://ideasign.com/~olamkatan/

Olam Katan (small world) is an Internet mailing-list discussion group for Jews in small communities, rural situations and small congregations. The mailing list is open to subscription and contribution by any Jews in rural areas, small Jewish communities and small congregations, those who have lived in those situations or who have an interest in Jews and Jewish communities in those situations. It is dedicated to enhancing Jewish life in those settings.

Not all Jews live in the major cities of the United States and Canada and have access to the resources of these metropolitan centers. This site is an effort to reach the small communities and join in sharing their trials and tribulations. It is also viewed as a means of overcoming their isolation and finding resolution to their common problems.

Several years ago I published a CD-ROM entitled *The First Electronic Jewish Bookshelf.* I was astounded by the number of inquiries and sales that I received from small communities around the United States (and throughout the world). Jews living in these small communities are afflicted with a deep sense of isolation.

Palo Alto

http://www.paloaltojcc.org/

"Welcome to our corner of cyberspace: the Albert L. Schultz Palo Alto Jewish Community Center Home Page. We offer a wide variety of programs for people of all interests, ages and backgrounds. We feature a full service health & fitness center, preschool, day care, international entertainers, programs in performing and fine arts, senior services and more."

This site represents more than just the JCC listings indicated by the welcoming page. It reveals a lot about Palo Alto, which has an interesting Jewish community. Many of its Jewish inhabitants came from the Northeastern U.S. There are also computer programmers and scientists from Silicon Valley and the aircraft industries, and representatives of most professions and trades in the United States. You'll find a page for the Russian Department of the JCC which caters to the needs of America's newest Jewish immigrants, those coming from the former Soviet Union. This site gives you some understanding of the problems that Jewish communal institutions have in servicing the varied interests of their constituencies and how they overcome them.

A Guide to Jewish Philadelphia

http://www.shamash.org/places/phila/jfgp/guide/

Philadelphia is home to a very sizable Jewish population, and is one of the oldest Jewish communities in the United States. It houses a number of national Jewish institutions, such as The National Museum of American Jewish History and the Balch Museum of Ethnic Studies and was the focus of early Jewish life in the Colonial period. The site contains information about Jewish services in the area.

Unfortunately, the site does not reflect the vitality of the community, nor does it have any strong identity of its own. It is merely a series of lists of organizations and the workings of the local Federation which sponsors the site.

For more information on Jewish activities in Philadelphia, you would do well to look at the home page of the *Philadelphia Jewish Exponent*, one of the finest Jewish papers in the country. Their site is:
http://www.libertynet.org/~exponent/960516/960516.html.

The Exponent's site is not updated every week. But it is worth looking at anyhow. It gives you the feel of the pulse of the Jewish community in Greater Philadelphia.

Reading

http://www.berksweb.com/jcc/jewhist.html

The best part of this Web site is the early Jewish history page by George M. Meiser IX and Gloria Jean Meiser. A quote from this work puts Reading, Pennsylvania's Jewish history in perspective:

> "It is highly probable that there were Jews residing in Reading as early as 1753—or earlier. There may have been more than we'll ever know, as those who came into Berks during the early years were nearly all German Jews who, by name and language, were not readily distinguishable from their Pennsylvania Dutch neighbors. From the tax lists of the 1750s, we can be certain only of Lyon Nathan, Meyer Josephson, and Moses Heyman.
>
> "Christopher Sauer's Germantown newspaper for July 8, 1758 carried an ad stating that "Myer Josephson, formerly occupying Moses Heyman's store, Reading, has opened a new store in Steinmetz's house, at the Market Place."

The fortunes of the Jewish community have changed with the times and the migration of its Jewish inhabitants to other areas of Pennsylvania and other states as well. Reading is probably typical of the smaller and midsize Jewish communities that popped up all along the Eastern seaboard.

The modest number of links on this site accurately reflect the state of the Reading Jewish community.

St. Thomas Hebrew Congregation

http://www.usvi.net/caribcat/hebrew.html

The only resources on this site are: the history of St. Thomas by its author; a few links; and some colorful pictures of the Jewish congregation. The lively history section, written by Vivian Williamson-Bryan, is worth a read. Here's a bit of it:

> "As things go in St. Thomas 200 years is not breathtakingly old—after all, Columbus did stumble upon these islands in 1493... St. Croix was actually colonized before us but in 1671 a permanent settlement was established in St. Thomas by the

Danes (the Danish flavor is still quite evident—we may be owned by the U.S. now but it's obvious they weren't the first). Being rather literally minded souls, they named the town Taphus since it was party headquarters for the area's pirates (always a colorful, fun-loving lot) and also provided a big night out for the island's planters. Over time, though, things became more staid (sounds kind of like life, doesn't it?) and religion gained a foothold. There were a number of houses of worship established in the 18th century and 1796 was the year for the Hebrew Congregation. Things did not exactly start with a bang—records show that in 1801 only 9 families belonged. But the island's sugar, molasses and rum trades were a draw for Jewish merchants, ship chandlers (those pirates needed supplies) and traders so things were bound to grow. Today there are approximately 600 members—not a huge amount when compared to the Lutheran or Moravian churches (the Lutherans, of course, had a big boost from the Danish settlers and the Moravians were the first to send missionaries to proselytize among the slaves) but it's always been a very influential group. Probably the most famous member (there have been a couple of Virgin Islands governors and at least one U.S. senator but unless you're from here I'm sure you've never heard of them) was Camille Pissaro, the father of French Impressionism (yes, he's a born Thomian—our world-famous native son)."

Jews in San Diego
http://www.jewishinsandiego.org/

Both San Diego and its adjacent community of La Jolla represent a lifestyle different from anything else you will experience in the United States. As of this writing, the Web page was newly up and running. Sponsored by the United Jewish Federation of San Diego, it has listings of agencies, a community calendar, and lists of schools, congregations, and other local Jewish organizations and stores.

Jews In Seattle
http://www.jewishinseattle.org/

The first Jewish settlers came to Seattle in the 1860s. It was a slow beginning, but the community increased with

Alaskan gold discoveries at the turn of the century. Seattle was a port of embarkation for the Yukon and Klondike, and Jewish merchants from all parts of the country converged on Seattle to become a part of the gold rush. Seattle has become a vibrant Jewish community, and has added a large population of Sephardim who came to Seattle from Turkey and the Island of Rhodes early in this century. Today the children of 19th-century merchants are employed in Seattle's aircraft and computer industries. While the Seattle Jewish community is not large, it is well organized and vibrant.

The site, sponsored by the Jewish Federation of Greater Seattle, contains a great deal of information about Seattle's Jewish community, and also has interesting links to the general community. Inasmuch as Seattle is an important hub for the computer and aerospace industries, it gets a lot of interest from young professionals. To serve one of the needs of these newcomers, this site offers a registration service for Jewish families interested in moving to Seattle—a neat touch!

Shalom Tucson

http://www.tucson.com/JewishFed/JewishFed.html

The Tucson area is the home of some 20,000 Jews. It is an active community and has extensive Jewish resources, including a large Jewish Community Center, a day school, synagogues of all persuasions and a Hillel presence at the University of Arizona.

One of the most interesting institutions in this communal network is Handmaker Jewish Services for the Aging. This center has a wide variety of services and programs for the elderly. It includes a rehabilitation center, apartments, and even a hospice.

The Jewish Federation of Tucson site also lists the Jewish Community Foundation and other community and Jewish links.

Washington DC Metro Area Jewish Community Pages

http://www.dcort.org/

The area covered by this site includes both Washington D.C. and surrounding communities including: Arlington; Alexandria; Falls Church; Bowie; Burke; Gaithersburg; Germantown; Fairfax; Laurel; Olney; Potomac; Prince George's; Reston; Rockville; Silver Spring; Temple Hills; Wheaton; and White Oak.

The D.C. area is beautiful and of great interest to Jews throughout the United States. In addition to being the capital of our nation, it is also the home of some major Jewish institutions, not the least of which is the U.S. Memorial Holocaust Museum, which draws visitors from every part of the world. In our museum chapter we also list several other Washington-based Jewish museums, including: The Jewish War Veterans National Museum of American Jewish Military History; The B'nai B'rith Museum; and the Lillian and Albert Small Jewish Museum, none of which should be left off a visit to the nation's capital.

The site contains a very useful "clickable" map of the entire area, and there are local maps for each of the regions. If you know anything about Washington, you know the Beltway that surrounds this metropolitan area is a navigational challenge to the visitor. Thus, the maps on this site make it very worthwhile. The site is usually updated quite regularly. However, during the summer months, the Webmasters seem to be a little slow in updating, perhaps because official Washington is pretty quiet during the summer and the area's several campuses are without their large student body.

In addition to the distinctly Jewish sites in museum, you should note that Jewish contributions to Washington are to be found in literally every corner of every major institution of the city. You'll find them at The Smithsonian; in the National Portrait Gallery that contains hundreds of famous

Jewish portraits; at the Hirschhorn Museum, which was donated by a well known Jewish art collector; The Library of Congress with its vast Judaica collection; and many others. Jews have played a vital part in the development of this country and you can feel it in many places in D.C.

Vancouver's Jewish History

http://www.interchg.ubc.ca/jfgv/

> "The Jewish population in Greater Vancouver has grown dramatically over the last 100 years and is now the third-largest Canadian Jewish community after Toronto and Montreal. From a community with the majority of its citizens residing within walking distance of each other in the East End (and a few wealthier ones in the West End), Jews now live from Lion's Bay to the United States border, and from the University Endowment Lands to Chilliwack. From a community of peddlers, small trades and craftsmen, it has become a community of managers, business persons, and professionals."

This Web site contains information about Vancouver's vibrant Jewish community. The site itself is still under construction by the Jewish Federation of Vancouver. When it's completed it will contain information on community resources, education, a focus on youth, a community hotline, a Jewish library, information for newcomers to Vancouver, Jewish festivals, a Jewish community calendar and more.

Another Vancouver site is of interest:

The Sephardic Community

http://www.direct.ca/burton/bethhamidrash

This site includes a history of the Sephardic community of the city as seen through the eyes of its Sephardic congregation, Beth Hamidrash.

"Our community became organized as a functioning body in the late 1960s. It is a traditional, heterogeneous congregation comprising Jews from India, Shanghai, Kobe and the United Kingdom. Beth Hamidrash congregants are mainly of Iraqi origin as well as Moroccan, Egyptian, Yemeni, Syrian, Spanish-Portugese, Israelis and others.

"The diverse origins of our congregants have made our society and synagogue an exciting place for social, religious and educational activities and for culinary experiences. Despite our different backgrounds, a remarkable sense of harmony prevails."

This page also has links to a number of Sephardic Web sites.

Major Denominations within Judaism

Judaism has long been a fractured entity. The Bible is replete with arguments among our patriarchs and this practice has continued to the present. Visit even the smallest towns and villages in America and you'll often find an Orthodox and a Conservative synagogue and/or a Reform temple. In the larger cities you might also find a synagogue affiliated with the Reconstructionist, Traditionalist, or Humanist movement. All are vying for the attention of a limited Jewish clientele.

Historically, many Conservative and Reform temples started out as Orthodox institutions. Why? Because the vast majority of European immigrants who came to this country were Orthodox, as were their parents and grandparents and the generations before them. When the immigrants came to this country, they felt duty-bound to carry on the traditions of their ancestors. But for many of the immigrants and their children, Orthodoxy became anathema. It didn't seem to relate to their desire to become "real Americans." It also hindered their entrance into the mainstream of American life. "Real Americans" didn't keep kosher or observe the Sabbath. They didn't stay within their own fold and they didn't do things that marked them as being different.

Additionally, the immigrant Jews did not have a real support structure. The communal institutions that were the support system of their old towns and villages were nonexistent in America. The language barrier between the young and the old complicated issues even further.

Finally, the Jew in America was a minority member of a larger society. He couldn't fall back upon his Jewishness.

But as the Jews became a part of America, they began to realize that there was nothing wrong with being Jewish. Indeed, it was the thing to do. You went back to your roots and proclaimed your ancestry—unless it had already been separated from you by intermarriage and assimilation. At the same time, however, many sought a different type of Judaism than that which was practiced by their parents and grandparents. It had to represent the new realities of American life and times. Often by the time Jews realized their state of limbo between old country and new world, they had already disappeared from a chain of tradition that had linked their ancestors for many thousands of years.

Judaism in America today is in itself an interesting phenomenon. By all rights, Jews should have disappeared into the fabric of American society. It probably would have except for the external factors facing American Jews, namely the Holocaust and the emergence of the State of Israel. Both of these lent a sense of vitality to American Jewry and gave it a new impetus—a new lease on life. These events drew the Jewish consciousness back from the recesses of the American Jewish mindset to the forefront of his being.

In the process, American Jewry developed three major denominations or organizational and belief structures.

Orthodoxy is the most traditional of these denominations. It calls for the adherence to a belief system and a system of religious practice that dates back thousands of years. It views the Torah and its contents and commandments as divine. It requires a major commitment by its adherents, a commitment to the observance of the 613 commandments that are enunciated in the Five Books of Moses and the Oral Law as enunciated in the Talmud and its ancillary literature. From a theological standpoint, it requires adherence to the strict rules of the Sabbath and of Kashruth and of family purity. From an issue standpoint, it requires gender-separated seating in the synagogue, the observance of Sabbath practices, and the retention of the purity of the Jewish family.

Orthodox Judaism itself has an infinite number of varieties, based upon the birthplace and traditions of previous generations. These really fall into three categories: *Ashkenazim* and *Sephardim*, representing the Jews of the Western Europe and the Levant, and of *Chasidim*, representing Jews from Poland and Russia from the time of the birth of Chasidism as signified by the Baal Shem Tov.

With all their differences in customs, the religious beliefs of these groups are quite uniform. You can pray in a Chasidic synagogue in Jerusalem or an Orthodox Sephardic synagogue in St. Louis and feel quite comfortable with both the prayerbook and the philosophy and language of prayer.

The Reform movement represents a completely different mindset. There is no separation of the sexes in the synagogue. The laws of kosher food are generally not adhered to. Travel on the Sabbath and holidays is a matter of common and accepted practice. The basic belief in the immutability of Jewish law is far removed from the mindset of Reform theology, as is the concept of the oral tradition within the corpus of Jewish law. During the 19th century, the Reform movement made it very clear that it rejected the concept of a return to Zion, a hallmark of Orthodox Jewish belief. There was the rejection of many basic laws of Judaism and the adoption instead of an Americanized form of Judaism which in many ways was reminiscent of American Protestantism. It was also the easiest form of Judaism to follow. You didn't have to stand out either in form or dress. You could mix with the non-Jew by adopting his clothing and dietary habits and you could even intermarry with him. Reform Jews have not always remained in the Jewish fold for generations on end. Instead Reform Judaism has sometimes acted as a stepping stone into full absorption by American society. The most telling of Reform Jewish practices is the acceptance of *patrilineal descent*—a Jewish lineage based upon the religion of the father rather than the mother. This is one of the major issues, if not the major issue, between other more traditional forms of Judaism and Reform Judaism. It is a departure from basic Biblical practice and threatens the traditional fabric of Jewish existence. Reform Judaism is also the largest Jewish denomination in the United States.

Conservative Judaism stands in the middle of this fracas. It recognizes the authenticity of the Torah and its traditions. Yet it deems it necessary to accommodate itself to the signs of the times. Most Conservative synagogues have mixed seating. In deference to the change in the modern work ethic, many Conservative synagogues have their major service on Friday evenings rather than on the Sabbath itself. Women participate in the service and, as of late, have even been granted access to the Rabbinate, which has been a traditional stronghold of men in Orthodox Judaism. The thrust of the Conservative movement is the preservation of basic Jewish concepts without the adherence to the minutiae of Jewish religious law. For many years, this theology propelled Conservative Judaism into the forefront of the American Jewish religious consciousness. In recent years it has also provided it with a great deal of difficulty. A major concern within the more traditional ranks of the Conservative movement has been the acceptance of the ordination of women. This has caused a defection from the movement by many of those minds which have lent the most theological credence to the movement itself.

Aside from the thorny theological issues involved, the Conservative movement has also had to come to grips with the polarization of American Jewry and religious practice—a polarization which has on the one hand seen Orthodox Judaism veer to the right, and on the other hand watched the Reform movement accept and embrace Israel and the Hebrew language which it all but abandoned just a century ago. In other words, Reform Judaism has become a bit more traditional, Orthodoxy even more strictly observant of religious practices and beliefs, and the Conservative movement has been left in a nebulous theological position.

Movements in Judaism

http://members.aol.com/jewfaq/movement.htm

This is a short summary of the differences among various Jewish denominations. It is one author's point of view. The author starts off with the following statement:

> "The different sects or denominations of Judaism are generally referred to as movements. The differences between Jewish movements are not nearly as great as the differences between Christian denominations. The differences between Orthodoxy and Reform Judaism are not much greater than the differences between the liberal and fundamentalist wings of the Baptist denomination of Christianity. "

While I cannot categorize the differences among various Christian denominations, I think it unwise to compare these differences with those of Jewish denominations. I think that many Jewish theologians would find fault with this reasoning. However, the article itself is quite good. It compares these divisions of Jewish theology:

- Movements before the 20th century
- Movements in 20th century United States
- Movements in 20th century Israel
- Movements in 20th century United Kingdom

Orthodox

Orthodoxy is the least centralized of the American Jewish movements. While each of the other major movements in America has a single synagogue union, seminary (although there has been a division recently within Conservatism's Jewish Theological Seminary), and Rabbinical association, the Orthodox world is a jumble of loosely knit and independent institutional organizations. A great description of the various movements within Orthodoxy appears at Professor Eliezer Segal's home page (http://www.ucalgary.ca/~elsegal/), and another worth a look is at http://shamash.org/lists/ scjfaq/html/faq/02-07.html.

The Orthodox Union
http://www.ou.org

The Orthodox Union is the largest Orthodox synagogue organization, serving approximately 1,000 congregations in North America. Its home page, called *OU Online*, is the equivalent of a polished cyber-press release. The OU is best known for its supervision of kosher foods. The OU Kashruth directory for Passover appears on this site.

Two very useful aspects of this site are its listing of synagogues and its large number of links relating to substantive Jewish knowledge. The synagogue listing includes links to Web pages of Orthodox synagogues all over the world, whether OU affiliated or not. It's clear when viewing this page, however, that most Orthodox synagogues are not yet linked up. On the other hand, there is a nice on-line facility to register your Orthodox organization and get a free, very basic listing.

The links to Jewish information include Torah commentary, Jewish law (e.g., in-depth writings on kashruth and various other rituals), and viewpoints on current events. You can even arrange for a message to be placed at the Kotel (Western Wall)—an interesting mixture of technology and tradition.

As a nice touch, the front page lets you choose whether you want subsequent pages with or without frames and extensive graphics. This site has just undergone a major revamping.

National Council of Young Israel
http://www.youngisrael.org.il/

The National Council of Young Israel (NCYI), founded in 1912, serves as the national coordinating agency for nearly 150 orthodox congregations throughout the United States and Canada. This site has links to other NCYI branches, as well as a complete congregational directory.

The Young Israel movement made an early name for itself with its campus programs. The Young Israel House at Cornell University was the first kosher university dining program in the United States; during the Second World War and the Korean and Vietnam conflicts, it enabled Jewish soldiers to gain access to kosher food and Jewish facilities.

The organization's goals are encapsulated in this quote from the site:

"The aims and purposes of the organization shall be to foster and maintain a program of spiritual, cultural, social and communal activity towards the advancement and perpetuation of traditional Torah-true Judaism; and to instill into American Jewish youth an understanding and appreciation of the high ethical and spiritual values of Judaism and demonstrate the compatibility of the ancient faith of Israel with good Americanism."

Yeshiva University
http://yu1.yu.edu/

Yeshiva University in New York City is America's oldest and most comprehensive institution of higher education under Jewish auspices. The Rabbi Isaac Elchanan Theological Seminary (RIETS), an affiliate of YU, produces the largest share of Orthodox rabbis of any school in the United States RIETS claims to be the western hemisphere's largest center for higher learning in the Orthodox tradition. In addition to the rabbinical ordination program, RIETS has a school of Jewish music, and graduate and post-graduate Talmudic studies programs.

Additionally, YU has undergraduate and a number of highly respected graduate programs, such as the Benjamin Cardozo School of Law and the Albert Einstein School of Medicine.

The site for YU is a bit sparse. Not all the schools have links, and most of those that do have only the essential information—with the notable exception of the Medical School, which has links to many other medical resources and affiliated hospitals.

Conservative

Jewish Theological Seminary
http://www.jtsa.edu/

This is probably the most attractive site of all the Jewish seminaries in the United States. Exquisitely designed, this site has a great deal of information regarding the school, its programs, press releases, publications, and more, including links to all Conservative affiliates and synagogues that have Web pages—all in an well-organized and pleasant presentation. The "What's New" section offers links to the current week's Torah Commentary (the chancellor's commentary is archived back to 1993), as well as commentary on current events.

JTSA, as its page on academic programs tells you, is not only a rabbinical school, but also offers graduate and undergraduate degrees, and houses the Miller Cantorial School. The Los Angeles branch has recently moved toward independence from the rest of the JTSA organization.

Most impressive are the search capabilities at this site, which allow the user to search through Web pages or four archived mailing lists that JTSA maintains.

United Synagogue of Conservative Judaism
http://www.uscj.org/

This is the organization of about 800 Conservative synagogues in North America. The site has links to the full slate of Conservative organizations (Men's Clubs, Women's League, USY, etc.), past press releases, etc. The design makes it a bit difficult to navigate, although there is an option for a frames version which is easier. The site has a link to all

Conservative synagogues that have Web pages, but, curiously, it is a different list than the one found in the JTSA pages.

Union for Traditional Judaism

The Union for Traditional Judaism
http://www.utj.org/business/home/

The Union for Traditional Judaism is the newest of American Jewish denominations. In terms of traditional Jewish observance, it is considered somewhere between Conservative and Orthodox.

It is evident from the Web site that UTJ is a new and still somewhat small movement. Nevertheless, they've done a nice job explaining what they are about—providing an FAQ section and a "declaration of principles." The declaration reads in part:

> "The Union for Traditional Judaism is an organization of lay people, educators, talmudic scholars, cantors and pulpit rabbis who are dedicated to the principles of Traditional Judaism. Through innovative outreach projects, we hope to bring the greatest possible number of Jews closer to an open-minded observant Jewish lifestyle."

Reconstructionism

The Jewish Reconstructionist Federation
http://shamash.org/jrf/

Reconstructionism is the second-newest, and probably second-smallest, Jewish movement in the United States (next to the Union for Traditional Judaism).

Like the UTJ site, this site also reflects on their modest size. It is a very basic site, but with links to a complete directory of Reconstructionist congregations, and other well-written essential information—including a definition of Reconstructionism.

"Reconstructionists define Judaism as the evolving religious civilization of the Jewish people. By "evolving" we mean that Judaism has changed over the centuries of its existence. The faith of the ancient Israelites in the days of Solomon's Temple was not the same as that of the early rabbis. And neither of those faiths was the same as that of our more recent European ancestors. Each generation of Jews has subtly reshaped the faith and traditions of the Jewish people. Reconstructionist Jews seek to nurture this evolution."

Reform

Reform Judaism Home Page
http://shamash.org/reform/

An exceptionally well-organized set of Web pages, this thorough site has links to the three major arms of the Reform Movement (HUC-JIR, the rabbinical school; the UAHC, representing the approximately 1,000 synagogues of the movement; and the CCAR, the rabbinical conference); as well as links to the full alphabet of other major Reform organizations and affiliates that are either closely related to, or actually under the auspices of, one of the three major arms.

A particularly innovative feature is the "Self-Guided Tour of the Reform Web Sites," which is a nice way to cruise the site, checking out the highlights, without having to use the time-consuming hit-or-miss method. Another convenient feature is a search capability that allows the user to search the entire Web site for particular subjects.

The Union of American Hebrew Congregations
http://shamash.org/reform/uahc/

As a union of congregations, the UAHC is dedicated to maintaining the synagogue as the very center of Jewish life. It is the synagogue that transforms individual members into caring, committed Jews, inspiring them to live Jewish lives. We also understand that our synagogues are the door through which our members encounter a larger entity, *K'lal Yisrael*, the people of Israel.

As the description indicates, the UAHC is the synagogue arm of the Reform Jewish community in North America, representing some 1,000 institutions. A table of links appears on the home page, laid out in an easy manner for you to jump where you need to go. There is a tremendous amount of information about the UAHC and its programs and services here.

The UAHC's directory of congregations is the best of the movements. Not only is each congregation listed (along with a link to those who have Web pages), but you can search for congregations in various ways (region, state, city, synagogue name).

Other notable features include a list of Jewish resources on the Net of interest to Reform Jews, links to important current and historical documents of Reform Judaism, and an excellent searching tool for the on-line catalog of its music publishing arm, Transcontinental Music.

Hebrew Union College—Jewish Institute of Religion

http://www.huc.edu/

HUC-JIR, founded in 1875, is the leading educational institution for Reform Judaism. Most prominent, of course, is the rabbinical school, and the School of Sacred Music (for cantors). But there are various other graduate and undergraduate degrees offered at their four campuses. One of the more unique offerings of the site is the ability to do an on-line search of e-mail addresses of HUC-JIR students, faculty, and staff.

The New York Kollel, an affiliate of HUC-JIR, is a model for what a school ought to offer at its Web site. This excellent site includes a complete course guide, descriptions of each class, and biographies of the instructors teaching them. Additionally, the Kollel offers a few Internet classes.

The Central Conference of American Rabbis

http://shamash.org/reform/ccar/

The CCAR is the rabbinical arm of the Reform movement. The site has links to the *CCAR Journal*, where the table of contents and a few articles are available, and the CCAR Press, which boasts a complete catalog and ordering information.

Most impressive are their plans to put Reform Responsa on-line. Currently only the index is available, but it is a rather large one (over 90K), and it is accompanied by detailed citations.

Another Web site of particular interest to Reform Jews is:

http://shamash.org/reform/uahc/resc.html#ref

This site provides links to a variety of Internet resources that are geared to Reform Judaism. Among the sites listed are:

http://shamash.org/lists/scj-faq/HTML/faq/18-index.html

and

http://shamash.org/lists/scj-faq/HTML/faq/18-index.html

The former is a question and answer page about Reform Judaism. The latter is an index to the Reform Judaism Reading List.

The Egalitarian Chavura

http://www.mit.edu:8001/afs/athena.mit.edu/activity/h/hillel
/www/EGAL/egal.html

"The MIT Egalitarian Chavura, associated with MIT Hillel, is a group started on the MIT campus during the summer of 1994 [to]... promote Judaism by combining the previous Reform and Conservative minyans into a group that can appeal religiously to a large portion of Jews on campus... provide a comfortable environment for meeting other Jewish students... draw in previously unaffiliated members of the MIT Jewish community.

World Union for Progressive Judaism

http://shamash.org/reform/wupj/

The World Union for Progressive Judaism was founded in London in 1926. In North America, both the Reform and Reconstructionist movements are affiliated with the WUPJ. In the rest of the world, various other incarnations of Reform, usually called the Liberal or Progressive movements, are the affiliates of the WUPJ. While this site is only one page, it is useful because it has a collection of links to Progressive sites and congregations around the world.

Chabad

My first brush with Chabad came some forty years ago. We had just moved to Crown Heights, in Brooklyn, New York. 770 Eastern Parkway, the internationally known address of the Lubavitch movement, was just a few blocks from my home On the way to Sabbath morning services, I would walk up Kingston Avenue with the Lubavitch Chasidim as they made their way up the avenue. At Eastern Parkway, they would turn left and head toward 770 and I would turn right and go to the Young Israel of Eastern Parkway.

Apart from the Sabbath greetings that passed between us there was little communication between our two worlds. Lubavitch represented generations of Eastern European Jewry that I knew nothing about. The Young Israel movement represented a completely different type of Judaism. The men wore natty suits and ties. The ladies dressed in the latest fashions. We attended Lithuanian yeshivot and then went on to colleges and universities. The Lubavitch reveled in a combination of Chasidism and mysticism and dressed the way my grandparents did when they lived in Russia a century before.

Indeed, Lubavitch disappeared from my mind until my college days. I was active in the first days of the struggle for the release of Jews from the Soviet Union. In the early 60s it was very difficult to keep Passover in Russia. There wasn't a lot of food to begin with, but kosher food and matzot were almost impossible to obtain. One day we were contacted by Lubavitch emissaries and asked to help send thousands of

Passover packages to our Russian co-religionists. We began to understand the nature of the Lubavitch movement. Since the advent of Communism in 1917, the Lubavitch had gone underground—but had not left the Soviet Union. They performed circumcisions, taught classes in Jewish subjects, married individuals who wanted to keep their Jewish identity. All this was done at great sacrifice, and many Lubavitch wound up in jail, the gulag, or worse. But they never forgot their brethren, wherever they were. In later years, I would hear of Lubavitch holding Passover services in Nepal for Jewish students who "happened to be there" during the spring vacation season. I remember a counselor of mine disappearing from sight and then turning up in Milan, Italy, where the Rebbe sent him to open a branch. One day shortly before Passover, I parked my car in the Haight-Ashbury section of San Francisco. When I came back to the vehicle, I found an invitation to join a Chabad Passover Seder that was to be held a few nights later. In the course of my travels I have found the Lubavitch in every nook and cranny of the world. They have done a great deal to reach out to their fellow Jews, and this is most commendable.

When one speaks of the Lubavitch movement, one cannot avoid discussing its leadership. Until a short time ago, the Lubavitch were led by a dynamic and charismatic leader, Rabbi Menachem Mendel Schneerson of blessed memory. I had direct contact with the Rebbe on just a few occasions, but they are clearly etched in my mind's eye. The first was when I had just graduated college and was working for a Zionist organization. The organization sponsored an American tour of the then–Chief Rabbi of the Israeli Defense Force, the late Rabbi Shlomo Goren. I accompanied Rabbi Goren to various meetings around the New York area. He always wore an Israeli Army uniform because in addition to being a rabbi, he was a paratrooper. (That is a story in itself.) But he didn't know what to do for his meeting with the Rebbe. Was he to wear a uniform or rabbinical garb? I don't know why he asked me for advice, but he did. And I told him that inasmuch as he was going to see the Rebbe in his capacity as the Chief Rabbi of the IDF, it was only proper that he wear his uniform. He looked at me and smiled. When I picked him up at the hotel, he was wearing his uniform.

We traveled together to 770 Eastern Parkway and were ushered into the cavernous hall where the Rebbe was conducting one of his periodical *Farbrengen*. The *Farbrengen* defies description: Thousands of Chasidim converged on 770 and waited for the Rebbe to appear. They sang in anticipation of his arrival, and when he finally came into the room, it resounded in joyful song. The Rebbe nodded for the assemblage to settle down and they immediately would. Then the Rebbe would go into a discourse that could last several hours. Periodically, his homily on a favorite topic was interrupted for a round of singing. Occasionally the Rebbe acknowledged the presence of a visiting dignitary by raising a small glass of vodka and nodding in his direction. In the meantime, a simultaneous translation and telecast was sent out to Lubavitch Chasidim throughout the world. It was all very carefully orchestrated.

When we walked into the room it was packed. How would we ever reach the rostrum? It wasn't a problem. One of the Rebbe's assistants simply nodded his head, and the masses in front of us opened a magical pathway. I had met the Rebbe on one previous occasion, but this time I was captivated by his presence. It was an awesome experience.

Physically, the Rebbe was not an imposing figure. He was of slight stature, quite ascetic looking with but one outstanding feature—his eyes. He had the ability to look out into a room filled with thousands of people, and have each one feel he was looking at them. The famed sociologist Max Weber used the term *charisma* to describe this phenomenon; it is rarely seen in real life. The late Lubavitcher Rebbe had charisma, but he was different from most people who were blessed with this unique phenomenon: He put it to good use! He built a worldwide network of educational facilities that sought to reach every Jew—no matter his or her religious persuasion.

I attend the giant COMDEX computer trade show that takes place every winter in Las Vegas. Hundreds of thousands of people attend this extravaganza, and many thousands of them are Jewish. In the early years you had to worry about Kashruth and the Sabbath. Today if you go into the main pavilions of COMDEX, you'll find a Lubavitch sign pointing to a booth offering kosher food at a cost comparable to the other food vendors on the convention floor. It's not a big thing, but it is indicative of the Lubavitch way of operating and caring for people.

The Lubavitch movement is not afraid of technology; it uses it to reach out to the world. A broadcast center located at Lubavitch headquarters beams its message far and wide. In recent years, the Lubavitch movement has moved to the Internet to spread its message. A glance at its sites listed in this chapter will give you some idea of the vast dimension of the Lubavitch enterprise and efforts.

Unfortunately, the Rebbe died in 1994, and no successor has been named to replace him. The organization has been caught up in a cult of personality and Messianic ardor. Many people have simply forgotten about the contributions the Lubavitch movement has made to world Judaism and have focused on this aberration. This chapter will put a little more focus into the efforts of the movement and show a measure of its efforts rather than its shortcomings.

Judaism on the Internet

http://www.chabad.org/

This is Chabad's major Web site. Chabad/Lubavitch organizations throughout the world maintain their own sites. However, most of them are links to this major address.

Its [Chabad-Lubavitch's] major thrust focuses on observing for
one's self and transmitting to others the beauty, depth, awareness
and joy inherent in the Torah-true way of life. Chabad-Lubavitch is
a Chasidic movement which revitalized Jewish life by intensifying
the individual's relationship to G-d, and deep sense of devotion
and love towards one's fellow man.

Chabad-Lubavitch philosophy has developed an intellectual
perspective which helps the individual live in full accordance
with the Torah-true way of life.

The Lubavitch aim to spread the word through concrete
deeds. They have focused on a series of *Mitzvot*, or positive
commandments, to implement their program. These consist of:

1. Ahavas Yisroel—The love of one's fellow Jew
2. Chinuch—Torah education
3. Daily Torah study
4. Tefillin—The donning of Tefillin on weekdays, by
   men and boys over 13
5. Mezuzoh—The Jewish sign
6. Tzedokoh—Giving charity every weekday
7. Possession Of Jewish holy books
8. Lighting Shabbos and festival candles
9. Kashruth—Jewish dietary laws
10. Taharas Hamishpocho—The Torah perspective on
    married life

This site dwells on each of these Mitzvot in detail. It also
has links to the following areas:

- Modern Technology and Judaism
- Questions on Judaism: You should know in advance
  that the answers you receive will be consistent with the
  theology of the Chabad. Don't expect Chabad to cater
  to your interpretation of Judaism. On the other hand,
  you should also know that the Chabad-Lubavitch are,

as a matter of principle, very open and nonjudg-mental. They accept you for who you are and hope that your exposure to their philosophy will help bring you closer to Judaism.

- Request for prayer or blessing: "The righteous are greater after their death than in their lifetime" [Talmud Chulin 7b]. Jews place great importance on the ability of past generations, and in particular of great scholars and saints, to intercede on their behalf before the Almighty. During his lifetime, the Lubavitch Rebbe paid a weekly visit to the grave of his predecessor. He found comfort and strength praying at his grave. Likewise, since the demise of the Rebbe, his tomb has become a place where Lubavitch Chasidim—and non-Chasidim—from all over the world come to ask for his intercedence on their behalf. The site tells you where to find the grave, how to write a message (*kvitel*) asking for assistance, and even gives travel directions if you are inclined to visit in person.

- Multimedia—Jewish art and Music On-Line: Links to sites on: Jewish art, photo gallery, Jewish Music, Chabad melodies, a cable to Jewish life, audio tapes teaching Hebrew, and ThinkJewish—Live Streaming Audio.

- Jewish Children International—Tzivos Hashem: "Tzivos Hashem is a global organization of Jewish boys and girls up to age 13. It is designed to serve as the umbrella of Jewish identity for every Jewish child regardless of background, family status, or orientation. Tzivos Hashem is dedicated to fostering continuity and a lifetime bond with Jews, G-d, Israel and Torah by building on the natural enthusiasm, curiosity and spirituality that are so abundant in children."

- Judaism Looks at the World: This site carries infor-mation on a variety of subjects, including conversion to Judaism, circumcision, the Noahide Laws and modern technology and Judaism.

- Links to more Chabad Web sites: Here are links to Chabad Web sites around the world. You'll even find a link to the Chabad Prison Chaplaincy program in Santa Barbara, California

- The Jewish Woman: We talked about this site in our chapter on feminism.

- Jewish Mysticism: "The mystical experience, in the wide sense of the term, is an integral part of the human experience. It is native to all people, without distinction of race or creed. With some more, with others less— yet, universal. The universality of mysticism is both fascinating and problematic." Here, Chabad examines Jewish mysticism.

- An Ideal World—The Era of *Moshiach* (Messiah): *From Exile to Redemption* is an on-line book that will give you an understanding of the Chabad-Lubavitch attitude toward the coming of the Messiah. It does not make for light reading, but it gives you a better understanding about the Lubavitch emphasis on the Messiah.

- Our Children's Corner: This page contains a number of Chasidic tales. Chasidic tales are not just folk tales. They have a message to impart. They are all beautiful, and children enjoy hearing them; they're not bad for grown ups either.

- Essays on the Torah—New Items Weekly: "The Long But Short Of It"—The Talmud relates: Said Rabbi Yehoshua the son of Chanania:

"Once a child got the better of me. I was traveling, and I met with a child at a crossroads. I asked him, 'Which way to the city?' and he answered: 'This way is short and long, and this way is long and short.' I took the 'short and long' way. I soon reached the city but found my approach obstructed by gardens and orchards. So I retraced my steps and said to the child: 'My son, did you not tell me that this is the short way?' Answered the child: 'Did I not tell you that it is also long?'"

Perhaps this best describes the material on this page. I can give you a short synopsis or a long one. The short one will be too short and the long one may persuade you not to read the page. I've reached a compromise that should make everyone happy: Please read it for yourself!

- The Chabad Philosophy: What is a Chasid? What is the Chasid's mission? How is he to go about realizing this mission in the context of Lubavitch activism? What is the role of the Rebbe in all this?

"The role of a Rebbe, then, is that of a soul-geologist who manifests the latent powers and treasures concealed in all, who seeks to awaken in everyone the potential he has. He is the generator that charges and a beacon that guides, in whom all the above is succinctly crystallized. His role as mentor and counselor, whose advice and blessing is sought in matters spiritual and material, is seen in the same context: the context of responsibility toward his people."

- Judaic Text Repository—Via Gopher: More information on Chasidic resources and texts.

- World-Wide Chabad Directory Listings: A list of Chabad institutions throughout the world. You can search it by zip code, country, or name.

Havienu L'Shalom

http://www.havienu.org/index.html

"Prayer—The world stands on three things: on the Torah, on the Service [of God through prayer], and on Deeds of Kindness. [Pirke Avos 1:2].

According to Chasidic teachings, the heightened spiritual sensitivity and perception (*daas*) which results from meditative prayer (*hisbonnenus*), has effects well beyond the moment. All of one's emotions are transformed: positively benefiting one's attitude and behavior throughout the day."

This site is a Lubavitch virtual synagogue. It makes for interesting viewing and is not as heavy as some of the other Lubavitch sites.

Material on this site includes: resources, a mystic's perspective, living with the times, running and returning, practical Halacha, Beis HaMikdash, and the Rabbi's study.

CHAPTER 6

Anti-Semitism and the Holocaust

For native-born Americans like myself, it is very hard to completely comprehend the Holocaust. We can read about it. We can talk about it. But we (thankfully) can't really experience it. My family came to this country from Poland and Russia at the turn of the century. They settled in New York as did millions of other Jews. They experienced hardships and turmoil, but were for the most part unscathed by the Holocaust.

My wife, on the other hand, is a Holocaust survivor. She came to Canada as a youth, but she grew up in a home where the Holocaust was the defining moment of their existence. There were no grandparents to remember. Aunts and uncles were scattered around the globe. Babies were born to bear the names of parents and grandparents, aunts and uncles, cousins and friends—all of whom perished in the Holocaust.

We made up our minds very early in our marriage that our children would grow up to know what the Holocaust was all about. It's not something that you can just "tell them." Instead, they have had to experience it for themselves in their own way. For one child, it was a visit to Poland and the Auschwitz crematoria. For the others, it was the sight of the tattooed numbers on an aunt's forearm and the stories that were sometimes told to them by their grandparents. The Holocaust bore into their consciousness and it is a memory and an experience that they will hopefully carry with them for the rest of their lives. Similarly, many of the Web sites in this chapter offer facts and documents without much interpretation. This allows each reader to absorb the phenomenom of anti-Semitism in their own way.

The sites included in this chapter reflect my personal choices. Why were they selected?

A number of years ago I took a collegiate group to Europe and Israel. We saw Holocaust memorials in France and Italy, as well as in Israel. Each of the participants on the group was affected by a different remembrance. To some, it was Yad Vashem and its haunting Hall of Remembrance. Others saw the tomb on Mt. Zion that displays plaques for each Jewish community that was obliterated by the Nazis. Each participant of our group could point to a particular site or experience that best helped define the Holocaust for them. And I can tell you that these impressions are still with them.

I thought that in doing this chapter I would try to relive some of these experiences wth you. I don't know what someone will find important to them. It could be the Protocols of the Elders of Zion or it could be one of the photographic sites. It might be the letters of Wolf Lewkowicz or the Auschwitz Alphabet. All I can hope is that somewhere in this chapter you will find the site or sites that will reach into your heart and soul. If you can manage that and in turn can pass this information and feeling on to someone else, then I have succeeded, and perhaps together we can improve the human value system.

Acknowledging the Holocaust without changing the underlying value system which leads to positive social action is meaningless. Alexander Kimel, in *The Creed of a Holocaust Survivor*, put this need for human improvement better than I ever could, and his words are a healthy counterbalance to the hatred seen on the Web sites in this chapter:

> I believe with all my heart,
>> That the Messiah and the Kingdom of Heaven will come;
>
> When man will conquer his destructive urge,
>> And learn how to live in harmony with nature and himself.

When all the preachers of hate will be silenced,
  And man will become his brother's keeper.

When man will stop killing man, in the name of God,
  And nation will not lift weapons against nation.

When it will be, I do not know, but
  Despite all the signs to the contrary.

In the dawn of a better World, I do believe.

Precursors to anti-Semitism and the Holocaust will be better understood after visiting some of these sites:

Classical and Christian anti-Semitism
http://remember.org/History.root.classical.html

Anti-Semitism does not develop in a vaccum.In order to understand it's manifestation you must also know the social, economic and religious conditions that accompany its apperances.

> The differences Jews had with their non-Jewish neighbors led to separate social and religious lives. Intolerance and suspicion of these differences led to fear and hatred. Classical anti-Semitism, Christian anti-Semitism and Modern anti-Semitism each have their own basis. In order for the Holocaust to have occurred, it required the perpetrators to have developed and spread the most virulent strain of anti-Semitism, whose roots can be traced back to ancient times.

History and Myth
http://www.dada.it/donnini/gesing.htm

Who was Jesus and what was the role of Jews in his death? The relationship between Jesus and the Jewish people has been a focus of thought for almost two thousand years. Judaism rebuffs the Christian claims both to the divinity of Jesus and the role that Jews played in his arrest and death. One truth remains self-evident—that the ancient Christian view of a Jewish role in the death of Jesus has caused Jewish blood to be spilled in many outbreaks of anti-Semitism.

On this site David Donnini offers a short, text-heavy summary of the essential points of his research work on this topic, "hoping it will be able to help develop a free and democratic confrontation on the religious subject, especially when religions seem still to put heavy obstacles on the process of comprehension and dialogue among different peoples of the world."

On the Jewish Question by Karl Marx

http://csf.colorado.edu/cgi-bin/mfs/24/csf/web/psn/marx/Archive/ 1844-JQ/index.html

> The German Jews desire emancipation. What kind of emancipation do they desire? Civic, political emancipation. The social emancipation of the Jew is the emancipation of society from Judaism.

These lines come from the beginning and the ending of a tract by Karl Marx, the father of communism, in *On The Jewish Question.* How much pain did this little volume cause? The entire volume is on-line at this site, which is a notable contribution to the understanding of anti-Semitism.

The Protocols of the Elders of Zion

ftp://ftp.std.com/obi/Rants/Protocols/ The_Protocols_of_The_Learned_Elders_of_Zion

The Protocols of The Learned Elders of Zion is one of the most virulently anti-Semitic documents ever written. It has been deemed the intellectual basis for modern anti-Semitism. *Protocols* claims to prove the existence of an international Jewish conspiracy seeking world power. The exact date of its writing is unknown. A likely source for this screed is the 19th-century Russian secret police. *Protocols* was embraced by anti-Semites in Russian and Germany and other countries as well. In the United States, it was popularized by the influential automaker, Henry Ford, in the 1920s. Next to Hitler's *Mein Kampf, Protocols* is the single most despised piece of anti-Semitic literature ever to have been written.

You can access the full text of this work on the Web at this site.

Hitler on the *Protocols*
http://www.igc.apc.org/ddickerson/hitler-protokollen.html

In *The Holocaust: The Destruction of European Jewry 1933-1945*, Nora Levin states that "Hitler used the *Protocols* as a manual in his war to exterminate the Jews" even though he knew that the *Protocols* were an absolute forgery.

This Web page offers Hitler's thoughts about the *Protocols* in both English and German.

The Nuremburg Laws
http://www.mtsu.edu/%7Ebaustin/nurmberg.html

When the Congress of the National Socialist Workers' (Nazi) Party convened in Nuremburg, Germany in September of 1935, on their agenda was the passage of a series of laws designed to clarify the requirements of citizenship in the Third Reich, assure the purity of German blood and German honor, and clarify the position of Jews in the Reich. These laws and the numerous auxiliary laws which followed them are called the *Nuremberg Laws*.

The Nuremburg Laws were the "legal" justification for the beginning of the end of European Jewry. This Web page enumerates these laws and auxilaries.

World War II in Europe—a Timeline
http://www.historyplace.com/worldwar2/timeline/ww2time.htm

The rise and fall of the Third Reich took less than a decade. It began with the day in 1929 that Hitler became leader of the National Socialist Party and ended on May 7, 1945 when Germany surrendered to the Allies. But what happened—and when did it happen? This well-crafted on-line time line covers every major historical event of each year of this era. This Web site gives one a historical perspective by which to measure the events of World War II. It doesn't evaluate or judge them. It just marks the dates, so that we can remember them.

The Holocaust: An Historical Summary

http://www.ushmm.org/education/history.html

This site shows chronologically, both by text and time line, how the killings of the Nazi regime spread.

> In 1933 approximately nine million Jews lived in the 21 countries of Europe that would be occupied by Germany during the war. By 1945 two out of every three European Jews had been killed. Although Jews were the primary victims, hundreds of thousands of Roma (Gypsies) and at least 250,000 mentally or physically disabled persons were also victims of Nazi genocide... More than three million Soviet prisoners of war were killed because of their nationality. Poles, as well as other Slavs, were targeted for slave labor, and as a result, almost two million perished. Homosexuals and others deemed "anti-social" were also persecuted and often murdered. In addition, thousands of political and religious dissidents such as communists, socialists, trade unionists, and Jehovah's Witnesses were persecuted for their beliefs and behavior and many of these individuals died as a result of maltreatment.

This time line and the one above overlap. One is more focused in the Holocaust aspect and the other on the overall aspects of World War II. Taken together, they are invaluable in showing the spread and collapse of Hitler's Nazi empire.

Dimensions of the Holocaust

gopher://www.shamash.org:70/00/holocaust/Summary

This file contains a short survey on the dimensions of the Holocaust, published by the Institut Fuer Zeitgeschichte (Institute for Contemporary History) in Munich, Germany, in 1992. It's quite clinical in its approach. Facts and numbers. No feeling. One quote is quite telling:

> One needs to differentiate by the furnishing of such gas chambers and the gassing actions carried out within them between the mass gassings of Jews in the extermination camps build for that purpose and the gassings of smaller scale in individual, already existing concentration camps (whereby patients, seized forced laborers, war prisoners, and political prisoners among others were also victims).

I have a problem in differentiating between the different types of camps. They all served the same purpose.

The Institut Fuer Zeitgeschichte is considered an authority on this issue in Germany, and has been used as a source of information on the Holocaust in various trials of Nazi war criminals there.

Holocaust Pictures Exhibition

http://modb.oce.ulg.ac.be/schmitz/holocaust.html

This site contains a set of black and white photographs relating to the Holocaust.

An old cliche says that a picture is worth a thousand words. How many words are these pictures worth? It's hard to say, because after you see these photos, you begin to realize that words simply aren't enough to describe the indescribable.

Auschwitz-Birkenau

http://remember.org/jacobs/

This Web site is an exhibit of photographs taken at the Auschwitz and Birkenau memorial sites by Alan Jacobs between 1979 and 1981. This is one man's attempt to come to grips with this monumental historical event. It isn't a major site. But it shows how even one individual can help the whole world remember

Still Photographs (U.S. National Archives)

gopher://gopher.nara.gov/ooh/inform/dc/audvis/stoll/ ww2photo.txt

Another excellent source for photographs on the Holocaust is the United States National Archives.

This site contains about 200 photographs relating to the Holocaust. These photographs are of a wider range of Holocaust topics and are of a higher technical quality that those found on the Holocaust Pictures Exhibition listed above, though both sets of pictures have a powerful emotional appeal. This site is not be missed.

Index of Riefenstahl

http://rubens.anu.edu.au/riefenstahl/

"This site, at the Australian National University, has many images from the two most (in)famous films of Nazi film-maker Leni Riefenstahl—*Triumph of the Will* and *Olympia*." The fact that they are essentially made-to-order Nazi propaganda is a part of their historical significance. They are a prime example of the misuse of art and artistry for sordid political ends. Riefenstahl was an extremely talented filmmaker, and unfortunately, she chose to use her talents to extol the virtues of Nazism in these films.

The Holocaust Project

http://www.ort.org/edu/holocaus/start.htm

How do students express themselves about the holocaust? Does it mean different things to people in different parts of the world? Is it a uniting factor for Jews wherever they live?

> This Web site displays the results of a project that asked school-children to commemorate the 50th anniversary of the fall of the Nazi regime, using any medium to express their feelings. The result was some very strong and touching work.
>
> The panel received about 90 works from many countries, including Argentina, India, Morocco, Italy, Uruguay and Israel, written in 5 languages (English, French, Spanish, Italian and Hebrew). These included essays, poems, stories, a play, paintings, collages and photographs. A video was submitted by an ORT Argentina graduate and an educational project was prepared by a teacher from Israel. Two schools from Israel (ORT Hatzor Haglilit and ORT Kiryat Tivon) submitted compiled works that their students prepared after visiting Poland.

The results of this project are really worth looking at.

Jewish Anti-fascist Committee

gopher://gopher.tamu.edu:70/00/.data/soviet.internal/
m1antfas.bkg

This Web site explains the bizarre story of the Jewish Anti-Fascist Committee, organized in the Soviet Union in 1942. The organization of this body was a diabolical act by Stalin, who was striving to gain access to the military resources of the United States. He decided to appeal to the Americans on the basis of the "anti-fascism" of the Jewish population in the Soviet Union. After 25 years of destroying Judaism and all its manifestations, he reincarnated Russian Jewry in the form of this committee.

This puppet group served the interests of Soviet foreign policy and the Soviet military through media propaganda (as well as through personal contacts with Jews abroad, especially in Britain and the United States) in order to influence public opinion and enlist foreign support for the Soviet war effort. In 1948, when its usefulness was over, the members of the Committee were banished or killed by Stalin. They included the cream of the remaining Soviet-Jewish *intelligentsia*.

The Wolf Lewkowicz Collection
http://web.mit.edu/afs/athena.mit.edu/user/m/a/maz/wolf/

If you want to understand life in prewar and wartime Poland, then these letters, all available to read at this Web site, are a must. The letters of Wolf Lewkowicz are comparable to more well-known personal journals to come out of World War II; they are quite evocative and powerful. This passage is taken from the site's introduction by Marshall L. Zissman and Sol J. Zissman.

> Between 1922 and 1939, Wolf Lewkowicz, of Konskie, Lodz and Opoczno, Poland, engaged in a lengthy and intimate correspondence in Yiddish with Sol J. Zissman, his deceased sister's son, who had been born in Konskie, Poland, and who had immigrated to the United States as an 11-year old boy... Wolf was 36 years old; he and his wife, Malke, and their three children lived in Lodz. At that time, Sol was 20, unmarried, and living in Chicago... Sol retained many of the letters he received from his uncle. There are more than 175 such letters. Many of them deal with confidential, personal and family matters. Some of them contain detailed information respecting the economic situation that faced ordinary Jews during this difficult period in Poland's history. There are also occasional references to anti-Semitism in Poland. Woven through all the letters, however, is the graphic

account of a desperate struggle to achieve economic dignity by a bright, articulate and insightful Polish Jew who, because of his lack of success as a breadwinner, judged himself a failure as a husband and as a father.

The situation in which we find Wolf as the correspondence opens in 1922 is precarious and, tragically, it deteriorates steadily throughout the rest of his life. His last letter, Letter 178, is dated in August, 1939, just before the outbreak of World War II. Wolf Lewkowicz died in Treblinka in 1943; he was 56 years old. Letter 179, written by two of his nephews in 1945 from what was then Palestine, contains a description of Wolf's final, tortured days. One of those nephews, Aaron Chmielnicki Carmi, escaped from the cattle car carrying the entire family from Opoczno to Treblinka, found his way to Warsaw and is one of a handful of Jewish Fighters' Organization members who survived the Warsaw Ghetto Uprising in 1943.

Holocaust—Understanding and Prevention
http://haven.ios.com/~kimel19/

The author of this Web site, Alexander Kimel, is a Holocaust survivor. The site reflects his experiences and his attitude toward his oppressors. It's not always very pretty. But it is a viewpoint which should be looked at and considered.

This excerpt conveys his ambition for this site. "The Holocaust is a tragedy for mankind. It is a precedence that increased the accepted level of violence. Without the Holocaust, the mass killings in Bosnia, Cambodia, Rwanda would have never occurred. The Holocaust is a warning to mankind that hatred is destructive, violence is contagious, while man has an unlimited capacity for cruelty."

This site is divided into a number of categories, some more complete and well-presented than others.

The Holocaust/Shoah Page
http://www.mtsu.edu/%7Ebaustin/holo.html

This site provides a wide variety of information about the Holocaust, including a glossary and chronology of the Holocaust—as well as information on the Nuremberg Laws, *Kristallnacht*, the T-4 euthanasia program (murder of the handicapped), Jewish losses in the Holocaust, and homosexuals and the Holocaust. This is a well-organized Web site, with a strong archive of useful facts and documents.

An Auschwitz Alphabet

http://www.spectacle.org/695/ausch.html

I thought I knew what the alphabet was all about. An Auschwitz Alphabet is a Web resource that gives one a whole new understanding of the ABC's. Each letter signifies a part of life in the Auschwitz concentration camp. It's a dizzying experience. The first entry is "A" for Arbeit or work. 'Arbeit Macht Frei' (Work Brings Freedom) was the sign over the gates of Auschwitz. It was placed there by Major Rudolf Hoss, commandant of the camp. This site has been the recipient of international praise for its construction and content.

Dachau: Principal Distinguishing Badges Worn by Prisoners

http://www.igc.apc.org/ddickerson/dachau-badges.html

In the Dachau camp, not all prisoners were treated equally—some were treated even worse. The badges each inmate wore made it easy to tell what type of prisoner the individual was: a political prisoner, a Jew, a Gypsy, a Homosexual, etc. If a picture is worth a thousand words, how much is such a badge worth?

On this Web site, you can see what these badges looked like.

The Pink Triangle Pages:The history of Nazi persecution of gay men and lesbians

http://www.cs.cmu.edu/afs/cs/user/scotts/bulgarians/pink.html

One of the lessons of this Web site, which details the persecution of homosexuals under the Nazi regime, is that there are no exceptions to hatred. Anti-Semitism is but one of bigotry's many ugly faces. The site contains a famous passage from Martin Niemoller which drives that point home.

They came for the communists, and I did not speak up because I wasn't a communist. They came for the socialists, and I did not speak up because I wasn't a socialist. They came for the union leaders, and I did not speak up because I wasn't a union leader. They came for the Jews, and I didn't speak up because I wasn't a Jew. Then they came for me, and there was no one was left to speak up for me.

David's Holocaust Awareness Project

http://members.aol.com/dhs11/remember.html

David, the creator of this site, is 11 years old and lives in Margate, New Jersey. This Holocaust summary is built from a school report, and has an impressive level of emotion and understanding. Why can an 11-year-old boy relate to this topic when so many older people cannot?

36 Questions About the Holocaust

http://www.wiesenthal.com/resource/36qlist1.htm

This is an on-line list of many common questions about the Holocaust, which the Wiesenthal Center of Los Angeles raises and to which it provides some answers. Understanding the meaning behind these answers takes time, but the clarity with which these fundamentals are spelled out makes this a very useful Web page.

The Janusz Korczak Living Heritage Association

http://www.lhs.se/ped/korczak/

This Web site, created by the Swedish Korczak Association, uses photographs and text to provide information about Janusz Korczak (1878-1942), a Polish pediatrician, author, and teacher who ran a Jewish orphanage in Warsaw. In the last days of the Warsaw Ghetto, Korczak—refusing all chances to save his own life—went to die with the orphans under his care in the gas chambers at Treblinka. Korczak epitomizes the sense of responsibility that one human being can have for another. Some of the material is in Swedish, and some in English. This site is a noble effort and deserves your attention.

Anne Frank Online

http://www.annefrank.com/

This site contains a bit of material on the life and times of Anne Frank. There used to be more material about Anne Frank available on the Internet. However, the story of this young heroine has become tangled in a tale of unfortunate circumstances regard the rights to publish material about her life. Now these resources are not available and the world is much poorer because of it.

March of the Living

http://www.bonder.com/march.html

This modest Web site documents the March of the Living, an annual journey in which thousands of primarily Jewish teens from around the world gather in Poland and Israel to mark two of the most significant dates on the modern Jewish calendar: Holocaust Remembrance Day and Israel Independence Day. The purpose of this trip is to give students a firsthand look at history and the evils of mankind.

Within this site, at **www.bonder.com/tour/index.html** is a moving and well-presented set of pages that give you a view through the eyes of a group of Jewish youngsters from Montreal who participated in The March.

Raoul Wallenberg

http://www.algonet.se/hatikva/wallenberg/

Raoul Wallenberg's extraordinary rescue operation during World War II, which saved the lives of many Hungarian Jews, has become widely known all over the world. This Internet site, with archives and pictures, has been created to honor Raoul Wallenberg and what he did, and to ensure he will never be forgotten. Wallenberg was captured by the Soviet army on January 17th, 1945, and has not been heard from since.

To save a Life: Stories of Jewish Rescue

http://sorrel.humboldt.edu/%7Erescuers/

This Web site offers the pages of *To Save a Life: Stories of Jewish Rescue*, a previously unpublished book in which personal narratives and photographs reveal how certain individuals, acting upon their own moral convictions while endangering their own and their families' lives, saved the lives of Jewish people from Nazi-occupied Europe. Amidst the documentation of the horrors of the Holocaust, it is useful to remind yourself of the selfless deeds of which people are capable.

Visas for Life: The Remarkable Story of Chiune and Yukiko Sugihara

http://www.hooked.net/users/rgreene/Sug.html

In life, people are tested in different ways. Only a few achieve greatness through simple acts of kindness, thoughtfulness and humanity. This is the story of a Japenese couple who, when confronted with evil, obeyed the kindness of their hearts and consciences in defiance of the orders of an indifferent government. Chiune and Yukiko Sugihara risked their careers, their livelihood and their future to save the lives of more than 6,000 Jews. This selfless act resulted in the second-largest number of Jews rescued from the Nazis. The Sugihara story is also told in picture form in The Holocaust Albm by Ron Greene. This was first viewed as a photographic exhibition at the Simon Wiesenthal Center in Los Angeles.

The Holocaust Album

http://www.hooked.net/users/rgreene/1Sugphoto5.html

The Story of Jan Zwartendijk and his Legacy to Judaism

http://remember.org/righteous.html

This site, created by David Krenzler, tells the powerful story of Jan Zwartendijk, a decent human being who saved thousands of lives. Zwartendijk was the director of the Philips Corporation in Lithuania during the war. He was able to use his position as acting Dutch consul in Kaunas (Kovno) to get travel papers for many Jews trapped in Jewish pockets of Lithuania.

Elizabeth Goldschläger: a story of courage

http://aleph.lib.ohio-state.edu/%7Edagalron/shoah.html

I can give you a dozen reasons to visit this page. But it really speaks for itself. You can't really understand what the survivors encounted in the horrific journey of death. But if you listen to their voices, you can begin to feel their pathos.

> "Shoah" it is a word that has haunted me as far back as I can remember. I always heard my parents conversing about the Shoah and my grandmother, but I couldn't figure out its meaning, or what she had to do with it. I always marveled at my grandmother's vigor and toughness, but I did not know what made her that way. When I was old enough to understand, my parents explained to me that the Shoah was the mass extermination of Jews in Europe during World War II, and that my grandmother escaped from the Nazis.

The Shoah Foundation

http://www.vhf.org/

Steven Spielberg may primarily be remembered for his great movie making. But undoubtedly he will also be remembered for the Shoah Visual History Foundation.

This major undertaking to record the testimony of the survivors of the Holocaust, wherever they reside, is one of the greatest oral history projects of all time.

"The archive will be used as a tool for global education about the Holocaust and to teach racial, ethnic and cultural tolerance. By preserving the eyewitness testimonies of tens-of-thousands of Holocaust survivors, the Foundation will enable future generations to learn the lessons of this devastating period in human history from those who survived."

Underlying Spielberg's efforts is the gnawing fear that the world will forget. This is his way of helping it to remember.

My Holocaust Experiences
by Charles V. Ferree
http://remember.org/chuckf.html

Charles V. Ferree, an Allied soldier remembers the liberation of Dachau. His memoir, which you can read on-line here, recalls the day of liberation. That day is still with him:

> After Dachau, I burned my uniform in a vain attempt to rid myself of the death smell. It's still with me, fifty years later. Only recently have I begun talking about the Holocaust. One reason is because I read that as many as seventeen percent of Americans recently polled expressed some doubts that it happened at all. The greatest tragedy in modern times. And some doubt it happened. Others compare the Holocaust with special interests, to fight this or that cause.

This denial and distortion is hard for many Jews to understand. But as the generations that survived and liberated these death camps age, it is more important than ever for sites like this one to bear testament to their experiences so that those who come later will know the truth.

Liberation of Buchenwald
by Harry J. Herder, Jr.
http://remember.org/liberators.html#Lib

This site is another of the moving memoirs of the Allied soldiers who liberated the death camps, in this case the notorious Buchenwald. The words of Harry J. Herder, Jr. are devastatingly evocative:

> Over fifty years ago, I went through a set of experiences that I have never been able to shake from my mind. They subside in my mind, and, then, in the spring always, some small trigger will set them off and I will be immersed in these experiences once more. The degree of immersion varies from year to year, but there is no gradual diminution with time. I note, but do not understand, that the events occurred in the spring, and the re-immersion seems to be always in the spring. This year I set those memories on paper, all of them, or at least all of them I recall. I hope for the catharsis. I do not expect a complete purging—that would be expecting too much—but if I can get these memories to crawl deeper into my mind, to reappear less vividly, and less frequently, it will be a help.

Just recently the media carried a story about a Jew from Russia and his Israeli sister. For more than fifty years, they didn't know of each other's existence. Finally, they found each other. The point raised by the successful conclusion of this quest is that nobody who has gone through the Holocaust can entirely believe in its finality. They feel that somewhere, somehow, somebody must have survived.

In the course of my own experiences, I have seen this joyous event repeated again and again. Brothers and sisters reuniting after more than 30 years does happen. Once, I was at a dinner in London, Ontario, Canada and was seated next to the cantor of the local synagogue. He told me that he had lost his whole family in the Holocaust. But he had heard that there was one survivor, a cousin living in Israel. However, he didn't know how to reach him. But the cousin was not in Israel! He was in New York at the time and he was a friend of mine. After dinner, I invited everyone to come to my hotel room and I then called New York. When my friend got on the line, I gave the phone to the cantor. I told him, "I think that you two might have something to say to each other." The thought of this scene moves me to this very day.

For years on end, Israeli newspapers and Jewish papers in the United States have carried messages from people looking for information about their loved ones. Now this effort has come to the Internet as well. The following sites show a sampling of these efforts to rejoin families torn asunder by war.

Search for Information on Golub-Dobrzyn (Poland)

http://connexus.apana.org.au/~mdobia/

This site's creators are looking for survivors of World War I and World War II from a particular area in Poland. It is one of a number of sites on the Web that seek survivors from WWII. It is like looking for a needle in a haystack. But sometimes there is a pleasant surprise.

Yad Layeled
http://www.macom.co.il/holocaust-children/

During World War II, many Jewish families entrusted their children with non-Jewish neighbors and with Christian religious institutions. Many of the survivors were lost to Judaism and were never heard from again.

Yad Layeled, the Museum for the Children, which is the newest addition to the Ghetto Fighter's House, opened its doors in 1995. It's in the Western Galilee, Israel. The Museum holds a unique department called the "Children Without Identity" division. The purpose of the department is to try to uncover the true identities of Jewish children who were born between 1936 and 1945 and were left orphans at the end of the war. These children were saved from Nazis, thanks to the nobility of character and kindness of Christians who sheltered them and kept them hidden in their homes, or in convents until the end of the war. For the sake of safety, the children were given a "new" non-Jewish identity. After the war, most of the children were returned and resumed their lives as Jews under their true "old" self. However, an important number of them, particularly in Poland, continued to live—and still do up to this day—under an assumed identity, not knowing who they really are. They do not know what their real name are and know very little, or nothing at all, about their whereabouts during the Holocaust. For many of those youngsters, the trauma caused by the separation from their parents and the painful memories associated with the Shoah created an emotional barrier, preventing them from seeking their true identity after the war. The new division at Yad Layeled was created to help people in this difficult journey into the past, to find out who they really are.

Munich Jews Memorial Book Project
http://www.writething.com/cybrary/munich.html

This page is an attempt to contact members of the pre-World War II Munich Jewish community, and to put together a complete picture of the tragic history of the Jews of this German city during the war:

> Since 1994 the archive of the city of Munich has been preparing a memorial book on a biographical basis about Munich Jews who were persecuted, expelled and exterminated by the Nazis. This project is an important attempt to determine the fate of the Munich Jewish community and its members during the Nazi period. To be able to realize a complete biographical memorial book, we are looking for any kind of valuable information, such as documents, pictures, testimonies and eye-witness accounts about the persecution of the Jews in Munich between 1933 and 1945.

It seems impossible that such an inhumane horror could have occured. How did it happen, and more importantly, why?

Art Spieglman's Maus: Working Through the Trauma of the Holocaust

http://jefferson.village.virginia.edu/holocaust/spiegelman.html

When is a cartoon not a cartoon? When it's a Maus! This page contains a fascinating psychological analysis of the famous Maus cartoon character created by Art Spiegelman, a son of Holocaust survivors. This is heavy reading, but is an insightful and provocative document.

Excerpts of Nazi Documents Relating to the Extermination of Jews

gopher://israel.nysernet.org:70/00/holocaust/Nazi_Doc

The following are excerpts from original Nazi documents, relating directly to the extermination of Jews and others carried out by the Nazis during World War II. The purpose of this collection is to offer these official Nazi documents in an easily accessible form, and to direct readers to the sources for more complete references.

Topics covered on this site include: medical experiments, the economic plunder, Auschwitz, *Kristallnacht*, verdicts of SS courts, and a miscellaneous category, which includes proof of many horrors: prosecution of a Jewish woman for selling her mother's milk to feed German babies, a letter about transporting to Germany "racially valuable children" whose parents were slain by the Nazis, Reichsfuehrer-SS Himmler describing Russians and Slavs as "human animals" to be used for work, Himmler's orders to kill and destroy everything in Nazi occupied Ukraine before evacuating it, and a detailed report about mass executions in the Nazi-occupied Baltics (the "Jager report").

We Were Only Following Orders
http://www.catholic.net/RCC/Periodicals/Crisis/judaism.html

This is an on-line essay which looks at the denial of responsiblity offered by Germans during the Nuremberg trials after the war and the long-term consequences of that denial for later generations:

> When the Allies decided to try the surviving Nazi leaders directly after the end of WWII...they also repeatedly broadcast the consistent theme of all the Nuremberg defendants until it was the only phrase people could recall from the mind-numbing testimony- "We were only following orders." So odious did that phrase become, that even now, the West is still reeling from the unintended consequence.
>
> Nuremberg effectively established, albeit unintentionally, the popular conviction that following orders is the road to unfathomable evil. It told us that true moral heroism lies in rejecting authority.

United Nations Year for Tolerance Statement by Mr. Simon Wiesenthal
http://www.wiesenthal.com/itn/wiesun.htm

> Simon Wiesenthal is the most famous Nazi hunter in the world. The story of his efforts to bring Nazi criminals to justice has been made into books and even a movie. Why did Wiesenthal devote his life to being a Nazi hunter? The answer usually given is that he suffered his own great and personal losses in the Holocaust. While this is true and should not be minimized, Wiesenthal is also trying to leave this world with a message: It can happen again. It is happening every day. In Bosnia and Nigeria, Lagos and China. Wherever there is a public that is not vigilant about the rights of others, then Nazism and other forms of totalitarianism can arise again.

This page, on the Wiesenthal Center's Web site, contains a message that he delivered to the United Nations. His words ring true and send a message to the world.

The Wiesenthal Center Web page also has other on-line resources worth a look once you've examined this speech.

Holocaust Denial and The Big Lie

http://www.remember.org/History.root.rev.html

One of the most insidious developments since the Holocaust is the persistent "denial" that it ever took place. On this site, the authors study each of the claims and refute them. As Holocaust-denial advocates put forth a sophisticated and relentless effort, the attempts to refute this have to be just as sophisticated and unrelenting.

Holocaust denial is a serious concern, and unfortunately it is a growing one as well. A scant half-century has passed since the close of World War II and the systematic extermination of European Jewry. But there are those who claim that the documented events of the Nazi era never took place. It's called Holocaust Denial and there are active proponents of this theory in even the most "civilized" of nations. Even those nations whose youngsters were sacrificed for the cause of democracy have people and Web sites that claim that the events never took place. If it weren't so tragic this would almost be comic. How does anyone deny the events that shook the world to its very foundation? If you don't believe that anyone actually could see for yourself.

The Nizkor Project

http://nizkor.almanac.bc.ca/

The Nizkor Project is not a single collection of Web pages. It is a collage of different projects, focusing around the Holocaust and the denial of the Holocaust, which is often wrongly called Holocaust "revisionism." The entire collection revolves about the attempt by the authors not to let anyone "revise" the Holocaust. Fact must remain fact and the passage of 50 or 500 years should not alter the lives and deaths of six million Jews and countless millions of other innocent victims of Nazi oppression.

The site's features are showcased collections of information about Holocaust denial and the Holocaust. Here you will find Nizkor's responses to the most frequently perpetrated myths regarding the Holocaust.

Holocaust Denial Information via Electronic Media, particularly the Internet

http://www.ase.on.ca/~ajhyman/legalp.html

Anti-Semitism takes on different garb in different countries and different times. This Web essay by Avi Hyman documents anti-Semitic efforts going on right now in America:

> Recent news reports have related suggestions that Ernst Zundel and other individuals who question the authenticity of the Holocaust are attempting to gain direct access to the Internet. Zundel, in particular, has a reputation for allegedly being the world's largest print publisher of Holocaust denial material. This paper will serve to evaluate the legal issues pertaining to the use of the Internet as a medium of communication for Holocaust deniers, in light of the recent reports. Finally, the generalist issues discussed herein will have import to those interested in the broader issues of racism and other -isms on the net."

Antisemitism: The Holocaust, Neo-Fascism, "Anti-Zionism," and Black Antisemitism

http://ucsu.colorado.edu/~jsu/antisemitism.html#genant

The subject headings on this site, including Farrakhan and Black anti-Semitism gives you a feeling of what you can expect to find at this site:

Anti-Semitism takes on many different guises. It exists—nay it thrives today, some 50 years after the Holocaust destroyed more than six million Jews. Who are the haters? What do they look like? How do they act? What hatreds do they espouse. You'll find them at this site.

Anti-Semitism still exists in many guises. Earlier in this chapter we referred to the Soviet Jewish Anti-Fascist Committee of World War II. Russia, both before the advent of Communism and since the overthrow of this philosophy, has long been a hotbed of anti-Semitism. The *Protocols of The Elders of Zion* was probably a result of the efforts of the Czarist police. Among the Web pages below is a *Time* article that reminds us that this prejudice continues to flourish, both in Russia and closer to home.

Plots, Plots, and More Plots

http://pathfinder.com/@@t9GgLAYAdvseblb9/time/magazine/do
mestic/1994/941121/941121.russia.html

Just when you think that democracy has come to Russia, Vladimir Zhirinovsky raises his head to show you that much is unchanged. Read what Zhirinovsky has to say and wonder about the figures lurking in the Russian shadows. anti-Semitism exists in Russia today, as it has for centuries.

The Hate Page of the Week!!!

http://www.owlnet.rice.edu/~efx/hpotw.html

This is a page put up by a 'Net surfer who has compiled links to some of the uglier sites he has come across on the Web:

> On my meanderings through the 'Net, I have come across many a homepage which offended my sensibilities. There were pages out there which so shocked and angered me, that I wanted the whole world to see...I urge you to read through some of these sites, and allow yourself to see that there is still a great deal to be done before we can live in peace.

The Dark Side of the Net
http://www.vir.com/Shalom/hatred.html

This is another collection of links to various racist and revisionist areas of the Internet, including: the Aryan Crusader's Library, the New Jersey Skinhead Page, the Stormfront White Nationalist Resource Page, White Aryan Resistance/Tom Metzger Web Page, Knights of the Ku Klux Klan, and Ernst Zundel's Voice of Freedom Web site.

There are also a host of FTP sites, Internet mailing lists, and dial-in Bulletin Boards that cater to anti-Semitism on the Net.

Cybrary of the Holocaust
http://remember.org/

The purpose of the Cybrary is to help future generations remember the Holocaust. The Cybrary collects materials on the Holocaust and provides them to educators and educational institutions to enable them to develop programs on the Holocaust.

It has sections of resources covering texts, images, and the Imagine Art Gallery of Children's Art about the Holocaust.

The Cybrary is very well-presented and it has a variety of materials. Much of the information in the Cybrary can be found elsewhere on the Web. The Cybrary helps you find this information without looking all over for it. It does a good job but is not foolproof, and with a little diligence you can find additional reference information on the Holocaust at other sites on the Web.

The Felix Posen Bibliographic Project on Antisemitism
http://www2.huji.ac.il/www_jcd/bib.html

The Felix Posen Bibliographic Project comprises three on-line databases containing about 24,000 items. New material is added on a regular basis. The databases are: an annotated bibliography (publications from 1984 to the present); a retrospective bibliography (from 1983 back to 1977); and the "Jewish Question" in German-Speaking Countries, 1848-1914.

Judaism Reading List: Antisemitism and Christian Relations

http://www.math.uio.no/nett/fag/judaism/reading-lists/antisemitism.html

The goal of the project displayed on this Web site is to build a comprehensive database of all published writings about anti-Semitism and the Holocaust. The database lists books, articles, dissertations and Master's theses published in many countries and languages. It contains approximately 15,000 items. Most of the material is gathered from the holdings of the Jewish National and University Library in Jerusalem.

A related bibliography is also worth referring to. From Felix Rosen's page (above), it's called "Demonization of the Jew and the Jew as 'other'" and is found at **http://www3.huji.ac.il/www_jcd/dem.html.**

Whosoever saves a single life...

http://www.cs.cmu.edu/afs/cs.cmu.edu/user/mmbt/www/rescuers.html

This bibliography lists works in English which discuss the lives and actions of rescuers during the Holocaust. Individuals, groups, and in the case of Denmark, almost an entire country, reached out. Bulgaria was also active in protecting its Jewish population. It leaves you with some faith in mankind.

Finally, there are sites for teaching about the Holocaust:

The Beast Within: An Interdisciplinary Unit
http://www.fred.net/nhhs/html/beast.htm

This site presents the on-line activities of students participating in an interdisciplinary unit called "The Beast Within," which studies the darker side of human nature as explored by the literature and history of 20th-century man; the essays, poems, and graphic art at this site include students' reactions to their visit to the United States Holocaust Memorial Museum. This site was prepared for 9th graders, but, it is suitable for students both younger and older.

The Holocaust: A Guide for Pennsylvania Teachers Table of Contents
http://www.jer1.co.il/holocaust/guide/bmenv.html

Why another guide on the Holocaust? Author Gary M. Grobman answers the question in the preface to his Web site.

The purpose of this guide "is not so much to provide the gory details of the Nazis' race war against the Jews as to permit students to understand the types of thinking and behavior which led to genocide during World War II. By understanding this thinking and behavior, students can develop the necessary tools to not only avoid this themselves, but to condemn such thinking and behavior of others."

The Net Gazette
http://www.infopost.com/gazette/index.html

This site contains an article that looks at how the Holocaust is taught in schools in Germany. It is not a very extensive article, but is particularly interesting because it shows Germany sensitivity toward teaching about the Holocaust.

"Whose Memory Lives When the Last Survivor Dies?"

http://www.english.upenn.edu/~afilreis/Holocaust/commemorations-how.html

This article from the *New York Times* by Gustav Niebuhr contains a very moving selection of words and thoughts about the Holocaust and humanity:

> "By themselves, monuments are of little value, mere stones in the landscape," James E. Young, a professor of English and Judaic studies at the University of Massachusetts at Amherst, wrote in *The Texture of Memory: Holocaust Memorials and Meaning*. "But as part of a nation's rites or the object of a people's national pilgrimage, they are invested with national soul and memory."

Our memories are our future.

CHAPTER 7

Genealogy

There are several basic reasons for studies of genealogy in Jewish tradition.

Genealogy was an important factor in determining the rights of the priests and Levites to their positions in the Temple. Only those with confirmed Levitical status could perform these rites. This was particularly important after the return of the Jews to the Second Temple. As a result of the exile, the records of the ancestors of individual Priests and Levites were lost. At the same time, the confirmation of genealogy also allowed individuals to lay claim to the lands their ancestors had title to in the period of the First Temple.

Genealogical roots also played a very important role in determining the ability of Jews to marry, inasmuch as there are rules concerning the suitability of marriages between priests and divorcées and those of "impure" lineage. It also played a powerful role in the determination of the lineage of kings of Israel.

In our own day and age, the question of patrilineal lineage has been the cause of great dissension among the various branches of Judaism. Reform Judaism's acceptance of patrilineal lineage versus matrilineal lineage was the first major break in the concept of Jewish lineage since biblical times.

In another sense, lineage plays little role in Jewish life. Some of the greatest figures of Judaism, notably Rabbi Akiva and Rabbi Meir, were from families with little or no genealogical significance. Still others were from families of proselytes. Indeed, Judaism endowed Torah learning and piety with greater significance than genealogical factors.

Genealogy lists were also a means of passing along ethnological records and information concerning the history of settlements of the Jewish people throughout long periods of times.

In America, genealogy also plays another role in Jewish life. As a nation of immigrants, we are very conscious of our ancestry, yet we know little about it. Our dearth of knowledge about previous generations is a cause of deep concern to many people. Where was your family from? What did they do on the "other side?" Who and what were we? Studying one's family history can answer many of these integral questions.

The problems of genealogy have been heightened by events in modern Jewish life. As a result of the Holocaust, many Jews lost their families and their family histories as well. Genealogy is an attempt to recapture the past. In quite a few cases, these lineage studies have actually led to the reunification of families. For others, it has brought some closure to their search for family and past.

In the 1990s, large number of Jews left the former Soviet Union for Israel and other countries. Many had abandoned their Judaism and had intermarried. Now they were coming to Israel. How were they to be treated from a genealogical point of view? Were their children Jewish or not? On the one hand, Israeli law requires that for a child to be considered Jewish his mother must be Jewish. On the other hand, a whole generation of people had lived in a land where intermarriage was the norm rather than the exception. This has caused a great deal of pain and anguish in Israel.

A second area of difficulty emerged with the arrival of large numbers of Ethiopian Jews to Israel. The Ethiopian Jewish community kept genealogical records and by and large could determine the "Jewishness" of its members. This, too, has presented problems to Israeli society. In both the Soviet and Ethiopian cases, a great deal of ingenuity in the interpertation and application of Jewish Law has been used to ease the pain and integrate the immigrants into the mainstream of Jewish life. Lineage is especially important in Israel, where religious law is the determinant in the areas of marriage and divorce.

There are a number of incredibly useful resources in this chapter for aspiring Jewish genealogists. The quality of some of these sites (mostly done by volunteers) makes it clear that there are some very passionate and able genealogists out there waiting to help you.

JewishGen FAQ—Frequently Asked Questions

http://www.jewishgen.org/faqinfo.html

This site is a treasure trove for the potential genealogist interested in researching Jewish ancestry. It contains a wide variety of information, is very well organized, and answers questions for anyone from the neophyte asking how to get started to the experienced researcher needing to know what naturalization records exist at the National Archives. Even professional genealogists can benefit from the information here, as Jewish genealogy has its own unique issues and problems. View this site before going on to any other site in this chapter.

JewishGen: The Official Home of Jewish Genealogy

http://www.jewishgen.org/

The previous site is actually part of this tremendously valuable, award-winning resource. However, if you take our advice and check the FAQs before you go to this site, you'll have a better understanding of the big picture regarding genealogical research.

Beyond the traditional resources often found at genealogical Web sites, this site includes on-line searchable databases, the "JewishGen College," where one can take E-mail courses, a mentor program, and a translation service. Among the databases are *shtetl* finders, and the Jewish Genealogical Family Finder. If you know your family name and the town of birth you may be able to find the names of others researching the same name or town. The site even offers a Web-based tour and tutorial. All in all, this is one of the most valuable sites on theWeb.

The Association of Jewish Genealogical Societies
http://www.jewishgen.org/ajgs/

You can't do all your genealogical research while sitting at your computer. At some point you will need to visit some archives—and you will probably also want to join a local Jewish Genealogical Society. Most have monthly meetings, a newsletter, and lectures (some have libraries) to help you with research in your area. The Association of Jewish Genealogical Societies (AJGS) is the nonprofit organization that coordinates over 60 local Jewish genealogical societies around the world.

You will be surprised at the location of some of these societies. You'll find them in Azerbaijan, Mexico, Holland, and Brazil as well as in many of the United States and Israel.

Avotaynu
http://www.avotaynu.com/

Avotaynu is the biggest name in Jewish family research. They are the largest publisher of Jewish genealogy material: books, maps, video tapes, microfiche, and their top-notch journal *AVOTAYNU -The International Review of Jewish Genealogy*. It is published quarterly and is a must for anyone seriously interested in Jewish genealogy. There is also information here about the burgeoning field of Russian archival searches—for a fee, professionals will search for information about your relatives during their next trip to the former USSR.

Not every problem encountered, or resource needed, by the Jewish genealogist is specifically Jewish. For that reason, the following three sites are important additions to any collection of genealogy Web sites.

Cyndi's List of Genealogy Sites on the Internet

http://www.oz.net/~cyndihow/sites.htm

This award-winning site has over 10,000 links, and continues to grow by leaps and bounds. The links are categorized and cross-referenced in over 60 categories—and all of this is put together in one of the best-looking sites on the Web. Few sites are useful, well-organized, and pleasing to the eye, but this is one of them. The amount of information here is staggering.

The US Gen Web Project

http://www.usgenweb.com/

The idea here is to maintain a site of genealogical resources—linked together state-by-state, and county-by-county. Each county has a volunteer coordinator, and, while many counties are "orphans," even those counties have a tremendous amount of information. This is particularly important because many records you may need exist only at the county level. For a particular state, simply type in *http://www.usgenweb.com/xx*, where *xx* is the state you're looking for. It's a fabulous resource. (Note: The home page has a rather large map of the U.S. and may take a while to load). The idea has spawned a World Genealogy Web Project (http://www.dsenter.com/worldgenweb/), but as of this writing, it is far from complete. If you need to do any research in the U.S., you *must* check out this site.

The Genealogy Home Page

http://www.genhomepage.com/

This is another site that offers an astounding number of links to every conceivable area of genealogy. Between this site and Cyndi's list, you should have everything covered.

Major Jewish Organizations

Jews have created and contributed to a vast network of organizations that offer everything from combatting anti-Semitism to lobbying in Washington to supervising the Jewish education of our children. The Web sites in this chapter represent just a few of these groups—the ones that have an on-line presence that is well-presented and offers significant information. Hopefully, updates of this volume will enable us to make additions as more groups take advantage of the nationwide and international reach of the Web.

The organizational life of Jews both in the United States and throughout the world plays a key role in protecting the quality of Jewish life. For the most part, this chapter lists national Jewish organizations, since local communities are covered in Chapter 3. We have also excluded religious organizations and educational institutions, which likewise have their own coverage in different parts of this book.

We have attempted to feature organizations which play unique roles in society. These include organizations which reflect specific needs—such as drug and alcohol addiction, anti-Semitism, vocational assistance, and anti-missionary organizations.

These listings are essentially descriptions of the groups and what services they provide. For more detail about the vast contents and links each site contains, just fire up your browser, go to our bookmark file, and check them out.

AIPAC's CyberCenter for Pro-Israel Activism
http://www.aipac.org/

The AIPAC CyberCenter for Pro-Israel Activism is a slick, well-organized site that explains the goals and programs of one of the most powerful Israel-advocacy programs in the United States. It offers you the option to view the Web site as text only, which speeds things up considerably.

"The American-Israel Public Affairs Committee is the national legislative advisory arm of America's Jewish community. You wake up in the morning and you read about a U.S. government policy toward Israel that irks you. What can you do about it? AIPAC has been working at this problem since the early 1950s... AIPAC reflects the use of the democratic process to impart the desires of America's Jews vis-a-vis Israel. AIPAC also plays a role in areas such as: foreign aid, the peace process, U.S.-Israel strategic cooperation, and the recognition of Jerusalem as the seat of Israel's government."

You can look at AIPAC's efforts and offices state by state, read about their legislative efforts, sign up as a member, and check out their coverage of the 1996 political conventions and elections. There is also a moving memorial area remembering the late Israeli Prime Minister, Yitzhak Rabin.

The Aleph Institute
http://www.aleph-institute.org/

On the rather spartan Aleph Institute site, you can find resources for lawyers, military personnel, chaplains, and correctional institution staff aiding Jews in their observances. Also available on-line are weekly Torah classes from Rabbi Sholom Lipskar.

"The Aleph Institute is a not-for-profit, national Jewish educational, humanitarian and advocacy organization that was founded in 1981. It has grown to become the world's foremost agency serving the needs of Jews of all backgrounds who are in prison, the military, or anywhere they and their families may become isolated from their heritage. Isolation is a terrible thing. It creates a state of limbo in which the individual loses his identity. When one is isolated from the Jewish community he stands to lose his Jewish identity."

Read this site and gain some appreciation of the things that we take for granted.

American Jewish Committee

http://ajc.org:80/

This is a lavish, but very slow-to-load site from the American Jewish Committee. It offers the AJC perspective on interfaith and interethnic issues, anti-Semitism, Israel, and Jewish identity, as well as press releases and membership information. The legibility of this site is hampered by their choice of yellow as a text color.

> "For nine decades the American Jewish Committee has been a vital force in the American Jewish community, a unique influence on the broader American society, and a guiding spirit in the worldwide campaign to enhance the human rights and fundamental freedom of men and women everywhere. Through careful research, strategic planning, and courageous social and political action in concert with effective leaders of a wide variety of like-minded ethnic, racial and religious groups, the AJC has contributed significantly to the reduction of intolerance and discrimination in American life and the enhancement of democratic values and pluralism."

American Jewish Congress On-Line

gopher://www.shamash.org:0/./ajcongress

The American Jewish Congress On-line carries a great deal of material about the Congress. It covers each area of the activities of the organization. Of particular interest are the activities of the AJC in the areas of financial aid to parochial schools, its legislative and litigation activities. It is:

motivated by the need to ensure the creative survival of the Jewish people, deeply cognizant of the Jewish responsibility to participate fully in public life, inspired by Jewish teachings and values, informed by liberal principles, dedicated to an activist and independent role, and committed to making its decisions through democratic processes... protect fundamental constitutional freedoms and American democratic institutions, particularly the civil and religious rights and liberties of all Americans and the separation of church and state; advance the security and prosperity of the State of Israel and its democratic institutions, and to support Israel's search for peaceful relations with its neighbors in the region; advance social and economic justice, women's equality, and human rights at home and abroad; remain vigilant against anti-Semitism, racism, and other forms of bigotry, and to celebrate cultural diversity and promote unity in American life; and invigorate and enhance Jewish religious, institutional, communal, and cultural life at home and abroad, and to seek creative ways to express Jewish identity, ethics, and values.

American Jewish Joint Distribution Committee, Inc

http://www.ort.org/communit/jdc/home.htm

The Web site for the JDC is only partially completed. There are a number of areas that haven't been fleshed out yet. Currently available are some details about their programs to help Jews live as Jews all over the world—Israel, the formerly Soviet countries, Eastern Europe, Africa, Asia, and Latin America, as well as a photolibrary of their efforts since the 1920s.

JDC was founded with the outbreak of World War 1, and was conceived of as a short term project. The combined efforts of American Jews to assist and rehabilitate the Jews overseas were seen as an immediate response to an urgent but temporary state of affairs. When the problems were solved, the organisation would dissolve. During the twenties, and even afterwards to some extent, the heads of the JDC continued to see the organisation as a provisional one. They had but to solve a few of the more pressing problems of world Jewry which still persisted. The belief in progress is so much stronger, aparently, than the memory of deprivation and suffering. So it was, in any case, among the Jews who founded the JDC.

The American Physicians Fellowship for Medicine in Israel

http://www.apfmed.org/

This Web site describes the many programs to improve the opportunities of Israeli physicians, both Jew and Arab, set up by the APFM (American Physicians Fellowship for Medicine). These include emergency aid programs, medical research projects, training programs, and their new focus areas—womens' health and technology-sharing on pathology.

> The American Physicians Fellowship for Medicine in Israel (APF) was founded in 1950 by a group of American Jewish physicians who wanted to show solidarity with their professional colleagues in the newly founded State of Israel. APF has been dedicated to assisting the development of Israel as a world-class medical center since that time. Through a variety of programs directed to the improvement of medical education, research and care in Israel, APF's broad-based membership has been in the forefront of establishing ongoing connections between the medical communities of Israel and North America. Not tied to any one Israeli institution, APF has striven to fill unique niches and create real people-to-people linkages with all of Israel's medical schools and many hospitals and other medical institutions.

ADL online

http://www.adl.org/

The Anti-Defamation League is an extremely prominent and aggressive enemy of groups and activities it considers anti-Semitic. Their site offers current events, summaries about a variety of dangerous activities, press releases, and archives. You can also read about their A World of Difference Institute, which sponsors diversity-training programs:

> The Anti-Defamation League, founded in 1913, is the world's leading organization fighting anti-Semitism through programs and services that counteract hatred, prejudice and bigotry. The mission of the Anti-Defamation League is "to stop the defamation of the Jewish people, to secure justice and fair treatment to all citizens alike."

B'nai B'rith Canada

http://www.bnaibrith.ca

B'nai B'rith Canada is a sister organization to American B'nai B'rith. It is quite different in that Canadian Jewry's organizational structure is radically different than is the structure of American Jewry. B'nai B'rith Canada plays a very important role in Canadian Jewry, especially in light of the ongoing conflict between the French- and English-speaking communities in that nation. It has played a very important role in the area of Holocaust denial. You can read all about this worthy group's activities and publications, and read the on-line version of their magazine, *The Jewish Tribune*.

JESNA

http://www.jesna.org

This is the home page for the Jewish Education Service of North America. It has on-line program banks, archives of their project agendas, links to other Jewish educational groups, and their on-line workbook for education:

> JESNA, the Jewish Education Service of North America, was created in 1981 by the Jewish Federation movement to serve as its continental instrument of Jewish educational planning and services. JESNA's mission is to enhance the quality and increase the impact of Jewish education in North America by strengthening the motivation, knowledge, and skills of lay and professional leaders and by encouraging concerted community action to expand and improve Jewish education in all its forms and settings.

The Jewish War Veterans of the United States of America

http://www.penfed.org/jwv/home.htm

You can read all about the history of American Jews in the military on this site. There is a time line of significant event for these warriors, and information about the Jewish War Veteran's Museum.

This is a rich legacy to read about. American Jews have borne arms on behalf of their adopted nation since their landing in New York (then called New Amsterdam) in

1654. Indeed, Jews have played prominent roles in every single military endeavor of the United States since before the founding of the nation in 1776. The JWV celebrates the participating of American Jews in these efforts. It has also represented the interest of the Jewish soldiers who have come home from the wars, not always an easy task. The first Jews who wanted to fight for their nation were turned away by Peter Minuit, head of the New Amsterdam community. They had to appeal to the Dutch West India Company to gain their right to become full members of the tiny outpost in New York. This was the beginning of the legacy of Jewish participation in America's efforts at defense of its democratic principles. Over time the Jewish War Veterans has expanded its mandate to include interests of American Jewry in regard to many other matters facing the community. It has been active on behalf of Soviet Jewry and efforts to fight anti-Semitism.

The Association for Civil Rights in Israel
http://www.nif.org/acri/

Much of the information on this site is a bit dated. It describes the actions of the ACRI, which is essentially an Israeli ACLU. You can read about their legal efforts to protect equality, free speech, human rights, Arab rights in Israeli territory, and due process:

> Israel is not a monolithic entity. It is a democratic nation, operating under restrictions based upon theocratic legal foundations and the newness of its democratic traditions. ... The purpose of this organization is to address legal issues facing Jews and Arabs living in Israel. The organization draws its premise from the diversity of the sources of Israel's legal system as well as the diversity of the inhabitants of the state. Israel, unlike the United States, does not have a written constitution. Additionally, it is a nation which has a state sponsored religious structure which is empowered in many areas of personal law. Oftentimes these conflicts come out in the open. The Association has a distinct viewpoint. It has also had to come to grips with issues arising from Israel's annexation of large amounts of territories from its arab neighbors as a result of the 1967 war.

This site presents an often unpopular point of view. You don't have to agree with it or disagree with it, but you should know that it exists.

Association of American and Canadians in Israel

http://www.aaci.org.il/

The AACI represents Americans, Canadians, and South Africans in Israel. Its Web site offers information about immigrant rights, employment opportunities, housing, education, and volunteer activities:

> The AACI was founded almost at the beginning of the declaration of Israel's statehood by American, Canadians and South Africans who migrated or made "Aliyah" to Israel. Immigrants from these nations presented and have differing problems and needs than do immigrants from other nations. One of the major differences between members of the AACI and immigrants from many other nations are the reasons for their immigration to Israel. For AACI members the reasons are based upon a commitment to the principles of Zionism and Jewish renewal. For many others Israel is a political and economic alternative to difficult situations under which they have lived for many years. ... AACI is a unique and integral part of the Israeli absorption system. Serving some 50,000 adult members currently in Israel and a further 3,000 newcomers yearly, AACI acts as advocate for the entire North American Community [and other English speaking immigrants] in Israel.

B'nai B'rith Interactive

http://bnaibrith.org/

This rich but very slow site details the activities of the B'nai B'rith, contains the *Jewish Monthly* on-line, and lists services and programs, press releases, a calendar, and job postings:

> We are the volunteers performing community service in your area. We are the emergency relief fund at work around the world. We are the venue where presidents and heads of state address Jewish concerns. We are the place where seniors turn for affordable housing. We are the focal point for singles and young couples. We are the center of Jewish life on campus. We are the youth group for Jewish teens.

This major service organization offers a wide variety of services to the American Jewish community.

Association of Jewish Family and Children's Agencies

gopher://www.shamash.nysernet.org:70//hh/AJFCA

This is a listing of Jewish Family and Childrens Agencies in The United States and Canada. It contains the names, addresses and phone numbers of the agencies. It does not have any further information on them. This is a very bare-bones list. Ideally, it should be much more functional. But it is there. If you have a need for any aspect of Jewish family or children's services, then you point to the appropriate state and start looking. In some cases, all the family needs are taken care of by a single agency. Other states will require you to look around. It is important for an individual to know he is not alone and that he has someplace to turn within the Jewish community, and this Web site is a beginning in conveying that.

The Coalition for the Advancement of Jewish Education

http://www.caje.org

This Web site is a rich resource for Jewish educators. It has articles from the *Jewish Education News*, a curriculum bank, and links to other Jewish educational sites on the Web:

> CAJE is the largest North American Jewish educators' organization, bringing together all who are engaged in the transmission of the Jewish heritage, across the ideological spectrum and at all levels of the career ladder. By enhancing the dignity and professional development of the Jewish teacher, CAJE works to elevate the status of Jewish education on the Jewish communal agenda.

Council of Jewish Federations
http://jewishfedna.org/

> The CJF is the continental association of 189 Jewish Federations, the central community organization which serves nearly 800 localities embracing a Jewish population of more than 6.1 million in the United States and Canada.

This Web site contains the addresses and phone numbers of all Jewish federations in the United States and Canada. The Jewish Federations support programs of service to the entire Jewish community. These include a vast range of services—social, educational, cultural, health and welfare, and community relations.

Hadassah—The Women's Zionist Organization
http://www.hadassays.org.il/

> Hadassah Women's Zionist Organization, the largest Zionist women's organization in the U.S.A, was founded by Henrietta Szold in 1912. The purpose of this nonpartisan organization is to provide medical and educational services for Israel "for the benefit of all, regardless of race or creed."

This minimal site has contact information, a history of the group, and links to Hadassah's Youth Services in Israel: Hadassah College of Technology, Hadassah Career Counseling Institute, and Hadassah Youth Center-Young Judaea's Home In Israel.

Jewish Vocational and Career Counseling Service
http://www.jvs.org/

This site is part of a nationwide network of vocational services aimed at helping find jobs and careers for members of the Jewish community. In these times of resizing and retrenchment, these services provide real assistance for many members of the community. It's a good place to keep in mind. It's also very helpful in aiding people who are not yet set on a career or who contemplate a career change. The services offered by the JVS can be of real assistance to them. The site has listings of JVS locations worldwide, links to other career-oriented and Jewish sites, and information on JVS internships and scholarship programs:

> Work defines how we feel about ourselves, how we support ourselves and our families, who we are in society. Helping someone become independent and productive through work brings the dignity of self-sufficiency, fulfills the highest Jewish value of Tzedakah, and builds our community by strengthening the individuals within it. We strive to: Foster full employment within the Jewish comunity, so that people with the desire and ability to work can find meaningful and productive employment.

Jewish GRAPEZINE: Jews in Recovery from Alcoholism and Drugs

http://www.jacsweb.org

The material on this well-made Web site deals with alcohol and substance abuse problems within the Jewish community. It has the text of the *Grapezine* magazine, excerpted below. It also has lists of substance recovery programs, stories of recovering addicts and their families, an on-line meeting place, writings from rabbis about addiction, and even cartoons on Jewish denial:

> A ship came sailing over the horizon when a sailor noticed a man in the water. A boat was lowered, the rescue was on. They saw waves breaking all around the castaway in an otherwise calm sea. He was holding onto a pintle of rock just breaking the surface, it was a miracle. How had he found his way on this uncharted ocean to this very spot where salvation was to be found? They threw him a ring on a rope, he put it around his neck. They pulled hard on the rope but they couldn't dislodge him from the rock. Was he caught fast? No! he was actually holding on. " Let go! " They shouted" "I can't" He replied.

MAZON: A Jewish Response to Hunger

http://www.shamash.org/soc-action/mazon/

This is the Web presence of Mazon, which combats hunger in America. You can read essays on hunger in America, the tradition of tzedakah, and information on Mazon grants:

> MAZON: A Jewish Response to Hunger builds a bridge between the abundance with which many of us are blessed and the desperation of millions of people who go hungry in the United States and throughout the world. MAZON (the Hebrew word for 'food') raises funds principally by asking American Jews to contribute a suggested amount of 3% of the cost of joyous celebrations such as b'nai mitzvah, weddings, birthdays, anniversaries—every joyous occasion, large or small.

National Jewish Committee on Scouting

http://shamash.org/scouts/

> The mission of National Jewish Committee on Scouting is to promote Boy Scouting among Jewish youth, to help Jewish institutions and local council Jewish committees to provide Scouting opportunities for Jewish youth, and to promote Jewish values in Scouting through program helps and the religious emblems program.

The site lists all the units (Boy Scouts, Cub Scouts and Explorers) in the entire United States. In addition, it has the Web addresses of Jewish-sponsored scouting units in the United States and throughout the world.

National Jewish Outreach Program

http://www.njop.org/

> The National Jewish Outreach program was founded in 1987, by Rabbi Ephraim Buchwald, in response to the urgent need to address the issues of Jewish assimilation and intermarriage. Since its founding, NJOP has become one of the largest and most successful Jewish outreach organizations in the world.

Believing that every Jew is entitled to a basic Jewish education, the National Jewish Outreach Program offers free, convenient and exciting courses to all members of the Jewish community. Through innovative advertising, NJOP has 'marketed' Judaism in a manner that has made it accessible to everyone. Participants in NJOP programs are introduced, many for the first time in their lives, to positive, joyous Jewish experiences in a way they never thought possible.

Jewish Singles Connection WWW Cyber Community

http://www.zdepth.com/jsc/

Marriage and family are integal parts of Jewish life. This site uses the Internet to hlp single Jews throughout the U.S. and Canada to get together.

> The Jewish Community used to be just that, centered in a few major cities in defined ethnic areas. At the end of the Twentieth Century, that model has broken down as a result of reduced anti-Semitism and increased personal mobility. The result is an increased scattering of Jews within cities and across countries, and the world. Jewish Singles Connection is an attempt to help reconnect young single Jews across the U.S. and the world to each other and recreate some of the community of yesteryear. To deal with the new community paradigm we see an opportunity to utilize the new communications paradigm... the Internet. We hope that our use of the latest technology and your interaction with it will bring personal rewards for you and indirectly the Jewish people. " How do you meet somone? This site gives you dozens of links to meeting individuals such as yourself- through-out the U.S.

Included on this site are several hundred listings of men and women interested in meeting a mate. This site offers no warrantees and you have to do all the checking on your own.

Jews for Judaism

http://shamash.org/judaica/answers/missionaries/jews4jud/about.html

> Jews for Judaism is North America's only full-time educational, outreach and counseling organization dedicated to countering the multi-million dollar efforts of deceptive missionary and cult groups that target the Jewish community for conversion. Our offices serve as Crisis Intervention Centers which help those in need and promote Jewish continuity. To date over 200,000 Jews worldwide have participated in Jews for Judaism's counseling and educational programs.

This is a handy address to have in hand. Often Jewish parents and children alike are confronted with missionary activities. What do you do if a loved one is contacted and courted by a missionary organization? It can be a very frightening experience. Jews for Judaism can help you gain a perspective on missionary activities and help you fight their efforts.

Louis S. and Molly B. Wolk Center for Jewish Cultural Enrichment for the Deaf at the Rochester Institute of Technology

http://www.infoshop.com/wolkcenter/

> The Wolk Center is a new exciting program designed to allow Jewish Deaf students to become familiar with and express their identity as Jews. We will have creative and entertaining programs including socials, cultural and educational projects, as well as national programs for Jewish students who have been previously cut off from such involvement in their past.

This site is not an end in itself. It is the beginning of a long voyage and a connection for the deaf and hearing impaired. Parents with children who are deaf are often unprepared for this affliction. Add to this the Jewish dimension and the problem becomes an even more difficult one. The Wolk Center attempts to tackle this problem. The site has links to many other programs for the deaf and hearing impaired.

Volunteers for Israel

http://member.aol.com/vol4israel/index.html

Wouldn't you like to spend your vacation living and working alongside Israelis, at an IDF army base, hospital, archaeological excavation or botanical gardens? Join the Volunteers for Israel and get an insider's view of the culture, lifestyle and pulse of Israel.

The Zionist Organization of America
http://www.zoa.org/

> The Zionist Organization of America is the oldest, and one of
> the largest, pro-Israel organizations in the United States.
> Founded in 1897 to support the re-establishment of a Jewish
> State in the ancient Land of Israel, its presidents have included
> such illustrious Jewish leaders as Supreme Court Justice Louis D.
> Brandeis and Rabbi Abba Hillel Silver. The ZOA was instrumen-
> tal in mobilizing the support of the U.S. government, Congress,
> and the American public for the creation of Israel in 1948.

The ZOA is a very energetic organization, and has been a
vocal supporter of Israel's Likud party since the days of
Menachem Begin. It is something of a gadfly among
Zionist groups.

Jewish Defense League Good Image Awards
http://www.jdl.org/96_picks.html

I must be crazy to include this site in our book. But it
makes sense! JDL's Good Image Award site includes the
pictures and mini biographies on a number of personalities
who are Jewish, at least by birth. Frankly, I didn't know
that Wynona Ryder's real name is Laura Horowitz. But I
am pleased to learn that I share a history with Kerri Strug,
Jerry Seinfeld, Roseanne, and Debra Winger. I could do
without Howard Stern, but he would probably say the
same about me.

From this page you can check out the JDL's main
home page, which has a ton of resources aimed at the
group's twin goals of empowering Jews and fighting anti-
Semitism. You can read about their activities in the on-line
JDL in Action Journal, check out neo-Nazi activity all over
the world, use their pages of Web links, and learn how to
contact or join this somewhat militant group.

PART II

The Jewish Year

The Calendar

The Jewish calendar is an extremely important document. It sets the cycle of the year and its events and governs a great many activities in Jewish life. The Jewish calendar is *lunisolar*, meaning that the months are in accord with the moon and the years according to the sun. The calendar sets the times for the holidays that take place during the year.

The Jewish calendar is very complex. It is amazing that our ancestors were able to make the necessary calculations without benefit of modern computers. Some of these complications are set forth in the Reingold site at the end of this chapter.

You might also want to look at the *Encyclopaedia Judaica* entry on the Jewish calendar.

Hebrew Date

http://www.doe.carleton.ca/doebin/dfs_dispatch?hebdate

Click into this straightforward site for today's Hebrew date, printed in black letters on a plain gray page: "The Hebrew date for today, [Roman calendar date], is [Hebrew calendar date]. And the Hebrew date for tomorrow is [Hebrew date]." Entries include the month, day and year.

If a holiday is approaching, you will find a section called "Upcoming Holidays." It provides a calculation of days until the first day of the holiday. For example, on one date early in December, the screen read "Chanukah 1 is in 3 days' time." But when there's no holiday rapidly approaching, the section disappears.

There is also a monthly calendar, complete with Hebrew dates, holidays and moon phases for Ottawa, Canada, but my computer couldn't access it.

If you want today's Hebrew calendar date, fast and easy, no muss, no fuss without the risk of getting lost in an interesting site you didn't really have time for anyway, this is the spot.

Calendar Maven Home Page

http://users.aol.com/calmaven/calmaven.htm

Calendar Maven is an ad for a Hebrew calendar software. "Hebrew Calendar is an invaluable low-cost computerized aid to any person or organization needing knowledge of Jewish dates or *halakhic* times of day…"

This mom-and-pop company has put together a rather complicated and thorough site marketing its product. If you're looking to buy, it might be worth a browse to see what the software can do, how it compares with similar products on the market, who is currently using it and what the answers are to frequently asked questions (FAQs). If you want to know more about the people behind the company, jump to their homepage, or correspond with them via e-mail. But if all you're after is basic information about the Hebrew calendar, try another site.

B'nai B'rith Calendar

http://bnaibrith.org/caln.html

Will Rosh Hashanah be early or late in the year 2000? Will my birthday be on Passover in 1999? If you are plagued by questions like these and must have the answer, check out this site. A simple but comprehensive Jewish holiday calendar laid out in a table format offers the day and date of every major Jewish holiday from 5757 (9/96-9/97) through 5765 (9/04-9/05). A basic description of each holiday is also provided. Note that this site is only legible if your browser supports tables.

Hebrew Calendar—AIR Project

http://www-syntim.inria.fr/htbin/air/hebrewcalendar2.pl

If you want to check a particular secular date and its corresponding Hebrew date or vice versa, the program on this page, called *Hebcal*, is the calendar for you. It is particularly useful if you're trying to figure out a birth-date or the date of a *Yahrzeit* (the anniversary of a death). The calendar can also list the *Parsha* (Torah reading of the week), and the day of the *Omer* (the period between Passover and Shavuot).

It has certain limitations. Dates are only valid before sundown on that secular date, Hebcal performs no checking for changes between the Julian and Gregorian calendar, so secular dates before 1752 are untrustworthy, and it cannot currently handle date computations before 2 C.E.

Jewish Communication Network
Jewish Calendar

http://www.jcn18.com/holiday/

The best of the lot, this calendar page is really quite neat. Select a month from 1996 or 1997 and it will pop up in calendar format on the screen. Hebrew and Roman dates are provided for each day. Special icons occupy the dates of Jewish holidays, like a tree for Tu B'Shvat or a menorah and a dreidel for Hanukkah. Click these icons and the calendar turns into a resource page filled with all kinds of information, children's games, humor, recipes, links to relevant sites around the Web and more!

A great tool, this site is operated by the Jewish Communication Network, "an on-line center where families, teachers, writers, Jewish professionals and organizations from around the world can create a vibrant digital Jewish community."

Edward M. Reingold's Calendar Book, Papers, and Code

http://emr.cs.uiuc.edu/~reingold/calendars.html

Most of us are happy just to find the Hebrew date now and then. But transposing the Hebrew date to another ethnic or religious calendar, say the Islamic, Persian, Coptic, Ethiopic, Bahai, Mayan, French Revolutionary, Chinese or Hindu calendar, well, that's another story.

But not for Ed Reingold, professor in the Department of Computer Science at the University of Illinois at Urbana-Champaign, or his colleague Nachum Dershowitz. Together they have written a book that explores these different calendars, how they evolved and how to jump from one to another. It also describes how to determine secular and religious holidays and how to calculate lunar phases, solstices, equinoxes, sunrise times and sunset times.

At this Web page, which is basically a very academic advertisement for the book (though it also includes some older papers and publications by Dr. Reingold), you can sample a chapter.

If you're really into calendars and have an academic bent, you'll enjoy this page. As for me, well, I have enough trouble keeping my secular/Jewish calendar dates straight.

The Jewish Holidays

A vast number of sites on the Internet have meaningful pages about the Jewish holidays. Since we could not possibly get all of them in this book, this is only a sampling of these sites. The four Web addresses listed here are the central addresses for top-flight sites that will give you details on most of the holidays and lead you to other sites on the Internet. These sites should be your primary holiday resources on the Web. Some of the highlights of these sites are found in the holiday-by-holiday listings throughout this chapter:

http://www.wzo.org.il/encountr/holidays.htm#yk

http://www.jewishpost.com/jewishpost/index.html

http://www.jcn18.com/hanukkah/index.htm

http://www.torah.org/learning/yomtov/

Holiday Overviews

Frequently Asked Questions and Answers on Soc.Culture.Jewish

http://shamash.nysernet.org/lists/scj-faq/HTML/faq/05-01.html

This site contains a short synopsis of each of the Jewish holidays. It is a good place to get your bearings on the sequence of the Jewish calendar year. You can find other calendar-oriented sites in Chapter 9, which is focused on the Jewish calendar. Another excellent general resource is the bibliography of the High Holidays found at *http://www2.huji.ac.il/www_melton/erosh.html.*

Rosh Hashanah

Rosh Hashana Postings

http://www.torah.org/learning/yomtov/roshhshn.htm

Rosh Hashanah, which falls on the first day of the first month of Tishrei, marks the beginning of a new year. The celebration of this holiday is marked with solemnity, as it is the day on which the whole world is judged for the coming year.

The postings on this site are all rabbinical essays. Topics include: The Month of Elul: Preparation and Customs; Rosh HaShana as The Epitome of G-d's Kindness; The Shofar: A Wake-Up Call; The Custom of Eating Symbolic Foods; the fast of Tzom Gedalya; The Ten Days of Repentance: Ideas For Inspiration; and Repentance: A Story.

You Won't Pass Out This New Year

http://www.haam.media.ucla.edu/regissue/newyear.html

"So, how was your Jewish new year? Have a great party? Drink lots of beer? See any fireworks? No??

Well, I didn't think so. The celebration of the Jewish new year is actually quite different than most other new year celebrations."

As you can see, some of this site's text is a bit tongue in cheek but it goes to the heart of the holiday—the Jewish New Year is unlike any other new year's celebration, and this site reminds you of that.

The Yo-Yo Diet Guide to the Jewish Holidays

http://www.extremely.com/yoyodiet.html

This lighthearted page is a bit of a spoof. This essay tells you which holidays you feast on and which holidays you fast on. It's not complicated, but it's funny.

Return to Creation

http://www.wzo.org.il/encountr/return.htm

This is a set of essays touching on Rosh Hashanah. Some of them are quite memorable. Here's a bit of one:

> On the eve before Rosh Hashanah late at night, the man cleaved to the shadows sliding his way to the rabbi's house without being seen. Crouched by the open window, he saw a single candle and two books. Reb Levi was peering into each one intensely much like an accountant checking columns and comparing them. Finally he closed both books, and holding them up in each hand, he called out from the depths of his soul, "Dear God: In my right hand is a list of all the bad things which we have done over the past year; in the left hand are all the bad things which you have done to us for the past year. They are both very complex and heavy. I'll make you a deal: Let's cancel both books and start out again. What do you think?

Also included on this site are discussions of other High Holiday topics: customs of Rosh Hashanah, a High Holiday survival guide, and New Year's resolutions.

The Book of Job

http://www.torah.org/learning/iyov/

The Book of Job is read during the Rosh Hashanah Service. This is a site about the Book of Job and the moral questions it raises. It offers the words of great scholars. For example:

> The Malbim, in the introduction to his commentary on this holy book, explains that the main purpose of the Book of Job is to expound upon one of the most perplexing phenomena in the human experience; the apparent lack of justice throughout history. All too often the righteous suffer and the wicked prosper. The underlying pain in this question has bothered the great thinkers in every generation including the greatest of all prophets, Moses.

The Teshuva Process During the Yamim Nora'im (Days of Awe)

http://shamash.nysernet.org/mail-jewish/
mail-jewish/rav/yom_kippur_94.txt

This Web page presents thoughts on repentence. It is a brilliant essay by a master teacher:

> According to the Rambam[Maimonides], teshuva[repentance] has a well defined and formulated structure. It is a process containing clear strata, involving recognition of sin, remorse, shame and resolve. There are guideposts in prayer that lead one to engage in this process, including vidui as well as much of the Yom Kippur liturgy. Teshuva is an all encompassing activity, engaging man's logic, will and emotion.

Days of Awe

http://user03.blue.aol.com/jewfaq/holiday3.htm

This is another on-line essay that aims to explain the intimate relationship with God that Jews attain during the High Holidays. You can judge the quality of this essay for yourself:

> One of the ongoing themes of the Days of Awe is the concept that Gd has "books" that he writes our names in, writing down who will live and who will die, who will have a good life and who will have a bad life, for the next year. These books are written in on Rosh Hashanah, but our actions during the Days of Awe can alter God's decree. The actions that change the decree are "*teshuvah, tefilah* and *tzedakah*," repentance, prayer, good deeds (usually, charity). These "books" are sealed on Yom Kippur. This concept of writing in books is the source of the common greeting during this time is "May you be inscribed and sealed for a good year."

News and Observations from Israel— Rosh Hashana Poll

http://www.mofet.macam98.ac.il/~izak/israel/a/0028.html

Every culture has a set of year-opening rituals. In secular countries, these are the beginning of a new calendar year and the resolutions that set goals for the new year. In Israel, the new year unofficially begins with a Rosh Hashanah poll of how Israelis feel about the coming year. It's very interesting and certainly puts things in perspective. This site puts together the results of this annual poll and makes some fascinating observations about it.

Yom Kippur

Yom Kippur
http://www.jtsa.edu/pubs/parashah/5756/yomkippur.html

This is a Web essay on the site of the Jewish Theological Seminary of America about the meaning of Yom Kippur, and it is written by JTSA Chancellor Ismar Schorsch:

> The High Holy Days don't play to our strength. The extended services put a premium on prayer, an activity at which we are no longer very adept. Yom Kippur asks of us to spend an entire day in the synagogue immersed in prayer. But we find it easier to believe in God than to pray to God. It is this common state of discomfort that prompts me to share with you a few thoughts on the art of Jewish praying.

It's No Contest for Faithful Jewish Fans
http://www.beaconjournal.com/10.2yomkip.html

This Web page has an amusing article about giving up baseball during the High Holidays, entitled "Tribe's opening playoff game tomorrow night just not in same league with Yom Kippur, holiest day of the year."

Holidays with a Twist—Yom Kippur
http://www.wzo.org.il/encountr/holidays.htm#yk

This site is a great source for holiday stories. One written by famed Yiddish writer I.L. Peretz starts this way:

> The town square...an ordinary day, neither a market day nor a day of the fair, a day of drowsy small activity...Suddenly there is heard, coming from just outside the town, approaching nearer and nearer, a wild impetuous clatter, a splutter and splashing of mud, a racket of furious wheels! In-ter-es-ting, think the merchants, wonder who it is? At their booths, at their storefronts, they peer out, curious.

If you're curious about the rest of the story, check out this site.

Yom Kippur Postings

http://www.torah.org/learning/yomtov/yomkppur.htm

This site offers Orthodox teachings on the ritual behavior and the lessons to be derived from proper Yom Kippur worship. Topics include: Understanding Our Special Conduct, Yom Kippur: A Lesson For Life, and Yom Kippur: Interpersonal Relationships.

Yom Kippur as Sacred Theatre

http://www.jtsa.edu/masoret/vol5/iss1/sacredth.html

This is a page from the on-line version of the Jewish Theological Seminary of America's publication *Masoret*. It describes the drama of the Yom Kippur observation:

> No day of the Jewish year is as dramatic as Yom Kippur. We sense the anticipation of the throngs crowding into the synagogue, and draw in our breath at the first haunting notes of Kol Nidre.

We Must Retrieve our Covenantal Relationship with God

http://www.jewish.com/bk950929/comm1.htm

Rabbi David Hartman's opinion piece in the *Jewish Bulletin of Northern California* is an excellent essay about the underlying theological importance of the High Holidays and how some modern observances have gotten away from that core concept.

Sukkot and Simchat Torah

Materials on Succot in the Pedagogic Centre's Collection

http://www2.huji.ac.il/www_melton/esukkot.html

This bibliographic listing of printed materials that are available for this holiday is posted by the library of the Melton Center for Jewish Education in the Diaspora at Hebrew University. It can be quite useful if you are trying to find written resources on Sukkot.

Holidays with a Twist—Succot

http://www.wzo.org.il/encountr/holidays.htm#succot

This is one of many essays about the Jewish holidays on this Web site by journalist Eli Birnbaum. Birnbaum has a humorous yet incisive way of connecting observances to everyday life:

> Golf and Succot have a lot in common, really. First there's the above title, which I'll deal with below. Then of course, both are held outdoors; third, both have people walking around with some kind a of stick and ball waving them around, with the rest of us trying to figure out what they're doing. Both are cancelled on account of rain. Both have a lot to do with green. Did you ever think of why there are 18 holes? Sure: 18 in Hebrew is "Chai" - life. Which brings us to the next point that they are both holy. Lastly my wife says I putter around too much decorating the succah. This is really terrible, but now that I got your attention...

You can read the rest of this story on the site. Also about Sukkot are "Happiness Is... a Cozy Succah," "The Small Succah—A Yiddish Folksong," and "Futility and Cockroaches".

Hannukah

The Jewish Communications Network Celebrates Chanukah

http://www.jcn18.com/hanukkah/index.htm

This is the best Hannukah site on the Internet! It tells the story of Hannukah, which is not unusual, but what is unusual is the other slickly programmed Hannukah material, including the world's first virtual dreidl, the top twelve reasons we like Hanukkah, and a bunch of appetizing-sounding holiday recipes. Another excellent, though less visually impressive, resource is "A Happy Chanukah," at http://w3.trib.com/~dont/chanukah.html, which relates the story of the miracle of Hannukah and provides links to other on-line resources about this holiday.

The Story of Chanukah in English and French

http://www.webcom.com/rel/chanuk2.html

This bilingual Web page from a Sephardic site in Montreal offers a short version of the Hannukah story, including rabbinical essays, in both English and French. It is well presented and part of a growing body of resources for French-speaking Jews.

Women and Chanukah by Eliezer Segal

http://www.ucalgary.ca/~elsegal/
Shokel/931209_In_the_Miracle.html

Journalist Eliezer Segal has put more than 100 of his essays, most of which originally appeared in the *Jewish Free Press*, on-line at his Web site. This particular essay looks at a fascinating issue I had never given much thought to previously—the role of women historically and today in the Hannukah celebration:

There is little in the major themes of Hannukah that would characterize it as a distinctively female holiday. Women do not figure prominently in either the military victories or in the miracle of the jar of oil. And yet Jewish tradition has emphasized that women have a special connection to the celebration, and in some communities they are accustomed to refraining from work while the candles are lit.

No my dear...Chanukah is not the Jewish Christmas!
http://w3.trib.com/~dont/chanukah.html

This whimsical illustrated site created by Don Tolin offers an overview of what Hannukah is—not just what it's not. Hannukah is not simply a transplantation of Christmas into Jewish terminology. It is a uniquely Jewish holiday that is celebrated for reasons that are important to Jews and Judaism. The text discusses the history and traditions of the holiday and has links to many other Hannukah Web sites. The title merely gives a hint of this site's perspective.

Chanukah—Supremacy Over Greece and Rome
gopher://israel.nysernet.org:70/00/judaica/tanach/
commentary/oxford-judaism/chanukagreece

This is a plain-text article that gives an unusual amount of detail about the politics of the Middle East after the destruction of the first commonwealth and about the event referred to as "the miracle menorah." Another look at the historical basis of the Macabee revolt can be found at *http://www.jcn18.com/hanukkah/strass1.htm.*

Fast of the Tenth of Tevet

Fast of 10th of Tevet
http://www.torah.org/learning/yomtov/tevet.htm

The Fast of the Tenth of Tevet is observed to recognize the beginning of the siege of Jerusalem by the forces of

Nebuchadnezzar and is thus connected with the destruction of Jerusalem and the Temple.

This page contains rabbinical essays about the Fast of the Tenth of Tevet and the power of prayer.

Tu B'shvat

JCN's Tu B'Shvat Home Companion
http://www.jcn18.com/

This site is a very interesting resource. It includes a Tu B'shvat Seder and Haggadah and talks about the relationship between Judaism and the environment:

> Tu B'Shvat, literally the fifteenth day of the Hebrew month of Shvat, is called *Rosh Hashana La'Ilanot* [the new year for the trees]. It marks the point when rabbis say the fruit of the trees— nourished by winter rains—begins to form. Israeli school children plant trees on Tu B'Shvat, as part of a hundred year old effort to reforest the country, an effort urged particularly by the Jewish National Fund.

Tu B'shvat from Project Genesis
http://www.torah.org/learning/yomtov/tubshvat.htm

This Web page is a rabbinic *parshat* on the *Mishna* explaining the reason for the Tu B'shvat holiday:

> The first Mishna in the tractate of Rosh HaShanah tells us that there are four "new years." One of these is the new year for trees... We follow the opinion of the school of Hillel, and we therefore celebrate the new year for trees on the 15th of Sh'vat. The holiday is called Tu B'Shvat because "Tu" is the pronunciation of the numeral 15 when spelled out (the letter "tet" and the letter "vav."). Hence, Tu B'Shvat means the 15th of Sh'vat.

Tu Bishvat (the Trees' Birthday): Stories about Honi Ha'Meagel
http://www.ualberta.ca/~yreshef/tuintro.htm

This Purim page contains stories about Honi Ha'Meagel. Honi is a Jewish folkore character, although some basis in reality for the stories is claimed. The truth or fiction of Honi is almost immaterial. However, the site gives you both versions, and the stories make nice reading for your children.

Tu Bishvat "For Man is as a Tree in a Field"
http://www.jajz-ed.org.il/tub96idx.html

In Israel, Tu B'shvat has become something of an environmental awareness event. This site from the Joint Authority for Jewish Zionist Education is an excellent resource for materials, activities, and projects for school children celebrating this holiday.

Purim

The Jewish Post Purim
http://www.jewishpost.com/holidays/purim/

This is part of the *Jerusalem Post* holiday Web pages, and it has a lot of child-oriented activities and information for one of Judaism's most festive holidays, including how to make a *gragger* (noisemaker), how to bake *hamentashen*, and masks children can print out and color to create Purim costumes. You can also read charming versions of the story of Purim and learn about Queen Esther, King Ahasuerus, Mordecai, and the hated Haman.

Another site with a number of fun Purim activities is found at *http://www.jcn18.com/holiday/purim/index.htm*.

This excellent resource from the Jewish Communications Network includes a number of unique activities, including a Java-powered Purim word-search game you can play over the Internet.

You may also want to check out *http://www.holidays.net/ purim/*, which has resources like an audio file of a *gragger* being twirled, stories, childrens activities, and recipes. One interesting thing to read is a fan letter about the site from Stephen Hakesberg, who describes himself as the only Jew in Greenland.

For more Purim recipes, try these two sites for appealing Hamatashen varieties:

> *http://www.fwi.uva.nl/~mes/recipe/usenet/ hamantashen.htm*
>
> *http://users.uniserve.com/~hostrov/recipe.html*

Purim, Parody, and Pilpul

http://www.ucalgary.ca/~elsegal/Shokel/
880219_Purim_Parody.html

In this short essay, Journalist Eliezer Segal explains why Purim has a special place in the Jewish experience.

> Ostensibly a commemoration of national deliverance from danger, we should have expected solemn ceremonies of thanksgiving such as characterize Passover and Hanukkah. The victory over Haman is, however, distinguished by a unique mood of high-spirited frivolity, coloured by high alcoholic content and a general tendency to make light of matters which would be treated more reverently at other seasons.

Megillat Esther on the Internet

http://www.613.org/purim.html

This Web site carries an audio reading of the Megillat Esther that you can play and download.

Vashti: A Feminist Heroine?
http://www.ucalgary.ca/~elsegal/Shokel/910301_Vashti.html

This plain text page presents the rabbinical debate over the story of Vashti, which is one of the more fascinating aspects of the Purim history. Here's the opening of the essay, put together by Eliezer Segal. Read the opinions and then make up your own mind about whether Vashti was a positive or negative character:

> Vashti has become one of the favourite heroines of the Jewish feminist movement. This much-maligned queen, the argument goes, should be appreciated as a positive role model, a woman who dared to disregard a royal decree that would have her displayed as a sex object before King Ahashverosh's rowdy drinking companions. Her ultimate downfall should accordingly be viewed as a martyrdom to the cause of sexual equality.

Passover

General Index on Pesach
http://www.jajz-ed.org.il/pes96idx.html

This site bills itself as the A–Z index of Passover. Believe it!

It contains a real wealth of materials on this holiday. It includes essays on the laws and customs for Passover and historical aspects of the Passover Haggadah. It even has Passover games and projects for children, including The Exodus—A Simulation Game. It's a very important site, and it is easy to search because it is organized alphabetically and by department. It can help make your Passover more meaningful.

A Passover CD-ROM
http://www.xpert.com/dee/passover.htm

If you've got everything else about Passover, you may want to check out the *Passover* CD-ROM, which is described and sold via this Web site. The CD-ROM includes games like Rescue Moses from the Nile, a pictorial tour of ancient Egypt, and recordings of traditional holiday songs.

Another commercial Passover Web site is *http://www.chabad.org/1800shmura/*. The Lubavitch Organization Web site tells you how to order Shmura Matzah, specially prepared for the Passover holiday (though the on-line order mechanism wasn't working when I tried to access it).

Holiday Guide to Passover from the Lubavitch Organization

gopher://gopher.chabad.org:70/00/guide/pesach

This is a practical but blandly presented guide to Passover. It contains the dates and times that the holiday begins. It talks about the order of the Seder, searching for and selling Chometz (items that are not permissible to be owned on Passover), the proper prayers for the lighting of the holiday candles, the significance of the various items on the Seder plate, and how to arrange the Seder plate.

Selling Your Chametz

gopher://chabad.org/00/texts/hagada.exp/contract

This one-page text site contains a "contract" for selling your Chometz to a non-Jew before Passover and describes how to execute the contract as well.

A Virtual Seder Plate

http://www.shamash.org/reform/uahc/congs/nj/nj006/seder/plate.html

Making up the Seder plate can be a bit confusing unless you have access to this nifty little site. These clickable pages tell you how to prepare the Seder plate, the significance of each item on it, and even how it should look.

The Jewish Communciation Network Passover

http://www.jcn18.com/holiday/passover/index.htm

One of the better Passover sites on the Web, this page contains colorful illustrations and some interesting and unusual material, including the JCN Interactive Internet Haggadah; The Anonymous Haggadah: A synthesis of the Passover ritual and liturgy with the Twelve Steps of Recovery (you can download this Haggadah as a Microsoft Word document); Passover for Food Lovers (there aren't a lot of recipes here, but you can learn to make a passover breakfast with Matzoh Brie); and the Rabbi Eliezer Incident (the story of a power struggle at the Sanhedrin, which was the ancient Rabbinical court).

Sometimes I think that the producers of the Jewish Communication Network enjoy the shock value of their rather eccentric contributions as much as they do the actual material contained therein. This is part of the site's charm, but it can be very disconcerting.

Passover—French Edition

http://www.webcom.com/rel/passover.html

This site was created by the Sephardic community in Montreal, Quebec, which is home to the largest French-speaking Jewish population outside France itself. It has French transliterations of prayers and an explanation of Passover rituals.

Passover on the Net

http://www.melizo.com/holidays/passover/

This is a colorful, well-organized presentation of the Passover story, an explanation of the Seder, the Four Questions, music you can play and sing along with, the results of their World Wide Web matzoh hunt, and a number of Passover recipes.

You can find more holiday recipes at *http:// www.marketnet.com/mktnet/kosher/recipes.html*, which has Web links to many recipe pages and a number of appealing recipes from Kosher Express—Passover granola, cream cheese brownies, and apple matzoh kugel, to name a few.

Passover Postings from Project Genesis

http://www.torah.org/learning/yomtov/pesach.htm

This site has detailed information about the Passover Seder. It is mostly text, and the material is not easy to read or digest, but the information at this site is of a very high quality, with essays on everything from "The Evil Son and the Importance of Unity" to a detailed breakdown of the Haggadah. You might want to look at this site for some very interesting thoughts on Passover, but only after you've viewed some of the more easy-to-read sites.

Passover—The Haggadah

I must admit to a partiality for the Passover Haggadah. No matter how many I acquire, I want more of them. I look forward to the months preceding the holiday to start scouring the Jewish bookstores to ask if any new ones have come out "this year." Invariably the answer is in the affirmative, and I go home with another Haggadah under my arm. Some of the earliest Jewish illuminated manuscripts were Passover Haggadot. You can find selections of these historic volumes in museums around the world. Illustrations from the 15th century Cincinnati Haggadah (seen on the front cover of this book) by Meir B. Israel Jaffe of Heidelberg can be found on the Internet at *http://www.emanuelnyc.org/seder/seder.html*.

Several thousand haggadot have been printed since the 15th Century. One of the oldest known was printed in Guadajara, Spain in 1482—before the expulsion of the Jews from that country ten years later.

In our time, the Haggadah has taken many different forms. Who could forget the Maxwell House Haggadah that found its way into millions of homes for the Passover Seder, a subtle reminder that Maxwell House Coffee is Kosher for Passover.

Several very different Haggadot are listed here. A few are very special. My own favorite would have to be the Rainbow Haggadah, not because of its artistry or commentaries but because of its expression of faith in a moment of despair.

The Rainbow Haggadah

http://www.jtsa.edu/pubs/parashah/5756/passover.html

Late in World War II, the American Army's 42nd (Rainbow) Division was fighting in Germany. These soldiers used local presses to print this basic Haggadah. It was the first Hebrew text printed in Germany since the end of 1939, when the destruction of Germany's Jewish population neared completion.

Read its story, and learn a bit about Jewish publishing in Hitler's Germany at this site.

Uncle Ely's Haggadah

http://www.ucalgary.ca/~elsegal/Uncle_Eli/Eli.html

The house had gone crazy, all turned upside-down, with everyone busily running around.

Mommy was screaming "Get out of the way!

You can't keep on lying around here all day!

Tomorrow is Passover. You don't look ready.

We have to remove everything that is bready.

Pack up the old dishes and pull out the new.

Prepare for the seder! There's too much to do!

So begins Uncle Ely's Haggadah for kids, found on this Web site. This is a novel Haggadah and a fun way to make children feel a part of the holiday and the Seder itself.

The Parnes Haggadah

http://www-personal.umich.edu/
~bparnes/HAGGADAH/seder1.htm

This beautifully written English-language Haggadah makes the Seder service understandable to all. It is not a traditional Haggadah because it contains no Hebrew except for some transliterations, but it deserves a look. You may want to incorporate parts of it into your own Seder.

The Rheingold Family Haggadah—You Don't Have to Be Jewish to Celebrate Freedom

http://www.cyborganic.com/People/ovid/haggadah.html

> Passover is a Jewish holiday, but it isn't just for Jews. We welcome our non-Jewish brothers and sisters to our celebration of liberation. Liberation from oppression is always a deep concern of Jews, because of our history. But Jews are not the only people who suffer under the yoke of oppression. We invite our friends and family to share this night with Jews all over the world, as we take this opportunity to celebrate our freedom and pray for the freedom of all those who suffer, wherever and whoever they may be.

Howard Rheingold is trying to accomplish the same task, and this Haggadah is part of his effort. It's a text-only Hagadah, with some Hebrew. Unfortunately, it is only readable as a single long scrolling page, which does not take advantage of the World Wide Web's presentation features.

Passover Seder—Congregation Emanu-El of the City of New York

http://www.emanuelnyc.org/seder/seder.html

This well-crafted and heavily illustrated site includes a Reform Seder service. It also has images of a number of ancient Haggadot, including the First Cincinnati

Haggadah (Germany, 15th century), the Second Cincinnati Haggadah (Moravia, 1717), and two others that date from the 1740s. The images are absolutely stunning

Chabad Passover Haggadah

http://www.chabad.org/sie/haggadah.htm

This English-language Chabad Haggadah is available as a plain-text version on line from a link to this site. It is also available in book form. It's simple and straightforward, with an anthology of commentaries and stories from the rabbis.

A Growing Haggadah

http://www.computergeeks.com/haggadah

This Haggadah from Rabbi Mark Hurwitz contains two very interesting documents within itself. The first is a listing of extant Haggadot. The Haggadah has been printed in more than 3,000 different versions. It is the only Jewish document to have this many versions. Some are simple and others are lavishly illuminated.

The second aspect of this Haggadah, which I find particularly interesting, is the juxtaposition of the Haggadah and the Last Supper of Christianity. The author of this Haggadah provides many historical details, and it's quite fascinating.

The Haggadah itself is quite tedious to go through on-line. You have to click to go to each page and it is a laborious task. You can buy the print version from the author. If you find it to your liking, that is certainly a recommended choice.

The Sarajevo Haggadah

http://www.vol.it/canal/haggadae.htm

This Web site sells the CD-ROM version of the historic Sarajevo Hagaddah. This is a very attractive and well-presented package which the vendor describes:

A multimedial navigation through the Sarajevo Haggadah, one of the most important Jewish illuminated Codices of the Middle Ages. This Haggadah on a CD-Rom has been prepared by the Italian Jewish community. The entire Codex is reproduced, it's history told and English and Italian translations are offered.

Haggadot Exhibition

gopher://chabad.org/00/currents/libagu

The Chabad Organization of Lubavitch offers a Haggadah exhibition every year at its headquarters in New York City. Look at this site for its schedule and a brief description of the collection.

The organization has some 200 Haggadot on exhibition, from a library of 2,000 Haggadot published since 1540. A number of Haggadot that are more than 300 years old (1540-1695) are on display.

The site also explains a bit about the Lubavitcher Rebbe's role in creating and annotating Haggadot and the history of Haggadot as publications.

The Omer

The seven-week period between Passover and Shavuot is marked on a daily basis by Sefiras HaOmer (the Counting of the Omer).

Sefiras HaOmer

http://www.torah.org/learning/yomtov/omer.htm

This is an on-line essay about the Rabbinic reasons for observing the counting of the Omer and why we observe it as we do. It also tells the story of Rabbi Akiva and his pupils:

> The Talmud... tells us that "Rabbi Akiva had 12,000 pairs of students... and all of them died in one period of time because they did not conduct themselves with respect towards one another... they all died between Pesach and Shavuos... and they all died a terrible death.

On the 33rd day of the Omer, which falls on the 18th of Iyar, we commemorate the occasion.

The great sadness of the preceding 32 days is overtaken with an immense celebration for the 33rd day. Marriage which may not be performed during the period between Passover and the 33rd day are now allowed and in Israel children are taken to the grave of Rabbi Shimon Bar Yohai in Miron to have their first haircuts.

Lag B'Omer

Lag B'Omer is the thirty-third day of the counting of the Omer. It is a day of celebration in Israel. According to tradition, the students of the great sage Rabbi Akiva, who had been dying in great numbers, stopped dying on this day.

A Journey to Meron

http://www.jerusalembooks.com/meron/index.htm

This is an unusual on-line photo album of a bus trip of Orthodox Jews who are going to visit the burial site of Rabbi Shimon Bar Yochai. It also has a number of songs about Meron and the Rabbi. The observance of Lag B'Omer is very interesting, and this site gives you a bit of the flavor of the holiday.

Go Jewish, Get Mystic

http://www.lia.org/mystic.html

This Web page on the site of the Jewish student group Lights in Action lends a mystical experience to Lag B'Omer and the traditions of Rabbi Shimon Bar Yochai. It explains his Kabbalist teachings and how they relate to quantum physics.

Yom HaShoah
(Holocaust Remembrance Day)

Yom HaShoah was established to remember the Holocaust and the six million Jews who perished. It falls on the twenty-ninth day of Nissan, the anniversary of the Warsaw Ghetto uprising.

Yom HaShoah—How to Remember the Holocaust

http://www.torah.org/learning/yomtov/holocast.htm

This set of essays written by Rabbi Yehuda Prero for Project Genesis explains how to commemorate the fallen on this day of mourning. It provides appropriate biblical readings, a story about Hannukah in Auschwitz, and makes the important point that the Holocaust was not the only or final incident of anti-Semitism, and that we must remain vigilant.

> Shoah is the Hebrew word for "whirlwind." It is the term used to described the conflagration that swept up six million Jewish souls between 1938 and 1945. A war was waged against the Jews in which unspeakable atrocities were perpetrated against a defenseless people. Men and women, young and old alike, were butchered at the hands of the accursed Nazis, may their name be eradicated for all time. Every year, on Yom HaShoah, we remember the martyrs who sanctified the name of God in the camps, the ghettos, and in the gas chambers.

Holocaust Remembrance Day

http://www.melizo.com/jewishpost/holocaust/

This slow but ornate site, called "Don't Let the Light Go Out" displays a number of animated movies, historical images, Quicktime movies and sound from the CD-ROM *Lest We Forget* to bring you a little closer to the horror that is and was the Holocaust. There are images of the camps in Germany, faces of the victims, film about the rise of the Nazis, and the decimation of the Polish Jews. There is also a Holocaust discussion board so you can offer your thoughts and feedback.

Yom Hazikaron

Commitment of a Lifetime

http://www.wzo.org.il/encountr/yomzik.htm

This is a passage about Yom Hazikaron from Robin Treistman on the World Zionist Organization site, which remembers Israel's fallen soldiers. She comments on the differences between Israel's solemn ceremony and America's celebratory Memorial Day.

A number of years ago I accompanied my wife and daughters on a trip to Mt. Herzl's military cemetery. We visited various sections of the deceptively quiet burial grounds of some of Israel's finest sons and daughters. We tramped from section to section. I could tell my children about this person or that one. They were not strangers. We shared a sense of history with them. Here Hannah Senesh was buried and there were the graves for the martyrs of Gush Etzion. (Their story is told at *http://www.jajz-ed.org.il/etzion3.html*). Each grave was a story. All of a sudden the still of the day was broken with a loud wail. In the distance we could hear a middle-aged woman crying. We didn't try to get any closer. We didn't want to interrupt her private moment with her loved one. It could have been her father or her husband, her brother or her son... It is on this one day of the year that we as a nation collectively mourn our loss.

Yom HaAtazma'ut (Israel Independence Day)

Yom Hazikaron is immediately followed by Yom HaAtzmaut. In the space of minutes a nation goes from mourning and despair to joy and happiness. The message is a simple one: Am Yisroel Chai, Israel, the people, the nation, the state lives on. The oppressors of this and every generation can inflict their wounds but they can't destroy our spirit and our being.

We are a generation sandwiched between two giant historical events of the Jewish nation: the Holocaust and the birth of the State of Israel. These two events, more than any other in the history of our people since the beginning of the Diaspora, have molded our national character. They have contributed to our every action as a people and they have profoundly affected the lives of millions of people. To some, the Holocaust is an abstract event. You can try to understand it, but you really can't comprehend it, for it is too staggering. Many books have been written about the Holocaust. They pose questions and give answers. But no answer is adequate. Some survivors came away from the Holocaust devoid of faith. Others found faith.

Then along came the State of Israel. Its creation spawned even more questions and provided some more answers, but it also served another need. It rejuvenated a people and it gave millions of Jews a reason to want to go on. Israel has problems. What country doesn't? But ancient Israel also had problems. There is no time in the history of the Jewish people that we have been devoid of difficulties of one sort or another. At least with a Jewish state we can say, "It's ours." Criticize it all you want. Everything you say is correct. Every question is valid. But what is most truthful of all is the very existence of a Jewish state. *Am Yisroel Chai.*

Yom HaAtazma'ut (Israel Independence Day)
http://www.jajz-ed.org.il/atz96idx.html

This Web page contains the official prayer for The State of Israel. It is said in many congregations on the Sabbath and holidays as well as on Yom Ha'Atzmaut.

Materials on Yom Ha'Atzmaut in English
http://www2.huji.ac.il/www_melton/yom.html

This site, part of the Melton Center reference library of Hebrew University, contains material on teaching about both Yom Ha'Atzmaut and Israel. The extensive bibliography of books and videos contains a brief summary of each listing.

Yom Yerushalyim
(Jerusalem Day)

On June 7, 1967, Israeli troops crashed through the Arab defenses and recaptured the parts of the holy city of Jerusalem that had previously been in Arab possession. Yom Yerushalayim commemorates this victory, which reunited Jerusalem.

Yom Yerushalayim Postings

http://www.torah.org/learning/yomtov/jeruslem.htm

This set of pages from the Project Genesis teaching program offers rabbinical insights into Jerusalem's paramount significance to the Jewish people. Please note when you are typing in this Web address that you need to use their abbreviated spelling of *Jerusalem* (*jeruslem*) to reach these pages.

Reunification of Jerusalem: A Soldier's Talk

http://www.virtual.co.il/city_services/holidays/yomyer/soldier.htm

The following is an excerpt from the memoirs of Yisrael Harel, a journalist who served in the Israeli Paratroops during the Six Day War. It is a page from the Virtual Jerusalem on-line guide, which has a photo tour of the city, stories, a time line, a quiz, and upcoming events in the city:

> On the 28th of Iyyar, 5727 (June 1967), I ran with my unit, Battalion 28, Paratroops Brigade 55—or rather what was left of the unit after two days of combat—from the Lion's Gate to the Plaza of the Temple Mount. Though the battle for the Old City had nearly been decided, well-aimed snipers' bullets continued to wound and kill men from our ranks. Yet we still felt that we were floating on air as we headed from the very zenith of the achievements of the Six Day war: liberating the Temple Mount and the Western wall.
>
> And when we stopped, out of breath from both exhaustion and excitement, we heard, crackling from our radios, Colonel Mordechai Gur's now famous cry: 'The Temple Mount is in our hands! Repeat: The Temple Mount is in our hands!'"

Another interesting part of the Virtual Jerusalem site is a detailed history of Jerusalem that takes you from the arrival of Abraham though the various occupiers (Roman, Byzantine, Muslim, Crusader, Ottoman, and British) and up to the current Israeli state. One thing you learn on this site is that "The name of the city appears as "Urushalem", meaning "the foundation of the city of the god Shalem.

Shavu'ot

What Is Shavuot?

http://www.planet.net/peterr/shavuot.html

This is an on-line handbook about the observation and history of Shavuot, a major festival that marks the giving of the Torah by God to the entire Jewish people on Mount Sinai. This guide is not exactly easy reading, but it is quite thorough.

Shavuot on the Net

http://www.jewishpost.com/holidays/shavuot/

This portion of the *Jerusalem Post* holiday listings site includes a number of fascinating essays about Shavuot, including "The Story of Shavuot" and the "Day of the First Fruits"; "Celebrating Shavuot with the Legends and Customs of the Holiday"; and "The Receiving of the Ten Commandments at Mount Sinai."

Fasts of Seventeenth of Tamuz and Ninth of Av

Fasts of 17th of Tamuz and 9th

http://www.torah.org/learning/yomtov/fasts.htm

This is another part of the excellent Project Genesis rabbinical commentaries. It includes several parshat about the reasons and observances behind this day of fasting. It does a nice job of quickly summarizing what this holiday is all about:

> The fast of the 17th of Tamuz begins a three week period of mourning. This time of mourning ends with the fast of the 9th of Av. The reason we mourn during this time is because the 17th of Tamuz marks the date on which the walls of Jerusalem were breached during the campaign that ended with the destruction of the Temple on the 9th of Av.
>
> Tisha B'Av is the saddest day in the Jewish calendar and the Mishna (Ta'anit) tells us that five things happened to our forefathers on this day. They are:

- It was decreed that the generation of the wilderness should not enter the promised land
- The first Temple was destroyed
- The second Temple was destroyed
- Betar was captured
- Jerusalem was ploughed over

Napoleon and Tisha B'av

http://www.lia.org/mornjoy.html

This is an interesting historical tale from the Lights in Action Jewish Student Group home page:

> Napoleon once halted his Imperial procession outside a Paris Synagogue upon hearing a cacophony of wails and cries. Believing that some sort of massacre was taking place, he immediately descended from his horse and stormed inside. There, Napoleon saw hundreds of Jews in tears, sitting on the floor in torn clothing.

If you want to hear what he said on seeing this particularly dramatic observance of Tisha B'av, read the rest of the story on this Web page.

CHAPTER 11

The Sabbath

"Remember the Sabbath day, to keep it holy. Six days shalt thou labor and do all thy work; but the seventh day is the Sabbath to Hashem your God; in it thou shalt not do any work, thou, nor thy son, nor thy daughter, thy manservant, nor thy maidservant, nor thy cattle, nor thy stranger that is within thy gates; for in six days, Hashem made heaven and earth, the sea, and all that is in them, and rested on the seventh day; therefore Hashem blessed the Sabbath day and hallowed it" (Exodus 20:8-11)

How important is the Sabbath? The Sabbath is called "yesod ha'emunah" (the very foundation of our faith), as it is written, "Between Me and the children of Israel, it is a sign forever." (Exodus 31:17) Rabbi Yudan said that according to the ordinary custom of the world, the master tells his servants, "Work for me six days and one day shall be for yourselves." God, however, says, "Work for yourselves six days and for Me one day" (Pesikta Rabbasi 23:2).

But how do you prepare for the Sabbath? "One is obligated to prepare cooked foods, meat, oil and spiced wine for the pleasure of the Sabbath" (Maimonides, Mishnah Torah, Shabbat 30:7-10, Shabbat 118b, Beitzah 15b). The Sabbath makes everything different!

The Emperor Antoninus once asked Rabbi Yehuda ben Chaninah, "Why does the Sabbath dish give forth so appetizing a fragrance? Rabbi Yehuda replied, "We have a certain ingredient called Sabbath, which gives the food its pleasant fragrance." The Emperor said, "Let me have some of it." Rabbi Yehuda explained, "It is of use to him who observes the Sabbath, but for him who does not, it does no good" (Shabbat 119a).

Our sages taught us that in order to truly keep the Sabbath holy, we must remember it all week long and prepare for it. If you see something during the week that you would enjoy having on the Sabbath, by all means purchase it and set it aside for the Sabbath day. (Beitzah 15b)

The Sabbath is more than a physical day—the seventh day of the week. It is a state of mind and a state of being. The Sabbath is also a time for togetherness. You can best enjoy the Sabbath by sharing it with other people. If you're looking for a Sabbath experience, your local rabbi, synagogue, temple, outreach program, Hillel or Chabad house will be more than willing to help you find your way. In the following pages you will see how Jews celebrate the Sabbath.

The Nature of Sabbath

http://members.aol.com/jewfaq/shabbat.htm

This is a lucid and in-depth entry from the Judaism 101 site. It begins eloquently:

> The Sabbath (or Shabbat, as it is called in Hebrew) is one of the best known and least understood of all Jewish observances. People who do not observe Shabbat think of it as a day filled with stifling restrictions, or as a day of prayer like the Christian Sabbath. But to those who observe Shabbat, it is a precious gift from G-d, a day of great joy eagerly awaited throughout the week, a time when we can set aside all of our weekday concerns and devote ourselves to higher pursuits. In Jewish literature, poetry and music, Shabbat is described as a bride or queen, as in the popular Shabbat hymn Lecha Dodi Likrat Kallah (come, my beloved, to meet the [Sabbath] bride). It is said 'more than Israel has kept Shabbat, Shabbat has kept Israel.'

The joy of Shabbat, written by someone who clearly finds Shabbat joyful, is found here—along with some of the more technical aspects of Shabbat observance, clearly explained.

Shabbat
http://www.comsynrye.org/shabbook.html

This page also opens with the famous quote from the 19th-century writer Ahad Ha'am: "Even more than the Jewish people has kept Shabbat, so Shabbat has kept the Jewish people."

The site introduces you to the preparations for the Sabbath. It includes a "Shabbat Checklist," recipes for *challah* and *cholent* (a traditional hot meat and potato stew made without initiating any cooking on the Sabbath itself), and a small bibliography.

This is a fine place to start your journey into the Sabbath. As the page explains, "People pick and choose [various observances], remembering and observing Shabbat in their own special way. Shabbat is very unique and once the first step is taken—a Friday night Shabbat dinner with family, loved ones and/or friends, for example—you will grow to love it and build through it."

The Shabbat Seder
http://www.jtsa.edu/fjmc/fjmcsbat.html

The Federation of Jewish Men's Clubs offers a book called *The Shabbat Seder*. This site is a one-page overview of the publication. As the site describes the book, "[it] can also be used for self-study. In a straightforward, simple way, it maps out all the steps of the Friday evening ritual, describing how to perform them and explaining their meanings."

Unfortunately, the bulk of the material is in the book, not at this Web site. Viewing this site will either make you want to go out and purchase the book, or make you frustrated that you can't click on a link to read more.

Shabbos: Heaven on Earth

http://www.j51.com/~jrsflw/shabbos.htm

This is one of Aish HaTorah's Discovery classes. As usual, they take a very open and direct approach to their explanations:

"Most observant Jews will tell you that Shabbos is one of the greatest sources of inspiration. And, paradoxically, Shabbos is often the greatest hurdle to those testing the waters of Judaism... What is it about Shabbos that makes it so important, so powerful, and yet so mystifying to people who haven't experienced it?"

Sound intriguing? This is a good taste of what the Discovery series has to offer—and another excellent piece on Shabbat.

Shabbos Kodesh and the Rabbi and Wung Fung Tu

http://www.mja.net/neveh/price/price10.html

I won't tell you what the title means because, to fully appreciate it, you need to read this page yourself. What I can tell you is that it contains some very beautiful stories about the Sabbath and goes into many details about the observance of the Sabbath day.

This page is written from a very traditional point of view, and, for the most part, seems addressed to traditionalists—but not totally, and that is where the title of the site comes in.

Kiddush and Shabbat Zemirot of 613.org

http://www.613.org/shabbat.html

One of the sections of "613.org" (see the Education chapter), is on Shabbat. The materials here are in audio files—meaning that some of these files are quite large. But they are unique. They claim that "these *zemirot* [Shabbat songs] are the first free Jewish *zemirot* ever available on the Internet." Most of the contents of this page are songs and prayers, but there is also a 61-minute Introduction to Shabbat class.

Call it Shabbat or Shabbos or the Sabbath—it wouldn't be the same without music. Singing at the Sabbath table brings joy.

Challah—A Traditional Jewish Bread

http://www.acenet.auburn.edu:70/0/programs/family/
usenet_recipes/challah-1

Challah is a traditional Jewish bread. It has been used for centuries for all special occasions, which, of course, include the Sabbath and Jewish holidays. There are different shapes for different occasions and in different parts of the world. (For Rosh Hashanah, the Jewish New Year, for example, a round challah is traditional.)

On the Sabbath, two loaves of *challah* are used. They represent the two portions of manna that God gave the Jewish people in the desert in preparation for the Sabbath.

Throughout our history, the Sabbath table, its setting and its foods, have played a major role in Jewish life. The songs and stories told around the Sabbath table were used to impart tradition to the people. Tasty morsels that were often unavailable the rest of the week magically found their way to the table on this day. The mind was at ease from the travails of the workweek. The pauper became a scholar. His Sabbath table was now a treasured possession. The world was his. All the cares of this world disappeared in the flames of the Sabbath candles. The purple tinge of the wine reflected the glory of the Sabbath and the light of the candles themselves. And then there was the golden, delicious *challah*. No cake ever tasted so good! The whole house knew that the Sabbath was coming. The aroma of baking *challahs* found their way into every nook and cranny. You could sense the taste of the *challah* long before you entered the house or saw the table set in all its finery.

There is absolutely nothing as delicious in the entire world as a fresh Sabbath *challah*. This page includes one recipe. (Two others, in fact, appear at this site—simply replace *challah-1* with *challah-2* or *challah-3* in the Web address.) There are a host of others throughout this site.

Sabbath Candle Lighting Times

The appropriate time to light Shabbat candles is 18 minutes before Friday's sunset. The following sites can help you find the candle-lighting time in your area.

Virtual Jerusalem's Candle Lighting Times

http://www.virtual.co.il/city_services/candles/

Here you'll find candle-lighting times for 15 major cities around the world, brought to you from the folks at Virtual Jerusalem.

Hebrew Calendar

http://www.havienu.org/resrcs/hebcal.html

This is a powerful, impressive site that lets you specify what kind of a calendar you want to see on the Web. You enter a month and a year, and other options (including candle-lighting times for 54 cities around the world, most of them in the U.S.), press "Click Here To Make a Calendar," and *presto*—you're looking at a Hebrew calendar which contains information to rival the Jewish calendars you find at bookstores. It's an incredible resource.

Sunrise Sunset Calculation

http://tycho.usno.navy.mil/srss.html

What happens if you don't live in a major city? If you live in the U.S., this site from the Department of the Navy can take care of you. It will compute sunrise and sunset for

22,000 different towns and cities. And if that doesn't help, you can simply enter the latitude and longitude directly to get the information. But remember to subtract 18 minutes for appropriate observances (and/or add 48, or 72, or whatever your custom is, for the end of Shabbat).

For more selections of Sabbath facts, see also:

Sabbath and Holiday Observance
http://shamash.org/lists/scj-faq/HTML/faq/07-index.html

Food & Wine

Remember the ad from Levy's Rye bread which showed an American Indian biting into a slice of this obviously Jewish rye bread? The ad had just one line of copy: "You don't have to be Jewish to love Levy's."

When you think about it for even a fleeting moment, you begin to understand the nature of *kashruth*, or "keeping kosher". It is based upon tradition and law, and in many ways defines one's Jewish ethnicity. There are many people who will tell you that there is nothing like a real "kosher pickle" or a genuine "kosher salami." Chicken soup is considered a Jewish antibiotic and empirical studies have even attested to its medicinal value.

But what is Kosher all about? Deuteronomy sets out the concept of *kashruth*, or keeping kosher. It is based upon a number of statements (12:23, 14:7, 10-11, 21), and on two verses in Exodus (23:19, 34:26).

Essentially, the Bible divides the matter into two parts: setting forth the relationship between man and animal and specifying which foods or animals are considered non-kosher.

On the latter, the Bible is very clear. On the former, there is more room for individual interpretation, because according to Jewish Law, rules covering kosher or kashruth fall into the category of religious *chukim* (ordinances). Ordinances, by their very nature, defy explanation. You can explain away an ordinance. But it is merely "an" explanation—an expression of "your" understanding. It is not a definitive reason that necessarily meets logical criteria.

Why do Jews keep kosher? From a metaphysical point of view, man has a singular role to play in this world. In order for him to carry out this role he has to strive for a level of perfection. To do so, he must master both his mental and physical needs. Part of mastering the physical need is simply to watch what food he puts in his mouth.

Kashruth plays a social role as well. The role of kashruth in keeping the Jew apart from the general population is a very interesting one. Kashruth is not just about food. It is also about drink—specifically, wine, because it was used in idolatry and idol worship and because the use of wine causes inebriation. Inebriation often leads to social intercourse which in turn causes a familiarity to come about between the Jew and the non-Jew in a setting that blurs the differences between them. And this can lead to a too familiar relationship that is unacceptable from a traditional Jewish point of view.

Kashruth also plays another significant role—it differentiates between the permitted and the forbidden. There are certain things in life that are simply forbidden. Man accepts these things. He may challenge them, but by and large he accepts that there are things that he should and should not do. The Bible uses kashruth in part to accomplish this purpose—to set down the differentiation of what should and should not be done.

From a practical standpoint, observing the laws of kashruth effectively differentiates between the religiously observant and nonobservant Jew and between the Jew and the non-Jew.

The Bible sets out a few basic laws of kashruth, keeping kosher. Sages over the years have added to it and clarified it. For the most part, these laws fall into three categories: the eating of animals (certain animals and fish are prohibited, others must be slaughtered in a specified humane manner); mixing meat and milk products (which is prohibited); and special rules regarding wine or grape juice. (There is a fourth category relating to Passover, but we leave that for the Passover chapter.)

There is a great deal of misunderstanding about kashruth. Many non-Jews (and Jews for that matter) believe that the reasons behind the dietary laws have to do with health, and the problems of keeping or storing food in the desert. But do you really need religious rules for keeping people from eating contaminated food?

Keeping kosher has nothing to do with healthy food, but everything to do with taking a natural, animalistic urge—eating—and investing it with spirituality or holiness.

Note that except for the rules regarding wine and grape products, all of the laws relate to the eating or preparation of animals. While animals are certainly not as important as humans in the Jewish tradition, the sanctity of animal life is, nevertheless, an important consideration. In fact, some commentators view kashruth as a compromise to vegetarianism—noting that in the Garden of Eden, Adam and Eve ate only fruits and vegetables. In short, to a person who keeps kosher, eating an animal product is something that can not be done in a casual manner.

"So much of Torah is disciplinary in nature and self-discipline is vital in the religious life of observance. Kashruth undoubtedly projects sensitivity towards animal, and even plant life; a respect for God's creation, and due humility and thoughtfulness while being compelled to rely upon lower forms of existence for sustenance," writes one of the rabbis on the Orthodox Union kosher page (see below).

The rules for wine can be summed up briefly: Wine plays an important ceremonial role in Judaism and in many other religions, and the laws of wine (and grape products) sanctify the use of these products in light of their use in pagan religious practices.

America-Asian Kashrus Services

http://www.kashrus.org/

Ostensibly just a kosher supervision organization, America-Asian Kashrus Services bill themselves as having the largest kosher Web site, and the largest provider of kosher information on the Web. They're not wrong!

There is a great deal of information about kashruth here—starting with a well-written introduction to the subject called "Kosher Basics," and moving on to interesting essays on why to keep kosher and how to ease into it. One can sign up for their biweekly mailing list to get the latest in kashruth news. Among some of the more surprising entries: a complete list of all kosher candy and soda in the U.S.; the largest list of kosher supervision organizations and their symbols; and an incredible directory of "kosher fish." This is no fish story—this rather complete list was compiled by the Curator and Dean Bibliographer in the Department of Ichthyology of the American Museum of Natural History, and the Union of Orthodox Congregations. Hundreds of varieties of fish are listed here—an excellent idea.

The site also discusses ritual slaughter of animals and a treatise on the ins and outs of the kashruth of ice cream (there are more issues involved here than you might think); and a nice-looking page on current kosher literature—10 books and magazines that they recommend.

Is kosher food more healthy for you? Read *Food Additives: What You Don't Know Can Kill You!* written by Rabbi Eidlitz, a well-known author.

And, finally, the recipes—hundreds of kosher recipes for Chinese, Indian, Thai, Sri Lankan, Singaporean and other Asian cuisines.

All in all, this is one of the nicest looking and most informative sites in the area of kosher food.

Kashruth—Theory, Law and Practice

http://www.pswtech.com/~stevenw/jewish/kosher/

This is the beginning of a well-organized and easy-to-follow class on kashruth. It's quite logical in its approach and it isn't bogged down with a lot of minutiae. But it has essential information about keeping kosher and setting up and using a kosher kitchen. (Of course, to *kasher* your own kitchen you should consult your local rabbi.) This site is incomplete, and, actually, more than a year has gone by since the last update, but it is a fine introduction to the concept of kashruth.

Foods of the Bible
http://203.8.13.18/visions/biblfood/biblefd.htm

Parts of Phyllis Glazer's *Foods of the Bible* are on-line here. Her introduction:

> It was a good land, the Bible tells us, that the Children of Israel entered after 40 years of desert wanderings. Unlike Egypt, The Land was full of brooks and streams, grasses and trees; a land distinguished by fertility, and marked by foods like wheat and barley, essentials for daily life. Vines meant sweet fruit, grape honey, raisins and wine. Figs were not only food, but medicine. Pomegranate juice refreshed the thirsty, provided color for dyeing and inspiration for decorations ranging from the Priestly garb to ceramic crafts. The earth gave forth oil-bearing olives and honey—the first delicacies of mankind. These basic foods, most characteristic of the Land of Israel, and the staples of the ancient Hebrew's existence, are referred to as The Seven Species.

The chapters for two of the Species are included on this Web site: wonderful recipes centered around wheat and barley—from Biblical butter to Wild Wheat Salad, along with biblical sources.

The Kosher Mall
http://www.koshermall.com/

The Kosher Mall is an ambitious site, covering the areas of kosher services, products, agencies, and current news.

Some of the areas are quite worthwhile. There is an "Ask the Rabbi" page, and a list of kashruth supervising agencies, and companies that produce kosher food. On the other hand, its list of kosher services (hotels, retail outlets, etc.) is still anemic, and some topics, such as current news, are still under construction. It's a bit difficult to get around, and it is not entirely clear how to find out if a particular company makes kosher food, there being no index or search facilities.

Overall, the idea here is solid and the graphics are beautiful. But the frames-only site is not easy to navigate, and there just isn't enough here yet to make the site work for everyone.

Kosher food vendors can be found at the following sites:

Kosher at Sugarplums

http://www.sugarplums.com/kosher.html

"To many new to the kosher kitchen, Jewish cookery has meant only matzoh balls and cheese blintzes. Oy vey! Jewish cooking offers so much more... from Grand Chocolate Pizzas to satisfy a sweet tooth, excellent Napa Valley wines to imbibe, as well as mouth-watering recipes such as Creole Pot Roast piquant to savor at Passover."

This commercial site offers some recipes, Marilyn's Kitchen Madness, a few cooking lessons via RealAudio, a "food forum" (an interactive bulletin board), and some interesting links to some other kosher food spots on the Web.

Best's Kosher Outlet

http://www.bests-kosher.com/bessin/

Best's claim to fame is that its hot dogs are the "official" kosher hot dogs of the Chicago White Sox, Cubs, and a variety of other Chicago-based sports teams.

The history of the company is actually more interesting than most, as the company went through many transformations and had connections with many other companies since being founded as the Oscherwitz Kosher Company, by Isaac Oscherwitz in 1886. Isaac was a Russian immigrant, and had emigrated from Germany, where he had been a sausage maker. Some of the other companies it was connected with were Best, Sinai Kosher, Bessin, Sara Lee, Shofar, and even Manischewitz.

Their "What is kosher" page is an interesting description of the processes from the meat producer's point of view—particularly the added effort and expense incurred to stay kashruth.

Unfortunately, while you can learn about the products, you can't order any food here—you can only find out where to buy it.

Empire Kosher Poultry Products

http://www.empirekosher.com/

Empire is the Frank Perdue of kosher chicken—their products are found throughout the world. This site includes kosher recipes, an "ask us" site for questions on kashruth and nutrition of Empire products, a tour of their plants and even a form to fill out to get a free quarterly newsletter and coupons for Empire products. Where to get a kosher chicken in your area? Check out the state-by-state listing of all their distributors. Kosher foods have come a long way in the past several decades. This is quite an impressive site for a food wholesaler.

Farmhouse Kosher Cheddar

http://www.wdi.co.uk/ashley/kosheng.html

This English-made brand of cheese is manufactured and marketed by the Ashley Chase Estate. We include it here because many people are unaware of its existence or of the fact that it is a kosher product. The Web site is probably only interesting for cheese aficionados.

Good Eats Food Products

http://hlthmall.com/healthmall/goodeats/welcome.html

The Age of Aquarius meets Judaism? Good Eats specializes in organic, macrobiotic, environmentally friendly, cruelty free, and kosher products. While not all the products here are kosher, the ones that are kosher are clearly marked with their kashruth supervision. The best parts about the site are the wide array of products, from baby food to family-size commodities, and that you can order them all on-line.

King Oscar Sardines

http://www.kingoscarusa.com/kosh.htm

King Oscar Brisling products have long been kosher-certified, a fact which they emphasize on their Web site, adding that kosher is a quality endorsement few food products get. The site explains that all but one King Oscar Brisling product hold this status, curry being the exception due to the milk powder in the sauce.

Wines

Royal Wines

http://www.kedemwines.com/

Royal Wines, in addition to producing well-known brands such as Kedem and Baron Herzog, claims to be "the world's leading distributor of kosher wines and beverages." They also import many Israeli and other foreign wines. Their motto "Award winning wines that happen to be kosher" is backed up with a full description of the many awards that they have won. Some of the information here includes a full listing of Royal Wines distributors, and a fine catalog and description of their wines, which is filled not just with adjectives, but dryness and sweetness ratings and appropriate accompanying foods.

The Kosher Wine Institute, a nonprofit organization Royal set up to educate consumers about kosher wine, is also part of this site. Among its undertakings is a syndicated column called *Kosher Wine Talk*. Past columns appear here. The first issue notes "A common fallacy is that Kosher wine comes in only three flavors: Sweet, Sticky and Heavy."

Clearly, Royal and others are doing their best to overcome this perception.

Some of these pages take a while to load, because of the attractive but "heavy" graphics of their wine bottles.

Smartwine Online
http://smartwine.com/ap/9604/ap640405.htm

> "Mention kosher wine, and most people think of the sweet, syrupy Manischewitz served with matzoh for the Passover Seder celebration. Alexandra Allen stocked her market with 200 cases of Manischewitz when she began offering kosher wines 10 years ago.

> "But today, some of California's top-ranked cabernet sauvignons and white zinfandels fill the racks of Shenson's Delicatessen in San Francisco, and all of them are kosher."

This page, quoted above, reprints a cute article from *Smart Wine*, an on-line magazine, that explains how far kosher wine, and its perceptions, have come in the past several decades.

Hagafen Cellars
http://www.nauticom.net/users/judaica/Hagafen/

Hagafen Cellars, established in 1979, produces kosher dry table wines in Napa Valley.

The vintner of Hagafen Cellars' is Ernie Weir. He founded Hagafen "out of the desire to make premium kosher wines in the famous Napa Valley tradition." The site includes descriptions of each of the Hagefen wines, a small number of recipes and an on-line order form. If you think of kosher wines as being the prewar Malaga or Concord grape varieties, these California kosher wines may change your mind.

There's really not a lot of depth to this site—unless, of course, you are looking for a case of some serious kosher wine.

Wineries in Israel

http://www.agmonet.co.il/wines/menu.htm

This site has pages of eight major wineries in Israel, including Carmel Mizrachi, responsible for three-quarters of Israeli wine production. Information about vintners, history, tours, etc., are all here. Additionally, a critic rates some of the better varieties, by giving each one to four grape clusters, a brief description of the wine, and the appropriate food matches.

For instance:

Rothschild Cabernet Sauvignon '90 (two clusters)

Tasting note: a composed yet modern wine, with an intense fruity aroma and a clean, lingering, buttery taste.

Food match: rack of lamb.

Specialty Foods

New York Flying Pizza Pies

http://www.flyingpizzas.com

Your kosher pizza worries are over! "With 25 years of experience in the pizza business, brothers Ari and Eddie Fishbaum, owners of Broadway's Jerusalem 2 Restaurant in New York City understand the pizza consumers need for a quality product. Tourists have come to their restaurant in the center of Manhattan for years and lamented that they cannot get real New York pizza back home."

Now they'll even Federal Express a kosher pizza to your home.

It should go without saying, but if you have any questions about specific products or the validity of the various supervisory organizations we list here, contact your local rabbi.

Kosher Supervision

America-Asian Kashrus Services
http://www.kashrus.org/

A stupendous Web site—see the first entry in this chapter for a more elaborate description of the many resources it provides.

The Orthodox Union—Thinking Kosher
http://www.ou.org/kosher/

The Orthodox Union, which is discussed in the first section of this book, is well known for its OU symbol certifying kashruth—the most recognized and accepted emblem in the field. This site is much more than a description of the OU certification. The primer on kashruth is probably as detailed as any you can find on-line. Additionally, they have an "Ask the Vebbe Rebbe" page—where you can direct your kashruth question to a halachic authority.

Kosher Overseers Associates of America
http://kosher.org/origins.html

This is the site of a private-label kosher supervision agency. The most interesting part of the site is the history of the agency itself. In the history section, they claim to be " the oldest continuous kosher endorsing agency in the USA."

United Kosher Supervision
http://www.j51.com/~yspivak/spivak2.htm

United Kosher Supervision, in addition to certifying kashruth status, also provides speakers, and has an e-mail hotline to answer questions. They also offer an on-line subscription form for *The Kosher News*, which at the time of this writing is still free.

Kashruth Division of the London Beth Din
http://www.kosher.org.uk/

This site contains the official list of England's kosher licensed caterers, restaurants and hotels, but does not contain information on kosher products in England or a hot line page listing new products introduced, and their kosher status. The *London Jewish Chronicle* does print an annual edition of kosher products; information about its purchase, as well as when the next update is to be published, is available on this site.

Recipes

Not all the recipes in this section are kosher. Some include milk and meat products, others include prohibited food. Remember to use milk and/or other substitutes where applicable.

N O T E

Ethiopian Jewish Foods
http://www.cais.com/nacoej/13.html

While there are just few recipes at this site, it is probably the only place where you can get a taste of "Beta Israel" (a.k.a. *Falasha*) cuisine—the food of Ethiopian Jewry.

Asian Kosher Recipes
http://www.kashrus.org/recipes/recipes.html

This award-winning site (part of the Asian-American Kashrus Services page mentioned at the top of this chapter) contains hundreds of kosher Asian recipes—ranging from well-known cuisines like Chinese, Indian, and Thai, to the more exotic foods of Sri Lanka and Singapore. (You can find three different kosher recipes for Pad Thai!)

Recipes from the Arab World

http://www.hiof.no/almashriq/base/food.html

This site contains quite a number of Arabic recipes. The entire text of *Food from the Arab World* (containing 130 recipes), a page full of links to Lebanese recipes, and over 50 recipes from *The Middle Eastern Cook Book* (recipes from Iraq) can be found here.

Moroccan Recipes

http://maghreb.net/morocco/cuisine/

This site describes Moroccan cuisine and the culture sur-rounding a traditional meal, along with nine "main specialties of Moroccan cuisine." It has some mouth-watering recipes—you can tell by the delicious-looking pictures.

Turkish Cuisine

http://www.metu.edu.tr/~melih/recipes.html

This well-organized Web site has a nice overview of Turkish cuisine, along with a generous collection of recipes. Recommended recipes are the Moussaka and the Eggs Turkish style

If you're looking for strictly Jewish recipes, give the following sites a try:

Jewish-food Recipe Archives

http://www.eskimo.com/~jefffree/recipes/

This is an index to the Jewish-food e-mail list archives, covering close to 2,000 recipes! These recipes have been contributed by subscribers to the Jewish-food list. Also on this site are recipes appropriate for Pesach, Chanukah and Purim meals.

Mimi's Cyber Kitchen

http://www.cyber-kitchen.com/pgjewish.htm

Mimi's Cyber Kitchen has a huge number of links to other kosher-recipe pages. While there are no recipes here, the number of links makes it a worthwhile page to bookmark. Unfortunately, there are a number of dead links on the page.

Jewish Holiday Recipes From Joan Nathan's Kitchen

http://www.epicurious.com/e_eating/e06_jewish_cooking/
nathan_home.html

This Web site offers selected recipes from Joan Nathan, a well-known Jewish cookbook author, including a few recipes for each holiday. Some selections include an entire holiday menu.

Sephardic Recipes

http://www.direct.ca/burton/bethhamidrash/recipes.html

This page is from the Web site of Beth Hamidrash, a Sephardic synagogue in Vancouver, B.C. It holds a number of excellent Sephardic recipes.

The main listing for Passover can be found in our chapter on holidays. That chapter contains information about keeping a kosher kitchen during Passover and the various laws that apply to Passover. The Web sites listed below focus as much on the cuisine as the religious details.

Kashrus Conscience

http://www.jewish.org/kashrut.bulletin.html

This is a reprint of an entire booklet from the Los Angeles Kosher Information Bureau. It might as well be titled Everything You Wanted to Know about Kosher for Passover Laws in the L.A. Area. Not only is general Passover law explained in great detail, but so are the rules regarding medicines, as well as a huge amount of product-specific information. While most of the information is useful, the site hasn't been updated since Passover of 1995. To the extent that ingredients in products change, the information will be outdated. Nevertheless, the site remains an excellent resource for generalized Passover kashruth information.

Mimi's Cyber Kitchen
http://www.cyber-kitchen.com/pgjewish.htm

Although Mimi's Cyber Kitchen was mentioned above, it rates a repeat mention here because there are links to over a dozen kosher-for-Passover-specific Web sites—including the unindexed but voluminous "Usenet Passover recipe archives."

Kosher Recipes from Kosher Express
http://www.marketnet.com/mktnet/kosher/

The Kosher Express Web site has a collection of kosher recipes from contributors around the world, mostly for Passover foods.

Kosher Express also brings you the Matza Market, "your Internet source for Kosher for Passover delectables!" A complete catalog is on-line, where you can order everything from matza to chicken soup to cake mix—all kosher for Passover.

Miscellaneous

A Gefilte "Fish Story"
http://sdb.bio.purdue.edu/SDBEduca/Gefilte.html

This Web site contains a photograph of the legendary "Gefilte Fish" embryo. If you don't have a sense of humor, please don't visit this page.

The Kosher Restaurant Database

http://shamash.org/kosher/krestquery.html

This database attempts to tell you the location of kosher restaurants nationwide. I would be very happy to tell you that this database is up to date, but it is not. The idea is sound—have users from around the country send information about kosher restaurants to a centralized database others can search—but the execution doesn't quite make it. The site *can* be useful as a starting point to finding restaurants if you are traveling, but you'll need to call ahead to make sure.

PART III

Jewish Culture

CHAPTER 13

Museums and Archives

The Jewish museums of the world have yet to embrace the idea of exhibiting their works on the Internet. At present, you may have to investigate a number of Web sites to get an idea of their contents.

If after this chapter you have a further interest in Jewish museums, you might want to read a book or two on the subject. Three good choices are *Jewish Museums of North America, A Guide to Collections, Artifacts, and Memorabilia* by Nancy Frazier (John Wiley & Sons, 1992); *The Museums of Israel* by L.Y. Rahman and Peter Larsen (Rizzoli, 1976) is outdated but interesting; and *The Israel Museum, Jerusalem,* by Martin Wey (St. Martin's Press, 1995).

Many leading American and European museums have significant Jewish holdings. These include The British Museum and The Vatican Museum, as well as the Library of Congress and The New York Public Library. Additionally, there are significant exhibitions in Jewish institutions in such diverse communities as Venice and Amsterdam in Europe and Los Angeles and Dallas in the United States.

Along with the museums in this chapter, we've also included a number of exhibits and archives.

Exhibit of Judaica at Yale University Library

http://www.library.yale.edu/exhibition/judaica/

Yale has a proud tradition of collecting Judaica that goes back to its earliest days and continues into the present. This on-line version contains a complete listing of the contents of the exhibit, but only a very small selection of the items on display at the Sterling Memorial Library actually appear at the site itself. Some of my favorite items in the exhibit include *Ketubot* (marriage contracts) from the Beinecke Rare Book and Manuscript Library at the university. In recent years it has become popular to have special marriage contracts designed specifically for the occasion. Several the sites in this volume link to artists who actually design *Ketubot*.

Like many of the Web sites in this chapter, this site is a mere tease. Not only are most of the items unavailable, but viewing them on a 15-inch computer screen is no substitute for an actual visit. On the other hand, of course, we don't all have the resources to visit all of these museums. Another problem with this site is that the text is intermixed with some rather large graphic images, making the downloads fairly slow.

Scrolls From the Dead Sea: The Ancient Library of Qumran and Modern Scholarship

http://lcweb.loc.gov/exhibits/scrolls/

This Web presentation (brought to you by the Library of Congress), is a model that other institutions that display collections ought to follow. The home page presents an in-depth table of contents, each of which links sequentially to a "tour" of the collection. The tour consists of pages of information that have links to the graphics themselves, so you always know whether a page you are about to bring up is laden with large graphics or not. Thus the organization is excellent, although we must add that the presentation of text is strictly bare-bones.

The well-known story of the scrolls is fascinating and full of controversy. According to the site:

In 1947, young Bedouin shepherds, searching for a stray goat in the Judean Desert, entered a long-untouched cave and found jars filled with ancient scrolls. That initial discovery by the Bedouins yielded seven scrolls and began a search that lasted nearly a decade and eventually produced thousands of scroll fragments from eleven caves.

Where did they come from? What theological implications do they have? Who "owns" the rights to the scholarship? These questions and more are touched in the tour.

Additionally, the complete exhibit brochure appears here as well as an extensive bibliography.

The Reuben and Edith Hecht Museum
http://researc.haifa.ac.il/~hecht/

The Reuben and Edith Hecht Museum's permanent archaeological exhibition is based on the private collection of Dr. Reuben Hecht, which he donated to Haifa University. This site gives you some information about the museum and a few images, as well as table of contents for the museum's published bulletins. Dr. Hecht's private collection of paintings is displayed in the Art wing. It includes representative works from various art movements, with an emphasis on Impressionism and the Jewish School of Paris. Works of Monet, Pissaro, Soutine, Struck, and others are exhibited. A few of the paintings can be found on the site as well.

Overall, however, this site does not do a particularly good job of conveying the excitement or importance of the actual collection.

The Israel Museum
http://www.imj.org.il/

You would think that museum Web sites, of all places, would have attractive pages, but few actually do. The Web presence of the Israel Museum, however, is a striking exception, which befits Israel's showpiece museum. Among its holdings are the Qumran (Dead Sea) Scrolls and a host of objects in its Judaica and Jewish Ethnology wing. The

Art Garden holds sculptures by Rodin, Picasso, and other artistic giants.

The site contains some very fine images that are representative of each of the departments and exhibits at the museum. Additionally, there are up-to-date schedules of lectures and other programs of interest to the community. A text-based search feature, which is fairly unique among sites in this chapter, allows you to search the entire site.

The Israel National Museum of Science

http://www.elron.net/n_sci_museum/

This Web site presents a delightful picture of the Israel National Museum. At this museum you learn by doing, with over 200 hands-on exhibits and a whole host of other creative teaching displays. One uses billiard balls to explain the principal of a subroutine; in others, visitors create mechanical toys. "A visit to this Museum is not a 'spectator sport' but an invitation to explore and discover a new world—the world of science and technology. A series of lectures for the general public on topics of science and technology is a regular feature of the Museum's program."

Unfortunately, pictures of hands-on exhibits do little more than make you wish you could visit.

Museo Sefardi

http://www.servicom.es/museosefardi/

For centuries prior to their expulsion in 1492, the Jews in Spain enjoyed a rich and cultured life. This time period became known as The Golden Age of Spain. A few years after their expulsion from Spain, they were also expelled from Portugal. By the turn of the century, the entire Iberian Peninsula had become off-limits to Jews, and the Spanish Edict of Expulsion itself was not officially rescinded until 1968. Today the Spanish Jewish community is not even a shadow of its former glory. The actual number of Jews living in Spain today hovers around 10,000.

The collection houses exhibits related to the story of *Sefarad* (the old Jewish name for Spain) and to the culture of the *Sefardi* people (in Spanish). There is very little on this site, other than the location of the museum and a list of current exhibits.

The Project Judaica Foundation
http://www2.judaica.org/pj/

The Project Judaica Foundation is involved in "the rescue, rehabilitation, dissemination, and exhibition of Judaica." Its programs include a summer college course in Poland, the publication and sale of various CD-ROMS (such as *The Dead Sea Scrolls Revealed*), and, of course, mounting museum exhibitions in such places as the Smithsonian Institution, The Israel Antiquities Authority, Library of Congress' Hebraic Section (where *From the Ends of the Earth* broke all previous attendance records). The Foundation is involved in a ton of projects, and you can find out all about them here—with the help of a complete listing and a search feature.

Consistent with its goal, the foundation offers something unique—not only do all the images at this site expand to larger graphic images, but they invite you to download the images for your own personal use!

Franz Rosenzweig Essay and Exhibit
http://www.library.vanderbilt.edu/divinity/rosenzw/rosenart.html

In 1913, Franz Rosenzweig, a thoroughly assimilated Jew, highly educated in Germany, decided to convert to Christianity. In preparation, he thought it proper to attend Orthodox Yom Kippur services, which ended up changing the course of his life. Within a few years he was writing treatises on Jewish education and philosophy. This site claims that "along with Martin Buber and Abraham Heschel, Rosenzweig is one of the most widely read Jewish thinkers among Christians."

As does the physical exhibit at Vanderbilt University, this site contains the full and fascinating story of Rosenzweig, a bibliography of the philosopher, and a number of images relating to his life. It's a fine presentation and represents the type of site that should be created for the Web. Neither flashy nor flamboyant, it's a job well done.

The United States Holocaust Memorial Museum

http://www.ushmm.org/

The United States Holocaust Memorial Museum is this country's "national institution for the documentation, study, and interpretation of Holocaust history and serves as this country's memorial to the millions of people murdered during the Holocaust." But it is more than that. It is a symbol of the triumph of good over evil. It is a symbol to the world that the Holocaust indeed took place, and that here in the pantheon of the American people, Washington, D.C., an entire nation pays tribute to and remembers the millions of Jews and non-Jews who perished at the hands of history's cruelest oppressor.

Since it opened in 1992, several million people have taken a journey into the netherworld of the Holocaust. The building's architecture is striking in and of itself. Its presentation and contents are above reproach. It's a credit to both the founders of the Museum and to the nation in which it is housed.

Despite the fact that you can't actually view the exhibits, this is an extremely well-organized site that contains a tremendous amount of information. Slowly but surely, the catalog of holdings is coming on line, and it can be queried directly. Materials to help teachers incorporate a Holocaust studies unit into their courses are available. The site contains contact information about the museum and its projects and exhibits. It's a good starting point for any planned visit to the museum.

Yad Vashem
http://www.yad-vashem.org.il/

Vad Vashem is the original. The world's first Holocaust memorial, it was built in Jerusalem in 1953, and its architecture met the task of creating awe and a sense of reflection for its visitors. Here you will find information on the historical and art museums, the striking Valley of the Communities, and the other components of the Yad Vashem memorial.

The general archives have collected some 40 to 50 million pages of documentation and testimony, and a tremendous number of photos and videos.

A project to create a computerized list of names of victims is underway, but it is proceeding slowly. At some point, much of what they have will be available on line. Like the U.S. memorial, Yad Vashem also offers a vast array of resources to teachers and educators, including curricula and dissertations. Yad Vashem also runs The International School for Holocaust Studies, which offers month-long seminars on teaching the *Shoah* and anti-Semitism.

This site is an excellent introductory look at a landmark resource that has to be visited to be fully appreciated.

The Judah Magnes Museum
http://www.jfed.org/Mentry.htm

Although founded quite recently (in 1962), the Judah Magnes Museum in Berkeley, California, was the first to be accredited by the American Association of Museums and has grown to be the third largest Jewish museum in North America.

The site contains a directory of the museum's exhibits, some images, and a sound file of a *shofar*.

The Jewish Museum
http://ortnet.ort.org/communit/jewmusm/home.htm

London's Jewish Museum opens a window to the history and religious life of the Jewish community in the United

Kingdom. Founded in 1932, the museum has one of the world's finest collections of Jewish ceremonial art.

The Web site serves as a directory of the Museum's exhibits and services. It offers few images and little information about the exhibits themselves.

Jacob M. Lowy Collection of The National Library of Canada

http://www.nlc-bnc.ca/services/elowy.htm

The Jacob M. Lowy Collection spans the history of printed Judaica—3,000 printed books dating from the beginning of the printing press (the late 15th century). Here, too, you can find the Saul Hayes Collection of 200 original manuscripts in Hebrew and other languages, along with microform holdings of the manuscript collections of selected European institutions.

The general stacks of the National Library also contain both Canadian and foreign Judaica. One image on the site is that of a leaf of *The Talmud Yerushalmi* (the Jerusalem Talmud) of Venice, 1523. This is an important collection, which makes this Web site of interest. Unfortunately, the entire Web site consists of three pages: one introductory and two others with about six images each.

The Chagall Windows

http://www6.huji.ac.il/md/chagall/

It is nearly impossible for a Jew to think of Mark Chagall without thinking of the famous Chagall Windows, the immense and colorful stained glass masterpieces located at the synagogue of the Hadassah-Hebrew University Medical Center. The twelve windows depict each of the tribes of Israel, and Chagall drew inspiration from the Bible, particularly Genesis 49, in which Jacob blesses his twelve sons, and Deuteronomy 33, in which Moses blesses the Twelve Tribes.

The windows are available for viewing both as thumbnails and as larger images, which can be seen on your screen in full color. You can get a feel for the beauty of the artwork, although of course, it can not convey the true magnificence of the windows. For armchair museum visitors, however, it just might be the next best thing to being there.

The Jewish Museum (New York)
http://www.jtsa.edu/jm/

This important Jewish museum, located in New York City, does not yet have a Web site of its own. This page merely presents a description of the museum's operations. Hopefully, its administration will have a Web presence in the future—it certainly deserves one. You might want to look at this site if you're planning a trip to New York. Jot down the museum's phone number and call to find out what it's exhibiting. A visit to the Jewish Museum is always a treat.

Southwest Jewish Archives
http://dizzy.library.arizona.edu/images/swja/swjalist.html

The typical Jewish story in America is of Eastern Europeans immigrating around the turn of the 20th century, passing through Ellis Island, and settling, at least initially, in the New York City area. Indeed, until recently, there were more Jews in the New York area than in Israel.

But there are other stories to be told, those of Jews who predated the Eastern European immigrants by two centuries or more. A few became mayors and businessmen in the West well before the Eastern European influx (one such family was the Goldwaters, of whom Presidential candidate Barry Goldwater is the most prominent). These so-called crypto-Jews settled in the Southwest even before the *Mayflower* arrived. Before the *Mayflower*? After their expulsion from Spain and other areas of Europe, many fled to the New World, particularly South America. When the Inquisition moved there, many headed north to what is now Mexico and the U.S. Southwest (some even moved to what became Manhattan).

This site, while neither flashy nor particularly well organized, does have a nice index. It also seems to be one of the few sites that has useful links to other places with related information, as well as most of the articles from their publications. It is utterly fascinating.

The Mechelen Museum of Deportation and The Resistance

http://www.cicb.be/shoah/

Malines, Belgium was the starting point of a one-way deportation route to Auschwitz. More than half of the Jews who lived in Belgium before World War II became Holocaust victims. This museum grapples with this history, but "it is not only a museum about the deportation of Belgian Jews, but also about their resistance. Thanks to the support they received from the Belgian people, many managed to escape from their Nazi pursuers and their collaborators."

This museum tells the story of the Antwerp Jewish community before and during the Second World War. It is worth taking a look at. The brief stories on each of its pages reflect the lives of Jews in Belgium during this most trying time.

The Museum of Jewish Culture in Slovakia

http://www.savba.sk/blava/muzea/muzea-e7.html

The Museum of Jewish Culture forms part of the Slovak National Museum/Historical Museum. The museum's collections comprise several hundreds of items of Judaica. Noteworthy are two jugs of the Burial Society Chevra Kadisha at Senec from the 18th century, and historical books by the famous Bratislava Rabbi Chatam Sofer (Moshe Schreiber, 1762–1839). At this time, however, there are only two pictures at the Web site.

The Museum of Television & Radio
http://www.mtr.org/

The Museum of Television and Radio is not a Jewish museum, but the Jewish influence within its walls is tremendous: from Jack Benny on radio, to Mr. Television, Milton Berle, to modern stars such as Jerry Seinfeld. From time to time, the museum mounts exhibitions that reflect the contributions of Jews to American radio and television. For example, *One People, Many Voices: The History of Jewish Music in America* reflects the cultural diversity of the United States. Look at this Web site for other exhibits of this type.

The Jewish War Veterans Museum
http://www.penfed.org/jwv/museum.htm

Every museum has its own story to tell, its own tale to weave. The Jewish War Veterans Museum tells the story of American Jewry's participation in every conflict that this nation has fought.

This history started when America's first Jewish settlers in New Amsterdam fought to fight alongside other members in the community in defending itself against marauding Indians and against the French and English. It continues through Uriah Levi, a self-styled Jeffersonian, to Admiral Hyman Rickover, father of the nuclear Navy. This site tells you about the latest exhibits and gives you a small sampling of what you can expect to find.

Ein Hod Artists Village
http://www.interart.co.il/

This art colony is known throughout Israel and much of the Jewish world. The Web site shows selections from various artists of the colony. Each representation comes with a detailed analysis of the artist's work. The exhibits on the site usually rally around a single theme. The colony has a well-deserved reputation, and this site gives a good insight into the way it operates.

The site also houses the Jerusalem Artists' House, which functions as a contemporary art center. Its spacious galleries, illuminated with diffused natural light, house exhibitions both by local artists and artists from other cities in Israel and around the world. The Artists' House is also recognized as a center for young Israeli artists.

Touro Synagogue National Historic Site (Newport)
http://nimrod.mit.edu/depts/rvc/kidder/RI09.html
Rhode Island's Touro Synagogue, dedicated in 1763, is the oldest synagogue building in the United States. It is immortalized as the subject of a letter sent by President George Washington in which he wrote "...happily the Government of the United States which gives to bigotry no sanction, to persecution no assistance requires only that they who live under its protection shall demean themselves as good citizens in giving it on all occasions their effectual support."

This site is actually part of the Kidder Smith Images Project of the MIT Libraries and contains a few images of the stately building.

Jewish Historical Society Of Maryland
http://www.artcom.com/museums/vs/gl/21202-46.htm
Among its other claims to fame in Jewish history, Baltimore was the home of Henrietta Szold (the founder of Hadassah), a model night school for immigrants as well as a host of other Jewish activities. While the museum has some important and interesting exhibits and some fine permanent materials, the Web site is fairly sparse, with just a few images, but it has the essentials if you're considering a visit.

The Lower East Side Tenement Museum
http://www.wnet.org/tenement/
A fascinating concept: portray the immigrant experience by focusing on the tenants of a single building. From 1870 to 1915 hundreds of families lived at 97 Orchard Street in New

York City. While this site, sponsored by WNET, New York's Public Television station, is not strictly a Jewish site, it does tell the story of Jewish immigration to New York and the Lower East Side. This beautifully done site is an absolute delight. It contains images and stories. Visitors learn about the people who lived in the apartments and see their photos. You can "peel" the wallpaper off the buildings and see objects from the excavation of the site or watch a video. This site is one of my personal favorites, and is a must if you want to know how your grandparents lived when they came to America.

Face to Face: Encounters between Jews and Blacks
http://www.libertynet.org/~flower/face/

Face to Face: Encounters between Jews and Blacks is a photo-text work, available as a book and exhibit. The project paired Jews and Blacks in Philadelphia, collecting "their comments on their special relationship, as they see it, in particular and in general; as it affects them personally and as it shapes the world in which they live."

The site contains information about the book, as well as about the exhibit itself, a number of images, and most importantly a thoughtful and useful study guide about Black-Jewish relations.

The Balch Institute of Philadelphia
http://www.libertynet.org/~balch/

The Balch Institute for Ethnic Studies is a museum and library "dedicated to collecting and interpreting materials drawn from America's ethnic, racial, and immigrant experiences." They have also done community-wide programs, focusing on the common ground that almost all Americans share: immigrant ancestors. It is also home to the Philadelphia Jewish Archives Center, which collects, preserves, and organizes the records of the Greater Philadelphia Jewish community and makes them available to scholars, students, researchers, and the general public.

The site only contains a few images, but it does list exhibitions that might be of interest to you.

Oriental Institute Museum
http://www-oi.uchicago.edu/
OI/MUS/HIGH/OI_Museum_Palestine.html

This museum, which is part of University of Chicago, is a showcase of the history, art, and architecture of the ancient Near and Middle East.

The Palestine section, using that term as the Romans did in reference to the ancient land of the Philistines, covers the area of present-day Israel and Jordan.

The extraordinary objects at the museum date back to the 13th century B.C.E. Some of the pieces, such as a Canaanite statue, can be viewed at the site. While you're surfing, you also might want to look at the Virtual Museum section, which includes photographic archives and videos (provided you have the right software).

Ellis Island Museum
http://www.ellisisland.org

Most Jews in this country have ancestors who immigrated in the "great wave" between 1881 and 1920. Most of those who immigrated after 1892 came through Ellis Island, in the shadow of the Statute of Liberty. Certainly, this is not a unique story for Jews. Today more than 40 percent—more than 100 million—of all living Americans can trace their roots to an ancestor who came through Ellis Island.

Ellis Island has been transformed into an immigrant museum. An Immigrant Wall of Fame and the American Family Immigration Center are part of this effort. The museum also contains an astounding collection of immigrant artifacts. It is an important part of Jewish Americana. As such, you'd expect more information from this Web site, but there aren't even any pictures. Nevertheless, Ellis Island itself is one tourist site that no visitor to the United States should miss, and this site can help you plan a trip there.

Library of the Jewish Theological Seminary
http://www.jtsa.edu/library/libhtm/exhib.html

This famed library of the home of the rabbinical school for the Conservative movement often has exhibitions on the Web, and offers more images than most sites in this chapter (there were more than fifty images when I visited). The ancillary materials and the descriptions offered are well done. If you are into cyber-cruising museums, don't miss this one.

Additionally, you can find information on nine traveling exhibitions that are available from the library.

Music

Music has been an integral part of Jewish life in every stage of Judaism's development, from before the First Temple was built in Jerusalem, through the years in which music and musical instruments played an important part in the Temple service, and in the years of the Diaspora. Music has continued to play an ever-present role in Jewish life.

Music reflects the times and the temperament of the Jewish people—you can tell a great deal about our history by listening to our music. The mournful tunes recalling the death of Jewish martyrs; the sounds of repentance in the Kol Nidre; the effervescence of the singing for the holiday of Tabernacles; the joy of the Simchat Torah celebration; the beat of the wedding marches and the serenading of the bride and groom all have special musical meaning.

But if any music stands out for us in our time, it is the music that was engendered by the Chasidic dynasties that dotted Poland and Russia in the past several centuries. Vel Pasternak, famed chronicler of Jewish music (a Web site on this topic is http://www.jdwishmusic.com/artic102.htm), tells of the importance of song in Chasidic life. He relates the following story:

> "Regarding the tale of the death of Rabbi Joshe Leib of Sassov. The Rebbe took upon himself the duty of financially assisting poor brides and attending their weddings. At the nuptial ceremony of an orphaned bride, the processional melody played by the itinerant Jewish musicians impressed him and he openly expressed the wish that this same tune accompany his burial. Many years later the Rebbe died and hundreds of Chasidim journeyed from all parts

of Eastern Europe to accompany this sainted being to his eternal rest. At a crossroads, the funeral cortege beheld a group of musicians sitting on a horsedrawn cart. With unexpected suddenness the horses broke and galloped off into the distance. When the procession arrived at the entrance to the cemetery it was met by the same group of musicians. Because they assumed that the musicians had come to jest, the Chasidim were angered. Suddenly a very old Chasid remembered the Rebbe's wish of long ago that a specific tune be played at his burial. There was consternation among the group. For hundreds of years Jewish tradition proclaimed that no music be played at a funeral. A rabbinical court (*bet din*) was hastily formed and after serious deliberation issued its tradition-breaking verdict that the wish of the Sassover Rebbe be honored. The old Chasid was asked if he could recall the *niggun* (a niggun is sung without accompanying words) and he sang several bars to the musicians. They took up the strains of the melody and the Rebbe was laid to rest with the same tune that had accompanied an orphaned bride many years before.

Of all the stories related to Chasidic music emanating from the Masters, no other story has quite the force and emotional appeal for the musician as the one related above. The reason is that in this instance the musician's wish and dream that music indeed become paramount in all devotional and philosophic posture, is fulfilled in the existential encounter of man in the face of his ultimate position in life, namely his death. Thus, music for Chasidism is not only the accompanying motif of one's life but the companion of the Chasid's eternal journey. The soul, in returning to its original source, the Maker, is ascending to the strains of a melody.

It is in this light that we view the home pages that we present to you. Some of the music is Chasidic. Much of it is klezmer. I am not a musician but I would venture to say that klezmer music is another expression of Chasidic music. It tells of the joy and the trials and tribulations of a time in Jewish life, primarily that of 18th- and 19th-century Poland and Russia. Much of the joy of Yiddish has been lost to American Jews—*Mamma Loshen* (the mother tongue) is a language of the past (well, almost). But it's still here in music and it speaks volumes. You can hear it and feel it at any Jewish simcha.

We've also included the addresses and information on a number of other musical and dance forms. These include the New Israeli Opera and the Israel Philharmonic Orchestra. In many respects the Israel Philharmonic symbolizes the renaissance of Israel's cultural life after the Holocaust. Even in the darkest and leanest years of modern Israel, the IPO stood forth as a symbol of Israel's resoluteness. Who could ever forget the IPO playing the Hatikvah or the dynamism of Leonard Bernstein conducting "His" orchestra?

TARA—The World of Jewish Music

http://www.jewishmusic.com/cgi-bin/vsc/index.htm?E+tarashop

Tara is Jewish music. One of the premiere music publishing shops, Tara Publications is owned by Velvel Pasternak, probably the single most important figure in modern Jewish music. A music teacher who decided to become a music publisher, he is a great lecturer with a fine sense of humor and a monumental knowledge of Jewish music. Cantors and choir directors, teachers and experts—everyone calls Vel to answer their questions. And he always finds time to chat.

If you're surfing the Web for Jewish music sites, you will inevitably land here—many other sites have links to Tara. Thorough and extensive, these pages are divided into eight sections including Jewish Music Store, Artists' Home Pages, New Releases, Cool Stuff, Articles, More Jewish Music Links, and Contact TARA.

If you want to shop for books, recordings or videos, click into Jewish Music Store, an on-line catalog with over 1,000 selections. You can access them all at once; browse by subject, title or artist; search only coordinated book and recording sets; or stick with the editor's choices. Each item is accompanied by an image of its cover, a description, the price and the catalog number.

Artists' Home Pages, a great resource, offers photos, biographical information, professional history, lists of recordings, links to relevant sites and sometimes even sample recordings of over 30 musicians, including Debbie Friedman, the Klezmatics, Craig Taubman, Dudu Fisher, David Broza, Yehuda Glantz and Shlomo Carlebach—and the list keeps growing. All of the pages are created and maintained by Tara.

"Cool Stuff" is really a find. There, listening samples and free sheet music are available on-line. Keep in mind that your computer has to be properly equipped to take advantage of this feature, or you might get a message like: "No viewer configured for file type: audio/x-wav. How would you like to handle this file? Save to disk/Cancel transfer/configure a viewer."

Incredibly organized, easy to get around, visually pleasing and thorough, Tara is a perfect starting place to surf the Web for Jewish music.

Transcontinental Music Publications, New Jewish Music Press

http://www.shamash.org/reform/uahc/transmp/

Transcontinental Music Publications, the music publishing arm of the Reform Movement, offers a wide variety of materials for synagogue and home use. It claims to be the largest publisher of Jewish choral music in the world, "the single most important resource for all community groups such as schools, universities, churches and libraries."

Unfortunately, the site does not take advantage of the Web as a visual, hypertext medium. There are no graphic images except for a small harp inside a Jewish star at the opening of the page; the background is poorly chosen, making the text, already too small and too light, difficult to read.

You will, however, find plenty of information here. After a short description of the company, there is some information regarding the three types of catalogs the company produces, additional services the company provides (consultation and distribution) and special major publications.

Click into the on-line catalog (the only option available if you want to stay at this site), and you will find an invitation to browse through special holiday selections, along with the option to submit your own search query or use the subject index provided. Once you begin to browse the actual lists, you will find that they are long and impressive, and that the company does not limit itself to artists affiliated with the Reform Movement. Each selection includes composer, item, title, medium, language, comments and price.

If you're familiar with Jewish choral music and looking for something specific, you might want to make a quick visit to this site.

Arbel: Philadelphia's Young Adult Jewish Choir
http://www.cris.com/~llipkin/arbel.html

Something like a brochure, the Arbel Web site is a good public relations page. Opening with a large blue treble clef on a music staff, it announces its musical subject matter and offers a straightforward description:

> Arbel was started in 1973 by David Braverman in an effort to bring together young male and female Jewish singers in Philadelphia. Our name is a Hebrew acronym, alef-resh-bet-lamed, which stands for *Ahavei Rinah Bo'u Lashira*; that is, Lovers of Song Come to Sing/Rejoice. Over the years, membership has changed, but the group has thrived...

> Our repertoire includes Jewish music in many languages, including French, Hebrew, Yiddish, Ladino, and English. We perform works by artists ranging from the Jewish Italian Renaissance composer Salamone de Rossi to contemporary American musicians Debbie Friedman and Craig Taubman. We also do Israeli folk music, Chasidic tunes and sacred classical works by Bernstein and Bloch. Other composers/artists we have borrowed from include Harry Belafonte and J.S. Bach.

Arbel's members are pre-college. They have grown up with computers, and it is not surprising that their Web site is well-executed and includes creative links. For example, you can jump to home pages of individual members; to the home pages of the universities in the Philadelphia area where former Arbel singers are now students; to the composers whose work the group performs; to the *Jewish Exponent*, Philadelphia's Jewish weekly; even to Philadelphia's cyberspace Chamber of Commerce, Libertynet. And that's only a small sampling.

Geared toward members and prospective members, this is a casual site that promotes itself well, but also welcomes the unexpected guest.

Avrom's Jewish Music Page

http://www.geocities.com/TimesSquare/2923/jmusic.html

Who is Avrom and why does he have a Jewish music site? Avrom is a guy who wants to share his interest in Jewish music. He has a page because he can, and it's already looking good. He begins with an introduction and overview:

What do I mean by "Jewish Music?"

By Jewish Music I mean the music that I and other Orthodox Jews enjoy...namely Mordechai ben David, Avraham Fried and others. In Israel, this is usually referred to as *Musika Ha Chasidut*, or Chasidic Music, but I personally feel this is not all the time an accurate name as not all of the songs are sung by Chasidim or are Chasidic in composition. Upon occasion, I have also seen it referred to as 'Chasidic Rock' (hmm, I wonder where they got that one from?) In any case, I will refer to it as Jewish Music...

What do I intend to do with this page?

What I want to do first is make short sketches or biographies of some of the more popular singers, composers or groups and hopefully get pictures to go next to the text. Then, I intend to do "music reviews" of new releases, something a little like the *Chai* reviews in the Jewish Press, except I will be more critical. Finally, I might make outlines of all releases of the artists (by year)...[I am] not planning on covering klezmer, chazanus (cantorial music), Israeli music or singers I don't particularly enjoy or listen to...

So now you know who Avrom is and what he's up to, and you're ready to explore his site. He offers just what he promises, and he does it well, with a star rating system and full description. Our host has a fairly extensive knowledge of the artists he writes about, and definite opinions about the sound of their music. While only one group has been reviewed so far, more are promised.

Avrom reveals his biases and his goals early in the game. It's up to you to decide whether the page is your cup of tea. Along the way, Avrom shares enough of his personality to make the site fun; it's also one of those sites that is beginning to redefine how we get information and who determines what that information will be.

Dylan and the Jews/Bob Dylan: Tangled up in Jews
http://www.well.com/user/yudel/dylan.html

> This Web page is devoted to studying and collecting trivia relating to the Jewish religious and cultural odyssey of Shabtai Zisel ben Avraham, aka Bob Dylan.

For aficionados with an interest in the Jewish content of Bob Dylan's life and work, this site will be all you are hoping for and more. It is authored by Larry Yudelson, formerly of the *Jewish Telegraphic Agency* (the Jewish equivalent of the *Associated Press*) The site contains articles about Bob Dylan, highlights of his religious journey, photographic essays of his hometown, links to Yiddish writers who influenced him, analyses of lyrics and more.

Is this an important Jewish music site? Yudelson thinks so, and he reveals why in this Q&A excerpt from the site.

> Q: "Do you think Dylan's Jewishness is an important issue?"

> A: (Yudelson): "I do believe that Dylan's Jewishness has a lot to teach us. His spiritual searching has always been at the core of his music. But spiritual searching is not something the organized Jewish community is particularly comfortable with. The Establishment freaks out when the younger generations (which still

includes those, like Dylan, who have moved well past 50) make cracks about their synagogues, and tune out when they start to speculate that maybe we all indeed 'have to serve somebody.' Where Jewish leaders are preaching continuity, Dylan quietly raised five children, saw them to bar mitzvahs and Jewish weddings, but is most at home perpetuating the culture of Woody Guthrie and the old blues singers. At the same time, he has an intense desire for God and salvation, a tremendous awareness of man's sinfulness and an appreciation of how much compassion is required in this world. His is an intense, spiritual emotional message, very Chasidic, with much to teach the Jewish world."

If you're into Dylan or see eye to eye with Larry Yudelson, you may find this site insightful with much to offer. It's certainly idiosyncratic, but it is designed and organized quite well, as might be expected of an experienced journalist.

Debbie Friedman's Home Page

http://www.jewishmusic.com/dfr.htm

This page is linked to so many other Jewish music pages that bumped into it many times before accessing it directly. Maybe that's because it's a fun site. Or maybe it's because Debbie Friedman is so popular. In a world of Jewish music that is dominated by Orthodox, male singers, she stands out. Often considered the musical guru to the Reform and Conservative Movements, she has been profiled by many major Jewish papers and magazines, and she packed Carnegie Hall on one of the most snowbound nights of the decade.

Her Web page, maintained by Tara (see first entry in this chapter), offers this description:

> Internationally acclaimed singer and songwriter Debbie Friedman pioneered the distinctive development of contemporary American Jewish music. Since 1972 when her first album, *Sing Unto God*, introduced her unique musical style, Ms. Friedman's songs have delighted and inspired people throughout the world. Her work has been performed at the Israel Song Festival. It is being sung in synagogues, churches, schools, camps and community centers throughout North America and Europe.

At this site, you will find a photo of Ms. Friedman, details about her cassettes and CDs, scheduling information and samples of her music.

Hebrew Children Songs for Holidays
Zagit-Zviya Netter

http://www.well.com/user/zagit/shirim.html

This is the Web site of Zagit-Zviya Netter, one of the founders of Ein-Hod, an artists' village in Israel. A painter and a writer, she also composes children's music. The URL provided above will lead you directly to the music section of her Web site, which includes sheet music ready to be printed out, divided by holiday. Librettos are posted separately.

The site is simply done but very clear. It uses easy-to-read fonts and large black print. If you can't read music, you can still listen to her work, if you have a sound card and MIDI file—or print it out and bring it along to your next holiday gathering.

Israeli Folk Dance Written Notes

http://www.artsci.wustl.edu/~jclerman/folkdance/dances.html

Created in February, 1995 to disseminate Israeli folk dances, this site is a great idea. Its owner, Jeff Lerman explains:

> This page exists to help disseminate Israeli folk dances. I have noticed that often, people learn a dance once or twice, know the music, and *almost* know the dance, but don't quite remember it. Written notes can be very helpful in these cases; while they aren't a substitute for the real thing (a videotape or a teacher), written notes can be the difference between wishing you could teach/dance a dance you learned at that last workshop, and actually doing it.

Choose one of the 14 dances listed and you will pull up detailed notes describing every step of the dance, ready to be printed out. A section called "Other Stuff" follows. It promises, among other things, to post information sent in by visitors to the site, such as times and locations for Israeli dancing workshops, listed by city.

While the page taps into the vibrant Israeli dancing subculture that exists in many cities and has the potential to be a must-see Web page, Mr. Lerman hasn't visited the site since it was created. It has never been updated and there is nothing posted in "Other Stuff." Perhaps someone out there would like to pick up where Mr. Lerman left off?

The Klez Top Ten

http://www.well.com/user/ari/klez/klezlist.html

Dave Tarras/Yiddish-American Music, 1925-1956

http://www.well.com/user/ari/klez/tarras.7001.html

Ari Davidow's Klez Picks

http://www.well.com/user/ari/klez/index.html

So you already know that klezmer music is popular. But just how popular, you ask? Well, let's put it this way. There's a Top-10 list.

On these pink plaid pages, a fellow named Ari Davidow shares his extensive knowledge of klezmer music. A typographer who works in English, Hebrew and Russian, he recently left a job at Addison-Wesley to "consider the next generation of Web technology." In addition to the klezmer music site, he also maintains a Jewish Web conference called "The Well," a Web site for the Global Children's Organization and an electronic Hebrew user's group. Ari's pages are fun to surf, even if the pink plaid background doesn't always work so well.

The klezmer pages contain a wealth of information, particularly in the "reviews" section, but you will also find news, on-line vendors, bands arranged by area, festivals, music samples, feedback, articles, related pages and yes, the Top-10 list. Actually, there are two Top-10 lists. Check them out, and then visit the "reviews" section. Full of information and personality, it's the best way to learn about klezmer music and who's playing it. For instance, pull up the review of Dave Tarras' last recording. In addition to the usual CD cover image, there's a thorough write-up that offers plenty about the musician, the recording and klezmer music generally:

> Dave Tarras was one of the people who defined American klezmer music. Henry Sapoznik worked with Tarras before his death in 1989 to put together this collection of wonderfully cleaned up masters. Freed of the snap, crackle, and pop of unedited 78s, what emerges is soul music with swing. This is the music without which Emma Goldmann would have forsaken revolution. This music is life. It sings of melting pot and 2,000 years of recorded history. It dances. This is the real thing, complete with a couple of radio ads and other aural mnemonics.

You may want to spend some time at this site exploring. If you're into klezmer, don't miss it.

The Wholesale Klezmer Band

http://www.crocker.com/~ganeydn

Formed in 1982, the Wholesale Klezmer Band performs at Jewish weddings and in concert, and offers a full selection of educational programs for grade schools, high schools, colleges and adult education courses.

While the band plays mostly Yiddish and Hebrew music, its specialty is making the music accessible to the English-speaking world with translations, stories, explanations, visual aids and "the universal language that speaks to your feet and makes them want to dance." Band members write many of their own tunes.

The best part of this site is the band's guide to Jewish weddings. A fantastic overview, the guide explains everything from the *tish* (groom's reception) to the *bedeken* (veiling of the bride), from the chupah right through the reception—and there are musical suggestions at every turn.

There is also a guide to music for bar and bat mitzvah celebrations; a calendar of events; a section for recordings, listening samples and reviews; an explanation of the band's educational programs and an opportunity to meet the members of the band and get some basic background information.

The last option takes some effort because that section, "Who's Who in the Wholesale Klezmer Band," is visually daunting. The background is bluish-gray with purple diamonds, and the text is cornflower blue. But overall, it's a fine, informative site.

The band shares these pages with Peggy Davis, a calligrapher. If you're at this site for the Jewish wedding overview, you might like to browse through her section too!

Klezmer & Related Music
Recordings & Books

http://www.hmtrad.com/hmtrad/wendy/klezmer.html

The House of Musical Traditions is a retail music store in Washington, DC specializing in exotic, unusual and vintage instruments from the United States and around the world. It carries folk instruments, instructional books, song books and recordings of traditional music. The site is geared toward selling the company's wares, but among the 11 subheadings you will find sections for festivals, lessons, repairs and articles about music.

Klezmer music is Wendy's specialty, and she has her own subheading. Her page opens to a graphic box that says "Oy Chanukah!" over three Chanukah candles. Unfortunately, the extensive offerings are presented in list format, with only the most basic information provided—

title, composer/artist/author, catalog number and price. If you know what you're looking for, there's a good chance it's here. But if you just want to browse, you may be disappointed, especially since some of the creative touches around the site, like the House of Musical Traditions at the bottom of the page called "About HMT" don't find their way into the most important part of the page.

Hot Latkes Klezmer Band

http://publix.empath.on.ca/hlkb.html

A large black and white photo of this London, Ontario band making music and having a grand time sets a warm tone for the home page. So what if it's really a résumé page, advertising the band's availability for concerts, festivals, workshops, children's program, weddings and bar mitzvahs? This site will make you feel good.

The band was launched in the spring of 1993 and "has developed an extensive repertoire of klezmer and Yiddish theater music, much of it based on the work of luminaries of the past including Dave Tarras, Abe Schwartz, Molly Picon, Harry Kandel and Aaron Lebedeff. In addition to traditional Yiddish material the Latkes have delved into Ladino and Yemenite Jewish music as well as Greek and Gypsy music."

If you want to learn more about the individual musicians, check out the descriptions of all of the group's current members. You can even jump to the guitarist's own home page. But I would rather jump to the latke recipe. It looks mighty delicious.

Israel Zohar—The Philharmonic Klezmer

http://www/klezmer.co.il/

Israel Zohar specializes in playing klezmer music with philharmonic orchestras, and this is his home page. Like many of the pages that fall into this genre, if you are not interested in the particular individual or band, you may not find the page terribly exciting. However, this one is beautifully done and worth checking out as an example of how to use the Web as a public relations tool.

A pale orange sheet of music is screened onto the background. In the foreground is an impressive photo of Zohar posing with Itzhak Perlman, and Zubin Mehta looks on from the background. Just above the photo, the following quote appears, reprinted from *Good Morning Israel*: "In the Gala concert of the Philharmonic with Itshak [*sic*] Perlman and Zubin Mehta, the Klezmer Israel Zohar was revealed as a virtuoso of subtleties of soul—two degrees above every other jewish [*sic*] soul player know today."

Now that's how to open a Web site! And now that he's gotten your attention, you can follow the high points of his career, or click directly into "shows" or "disks." While "shows" is simply a list of performances, "disks" includes CDs, books and other recordings with a very effective visual touch: covers are cleanly linked together like postage stamps, with titles underneath.

If you're a Zohar fan, or if you're thinking of putting a résumé or an advertisement on the Web, check out this page.

Balladeer Music

http://www.balladeer.com/cat/international/country/international5.htm#isr

When you reach Balladeer's home page, look for the world beat stick figures banging on bongo drums and dancing to their music—they're on each new page of this Web site and they add a very upbeat, lighthearted note. They are also your first hint that Balladeer is not a run-of-the-mill music company. In fact, Balladeer describes itself as a "premier CD and cassette music store in Eugene, Oregon established in 1982...[that carries] a diverse selection of recordings that are hard to find and worth having...We are international, multi-cultural, vibrant, diverse and happening...From Umbuti pygmies to Frank Zappa's favorite Mongolian Band, Hun Hur Tu, we either have it or we'll make an effort to find it for you."

They're not kidding. Their catalog includes 19 categories of music, such as Celtic, bluegrass, Hawaiian, children's, blues and soul, African, Cajun, Brazilian—you get the picture.

Click into Israeli music and hold onto to your *sandalim*! I tried counting the selections, but I stopped at 58 and I was still in "A"! (Artists are listed alphabetically.) With hundreds of choices, if you're looking for Israeli music, this is the place. You may find the same items for less money at other sources on the Net, so shop around. But remember, the selection here can't be beat.

Jerusalem of Gold
http://www1.huji.ac.il/jeru/song_of_jerusalem.html

This is a whole Web site devoted to everyone's favorite song about Jerusalem, *Yerushalayim Shel Zahav* (Jerusalem of Gold). The song was "written in the year 1967 before the Six Day War, when Jerusalem was still divided. A few days after the song was first heard, Jerusalem finally united and the words of the song were changed to reflect this."

The lives and careers of singer Shuly Nathan and composer Naomi Shemer would never be the same. People clung to the tune and its words. It became the theme song of the Six Day War and the resultant reunification of Jerusalem. Very few songs have caught the national spirit and imagination the way this one has. Today, some 30 years after it was written, the song is still popular.

After glancing at the photos of Shuly Nathan and Naomi Shemer, you can listen to the original recording of the song. Unfortunately, my computer wouldn't allow me that much enjoyment. It just flashed me a message that read, "Format of the sound selected is not supported by any sound device on this computer."

The site is actually part of a cyberspace museum called Jerusalem Mosaic, designed in 1994 as a creative way to explore different facets of Jerusalem on the Web.

Perkins' Page

http://www.cyberscribe.com/perkins

Click into David Perkins' home page, and right at the top is an invitation to view the site in Pig Latin. And you really can. This is one of those sites that is full of the personality of its owner. It's up to you to see if you like it. Who is David Perkins?

> Whenever David Perkins blows into an instrument, magic comes out. Whether he's blowing shofar blasts to open Israel Independence Day festivities in Seoul, Korea, or jamming on a bamboo flute with Bedouin drummers at a Galilee folk festival or playing a klezmer gig with his band of top-notch musicians—treating audiences to his virtuoso sax and clarinet playing—David is first and foremost a musician par excellence.

A manufacturer of silver trumpets according to biblical design, Perkins also handcrafts flutes using bamboo or PVC piping and creates and collects percussion instruments. He's into world beat, klezmer, Celtic and New Age music.

At his Web site, you can wander through his picture gallery, read articles about him or sample his recordings. If you can't listen on your computer, the short descriptions accompanying each piece, such as "original soul music" or "traditional Romanian klezmer melody," offer a taste. If you wander through the picture gallery, don't miss the photo of David Perkins playing the flute underwater in Eilat. Now that's a first.

These pages are well-designed and easy to follow. The repeating graphic images are reminiscent of Andy Warhol's work and set a colorful, artsy tone. Brightly colored small squares are specially designed to match each section. Within each section, the design repeats itself, each time colored differently.

Come and meet Mr. Perkins, "Jerusalem's King of Klezmer." He works hard at expressing himself, and after all, that's what music is all about.

Klezmorim Interview

http://www.mhs.mendocino.k12.ca.us/Mencomnet/business/
retail/larknet/artklezmoriminterview

On this plain gray page with black text, you will find an interview with Kevin Linscott, a member of the band Klezmorim. The page is part of the Web site of Lark in the Morning, a Mendocino, California store specializing in hard-to-find musical instruments, music, and instructional material. Though the site boasts a "Top 5% of all Web sites" star, this particular page is clean and simple, with no graphics at all. You can find it at the URL above, or under "Articles" at the Lark in the Morning home page (http://www.mhs.mendocino.k12.ca.us/Mencomnet/business/retail/larknet/).

Feedback from customers and the impressive response to this band at a Lark music celebration prompted the interview. Linscott pontificates on the history and evolution of klezmer music, offers some technical tidbits and suggests what other music has benefited from the influence of klezmer.

You may or may not agree with his version of history—he doesn't believe klezmer music has any religious association, though I'm not so sure. Always used to enhance Jewish festivities, it was played by itinerant musicians at Jewish weddings. And if you wander back to the 16th century, you won't be able to ignore the connection between religion and klezmer music. But the interview makes good reading. And don't forget to check out the rest of the site.

Klezamir

http://www.saturn.net/~dschrag/klezamir

Klezamir, a Massachusetts-based klezmer band, must know that surfing the Web can be time-consuming and frustrating, because this site is focused and to the point. It's also rather humorous. Just underneath the group's logo and photo is an introduction: "Feast on Klezamir's banquet of Roots Rockin' klezmer music, jazz showpieces of the Yiddish theater, Hebrew love songs, lively Israeli dances, and original tunes. Klezamir also serves up jazz, R&B and rock for your wedding, Bar/Bat Mitzvah, or other occasion."

You don't have to scroll down to check out your options—they're all listed and highlighted at the first screen (debut recording, reviews, band member biographies, upcoming performances, school shows and booking information). But do it. It's worth it for the questions that precede each option. My favorite is the one preceding upcoming performances: "So do they play live or are they just a studio band like the Beatles?"

Special items include a listening sample at the recording page and a review by "Internet klezmer maven" Ari Davidow. All of the information offered is thorough and up-to-date. If you're trying to get a sense of who's part of the klezmer scene, you'll want to visit this site.

Bonnie Abrams/A Sudenyu of Yiddish Song

http://www.dynrec.com/bonnie2.html

Dynamic Recording Studios has created a home page just for singer/songwriter Bonnie Abrams' recently released recording, *A Sudenyu of Yiddish Song*. The site opens with an image of the CD cover, and offers information on the recording and on Ms. Abrams:

> "Fourteen traditional and contemporary Folk & Theater songs. In Yiddish with lyrics (and English translations) included in the oversized insert. A child of Holocaust survivors, Bonnie Abrams serves up a musical sudenyu (feast) in this tribute to her heritage. Many renowned musicians are guests on this recording which is also available at the United States Holocaust Memorial in Washington, DC."

All 14 selections are listed at this site, and if you like, you can sample three of them. Or, jump to Ms. Abrams' home page for more in-depth information on the artist, who has two other recordings out, sings everything from choral music to Broadway show tunes and performs programs of song and narration from a European Jewish repertoire at multi-cultural celebrations and Holocaust commemorations.

Though certainly not expansive, this site does make a fine stop if you're cruising the Web in search of Jewish music—especially if you can listen to the recordings on-line.

Magevet

http://www.yale.edu/magevet

Welcome to the home page of Magevet, "Yale University's Only A Cappella Singing Group Devoted to Singing Jewish and Israeli Music." Founded by eight male undergraduates in 1993 to fill the need for Jewish singing at Yale, Magevet has grown into a co-ed group of 13 including one graduate student and one member of the administration.

Magevet has performed on and off-campus, with other college music groups and with the late Shlomo Carlebach; it has even gone on tour throughout the Northeast and in Florida.

"Magevet's repertoire includes a diverse selection of Jewish and Israeli songs...[including] classical works by Rossi and Marcello, well-know arrangements by Aldema and Barnett, folk songs, liturgical works, pop, jazz and any-thing else that we can give a Jewish bent. Most of our music has been composed or arranged by members of the group."

This Web site is full of the flair and banter of bright, witty college students. For example, you may wonder why the group has named itself "Magevet," which means "towel." In lieu of an explanation, the group suggests that the visitor read *The Hitchhiker's Guide to the Galaxy*.

No matter where you go in this site, there's plenty of information and plenty of fun. Help Magevet name its second recording, or get information on purchasing its first recording, *Mem's the Word*. Pull up photos of the group in the recording studio and read through friendly, chatty captions, or jump to students' home pages. Whether you're interested in the group, college life, or just having fun, this a delightful site.

Hazamir—the National Jewish High School Choir

http://www.azc.com/client/sheri/hazamir/

This small site belongs to Hazamir, the national Jewish high school choir "started in 1993 by the cooperative efforts of Mati Lazar, Caroll Goldberg and the Zamir Choral Foundation...Currently, there are groups in New York, New Jersey, Boston, Philadelphia and Delaware. Every year, Hazamir hosts a Winter Festival in the New York area where all the groups come together for two days and sing."

Though the page begins promisingly with youthful fluorescent letters spelling "Hazamir" on a blacked-out box, too much information is missing. Where is the paragraph describing Hazamir's affiliate for adults, the Zamir Choral, an institution in American Jewish musical life? And how will visitors realize how widely the Winter Festival concert is attended by New Yorkers, tourists and alumni of both Hazamir and the Zamir Chorale? Where are the links to relevant sites and member home pages?

Hazamir's "Big Event," a first-ever, five-week trip to Israel, however, is well-publicized, with a flashing marquee that makes it hard not to want to click in to get the details. What's here is a good start. But Hazamir deserves more.

The New Israeli Opera

http://www.israel-opera.co.il

This site is still under construction and carries the message "Welcome to the New Israeli Opera on-line. After the curtain rises on our site we hope that you will find many items of interest."

Sing Jerusalem 3000
http://www.jer1.co.il/mall/sing-jer/jer_son.htm

This site is simply an advertisement for Ben Reuven's 45–minute English-language tribute to Jerusalem. There's no information on Mr. Reuven and there's no information on who maintains this site, except for a link at the bottom of the page to Virtual Jerusalem. But there is plenty of praise for the show: "A musical and poetic masterpiece that evokes the spirit and message of the Holy City as few works have done since the Psalms of David." And there is plenty of advice describing how to use it: "This show is suitable for Jewish and non-Jewish audiences of all ages and can be specially adapted for conferences, congresses, school shows or other special events." If you like, you can download several of the 15 songs that are part of the show, but I'd rather take advantage of the link to Virtual Jerusalem, "a starting point for navigation to Jewish and Israeli sites."

Tmu-na Theatre
http://www.pf1.co.il/tmu-na

"Tmu-na Theatre was established in 1981 by Nava Zuckerman with the aim of providing artists working in the fields of theatre, movement, music, painting and creative writing with the opportunity to develop and express their personal skills in a multidisciplinary environment."

Since performing *Tmu-na* at the 1982 Akko Festival, the group has continuously worked in two simultaneous modes, participating in workshops and creating plays based on them.

At this site, in addition to basic information about the group, you will find a list of performances since 1982, show schedules that were at least nine months old when this viewer visited, reservation information and the opportunity to send questions or comments.

Black headings with dark mauve writing are the best feature at this site. The colors create an illusion of velvet, and while the words aren't easy to read, the effect is dramatic.

Tzimmes

http://www2.portal.ca/~jsiegel/tzimmes.html

First, there's the image that opens the site. It's not a photo. It's more like a drawing in the sand of happy musicians with their instruments. Then there's the name of the group—"Tzimmes." How can you resist? If you don't know what it means, the following definition is provided:

> Tzimmes (pronounced: tsi'-mes) is a Yiddish word for a sweet culinary concoction made variously of stewed carrots, honey, raisins, and prunes; it is considered to be the perfect complement to the main course of a Jewish feast. In another, more humorous connection, Jewish people are warned not to complicate a simple matter, with the adage: "Don't make me a big Tzimmes!" (It is safe to say that the warning is usually ignored!) All in all, a Tzimmes seems to go in many directions at once—you can eat it, you can think about it, you can ask for the recipe, you can compare it with the one your grandmother used to make..."

The band, established in 1986 in Victoria, British Columbia, played for four years before disbanding, but was reformed in 1991 in Vancouver by two of the original members. Tzimmes now has two recordings out and continues to present Jewish music in its many facets.

> Tzimmes offers a program that emphasizes the tremendous diversity within Jewish music. Our songs range in style from European klezmer to Middle Eastern Sephardi to North American folk. And we sing in several languages: Hebrew, Yiddish (Judeo-German), Ladino (Judeo-Spanish) and English. New settings of traditional repertoire alternate with original creations which reflect an ongoing integration of new materials. Over the nine years of our existence, Tzimmes has performed for audiences of every description.

At the Tzimmes site, you can select "About Tzimmes," "Jewish Music," "Sample Music," "Discography," "Ordering" or "Other Links." The first option provides bios and photos of the members of the group, reviews in print and on the radio and a bit about the band's repertoire. Click to "Sample Music" to hear Tzimmes play, or switch to "Discography" to get details about the group's recordings. In this section, accompanying each tune there is a short flavorful description, such as: "A real hooked-on-love song, Yiddish style: 'Oh Yossel, I'm out of my mind over you.'"

The best part of this site by far is "Jewish Music." Here you will find a serious overview of Jewish music—call it the lecture outline for Jewish Music 101. Thorough and detailed, it includes diagrams and even a glossary. Every word that appears in the glossary is highlighted in the text. It's one of those treats you bump into unexpectedly on the Web—don't miss it!

The Cincinnati Klezmer Project

http://jazz.san.uc.edu/~mossja/

> "This page is devoted to making public domain klezmer and Jewish music arrangements available to people interested in starting klezmer ensembles."

Eye-opening in its simplicity, this site makes accessible what is already available. Created by a klezmer ensemble consisting mostly of students from the Hebrew Union College–Jewish Institute of Religion and the University of Cincinnati College Conservatory of Music, it's a wonderful site that puts the Web to work.

Three arrangements are on-line now, with more promised. You will also find a list of suggested books for budding klezmer musicians, and links to five related sites: TARA, Yahoo's Jewish music index, Professor Michele Gingras of the Clarinet Studio at Miami University of Ohio, Hebrew Union College and the University of

Cincinnati College Conservatory of Music. And, for those in the Cincinnati area or planning to visit, there's a current list of upcoming local events.

Reb Shlomo (Carlebach) Home Page
http://shamash.nysernet.org/judaica/rebshlomo/

"Welcome to the deepest and most *gevaldig* place on the whole Net!" These words grace the top of the Carlebach home page. If you ever met or heard Shlomo Carlebach you could almost chuckle. They personify him. And you could just see the twinkle in his eye as he would say, "The most *gevaldig* [great, unreal, special] place on the whole Net."

Few people have had as much influence on Jewish music as Shlomo Carlebach did. His friend Velvel Pasternak wrote (at a now-defunct section of the Tara Web site):

> ...his melodies, along with his performances and personal involvement with *amcha* (the ordinary people), exerted a major musical as well as Judaic influence on several generations of Jews worldwide... What was the secret of his success? Why did he succeed for so long while others failed after 'short runs?' The answer, I believe, can be found in his uncanny ability to strike an immediate responsive chord in the ears of his listeners. Even a seemingly banal-sounding melody became a hypnotic mesmerizing chant. The simplicity of his melody line, the intensity of his performances, the charisma of his personality served to create a worldwide musical following.

At this site, you can explore Reb Shlomo's life, music, teaching and even his death. "An On-line Memorial from Jemm" is particularly well-executed. There is information posted about some of Carlebach's students, special events, organizations associated with him and links to other Carlebach sites. These pages carry a warm but reverential tone. They are a tribute to Reb Shlomo, and they manage to capture something of his spirit.

Art

The Jewish relationship with art is complex. On the one hand, art has been used throughout Jewish history for the glorification of the performance of religious observances. On the other hand, using the likeness of man or beast in Jewish art has been strongly prohibited. This comes from two biblical prohibitions: "Thou shalt not make unto thee a graven image, nor any manner of likeness, of any thing that is in heaven above, or that is in the earth beneath, or that is in the water under the earth" (Exodus 20:4) and "Thou shalt not make unto thee a graven image, even any manner of likeness, of any thing, that is in heaven above, or that is in the water under the earth" (Deuteronomy 5:8).

The evolution of art during different periods of Jewish history is quite interesting. Most notable has been the use of art in religious documents since the Middle Ages. This can best be seen in illustrated *haggadot,* quite a number of which still exist, and in the use of *ketubot* (handwritten and illustrated Jewish marriage certificates). Other examples of Jewish art to be found are in religious articles, such as spice boxes, kiddush cups, and on tombstones.

Elaborate tombstones, some of the best examples of which can be found in present-day Polish cemeteries, tell the tale of vibrant communities and reflect the lives of the individuals they memorialize. Art historians agree that tombstone culture, especially the kind that flourished from the 16th to the 19th centuries in Poland, Bohemia, Romania, the Ukraine, and Belorussia, constitutes one of the most interesting areas of Jewish art.

The theoretical dispute over what is and is not permitted in Jewish art has been going on since antiquity and continues today. The source of the conflict is a difference in interpretations of the biblical prohibitions above: some Jews have felt the prohibition applied only to images intended for idol worship, while others have extended it to include all sculpture, or even all figurative art, treating the human face with particular suspicion.

The art of gravestones reflects this controversy. Among Ashkenazic Jews, human shapes do not appear on traditional tombstones, with very few exceptions. According to religious codes and customs, which were strictly observed by the Orthodox, it was permissible to use decorations that tradition had accepted on tombstones. These included animal motifs (lions, deer, bears, sheep, birds, etc.), plant themes (baskets with fruit, grapes, leaves, etc.), and symbols that have recurred for centuries in Jewish funerary art, such as hands the sign of the priestly class, the Levites' pitcher (used for washing the hands of the priests), the Shield of David, the seven-branched candelabrum, and a dwindling candle.

The inscriptions on some of these stones tell a great deal about the deceased. In Krakow, the tombstone of the ReMaH, Rabbi Moshe Isserles (d.1572), reads as follows:

> Light of the West, the greatest of the generation's wise men, Rabbi Moshe Shepherd of the flock of Israel. On the 33rd day of the counting of Omer among Israel. He spread righteous deeds and taught law to Israel. He spread Torah among Israel. He established scholars for thousands among Israel. From Moshe (Moses) to Moshe (Maimonides) there has not been such a Moshe in Israel. And this is the law of the sin-offering and of the whole-offering which Moshe set before the people of Israel the year 5332 (1572). May his soul be bound up in the knot of life.

In modern times Judaism has brought forth a wealth of artists of international renown. These include Yaakov Agam, Marc Chagall, Sir Jacob Epstein, Jacques Lipchitz, Amadeo Modigliani, Louise Nevelson, David Palombo, Camille Pissaro, Larry Rivers, Mark Rothko, Reuven Rubin, Ben Shahn, Raphael Soyer, Jakob Stinhardt, and Arthur Szyk. These artists have found a prominent place in collections at major institutions throughout the world, and you can view much of their work in the institutions featured in the Museums chapter.

This chapter offers a look at less established contemporary Jewish art and artists, as well as Israeli stamps and coins, an often overlooked window into the artistic culture of a country. Israeli stamps and coins reflect the art and history of the State of Israel in a unique and official way. Israeli stamps are popular representations of Jewish history and life, and the coins and medals are also sought by many collectors.

You can use the Web sites at the end of the chapter, which are not as comprehensive or attractive as one might hope, to find more information about Israel's offerings in these areas. If you find these interesting, you may also want to check out one of dozens of attractive, but more general, sites on the Web relating to philatelic services.

On-line galleries of Jewish art are listed first.

A Word of Art

http://www.netvoyage.net/~wordrtst/ketuba.html

A Word of Art specializes in original and individualized *ketubot* designed specifically for each couple.

The tradition of ornate *ketubot* persisted through the years of Jewish dispersion. Modern *ketubot* take as their basis the traditional mode of the *ketubah*, with both contemporary and traditional artwork. *Ketubot* make a beautiful wedding gift for the husband to give to his bride. In Jewish tradition, the *ketubah* is kept by the wife for the entire span of her marriage. Often, they are treated as heirlooms by future generations. Legally they are proof of a valid Jewish marriage.

Samples of the beautiful *ketubot* created by A Word of Art are found on this Web site.

Artistic Judaic Promotions

http://tucson.com/ajp/orderis.html

Artistic Judaic Promotions represents distinguished Israeli and American artists, many of whom are internationally known. Their work can be previewed in this virtual catalog.

"AJP offers you access to these exceptional artists from the stroke of a keyboard. Here you will find unique Israeli and Judaic jewelry, wearable art, mezzuzot, Ketubot and fine Judaica, all of which are outstanding values as gifts for either you or someone special to you. There are also several Jewish craft kits on this site. These kits enable youngsters to create their own Judaic arts and crafts items."

Many of the artists have unique and attractive styles, in a variety of media. Examples by each of the artists are shown on the Web site, which also lists prices. The *ketubot* are available with a variety of wordings—Traditional, Conservative (Leiberman), and Modern Alternative, each with its own English interpretation.

Many AJP products are not overly expensive and they are quite unusual. They are worth a look if you are shopping.

The Genius of Marc Chagall

http://www.logotime.com/arta/

The Arta Gallery has been granted exclusive rights by the Chagall estate to oversee production and sale of a small selection of Chagall works, including lithographs, Kiddush cups, candlesticks, and *mezzuzot*.

Personally, I can't offer a great deal of enthusiasm for the items in this on-line catalog. Despite the title, these offerings do not adequately convey the genius of Chagall. For Chagall buffs, though, this could be an unique opportunity to look for affordable Chagall reproductions for the home.

Givon Art Gallery

http://www.macom.co.il/interart/givon/

This Tel Aviv gallery has a very small Web site that highlights the works of artists in its stable, including featured artists Moshe Gershuni and Raffi Lavie. It also has catalogues on Lea Nikel, Ido Bar El, Gabi Klasmer, and Nurit David. As no prices are mentioned, you have to know the Israeli art market for this site to be useful for more than on-line window-shopping.

Andrew Berger's Museum of the Psalms

http://www.adadvantage.com/art/index.html

Andre (Moshe-Zvi) Berger has set himself the goal of creating a picture for every one of King David's 150 Psalms. In 1994, he released his first book, which contained the first 41 Psalms along with 41 pictures. Since then he has painted several more, mainly of Psalms about Jerusalem. He has also painted several murals portraying the east coast of the United States.

This Web site shows Berger's psalm paintings as well as several of his murals. It is an interesting concept in marketing, and I think the artist is using this Web gallery to get his message across.

Art Judaica

http://www.artjudaica.com/vend/svend

Art Judaica is a virtual gallery of unique Judaic art and traditional symbols.

A new artist is featured every three to six weeks. On the site, you can also have the gallery notify you when a new artist is featured.

The following artists were on exhibit when this chapter was written: Bonnie Yales, Richard Bitterman, Yankel Ginzburg, Dori Jalazo, Marilyn Louis, Dani Katsir, Frank Meisler, Georgina Rothenberg, Israel Rubinstein, Calman Shemi, Arthur and Wendy Silver, Marian Slepian, Mae Tupa, and Shirley Zwang.

You can preview the artists' work, some of it fairly well-known, on-line. Prices range from a few hundred to several thousand dollars.

Emes Editions Limited

http://www.netaxs.com/people/zalesjp/

The Emes on-line gallery features the works of Mordechai Rosenstein, which it describes in glowing terms:

Mordechai Rosenstein creates limited edition silk screen prints of award-winning, original pieces, reflecting the rich and ancient traditions of Judaism. Drawing upon the inherent grace and lyrical qualities of the Hebrew alphabet, this truly gifted artist embellishes the letters and gives them a special rhythm and excitement to make them virtually dance across the print.

Rosenstein does art shows as fund-raisers all over America. He also renders designs for synagogue interiors, such as Yahrtzeit and dedication walls, stained-glass sections, and wool tapestries.

Kosinski Galleries

http://www2.NetVision.net.il/~kosinski/

This Web gallery is one of my favorite discoveries. The text on the site is evocative of the beautiful pieces created by the artist:

Born in Scotland, of Polish parents, in 1952, Kosinski spent his formative years in the English Lake District, awestruck by the majesty of his natural surroundings.

Introduced to Israel and Sinai in 1982, he immediately fell in love with the wilderness. ... He discovers unusual perspectives of otherwise familiar sites.

It's a pleasure to view his paintings on this Web site. They are beautiful and quite reasonably priced. He also offers lithographs. I think that I'll look Kosinski up on my next trip to Israel. His artistry is worth it.

Melech's Mosaic Home Page

http://rtlsoft.com/mmosaic/

Melech Postavsky, a Polish artist now living in Israel, has put examples of his colorful mosaics on the Web.

The themes of his work range from reconstruction of mosaic pieces found in archeological excavations to reproductions of Chagall, Gauguin, and lesser-known artists.

He primarily takes his themes from biblical sources and ancient mosaics found in Israel, but has also included a number of mosaics depicting scenes from prewar Europe.

Tiroche Auction House
http://www.macom.co.il/interart/tiroche/

Tiroche Auction House was established in 1992 in Herzelia Pituach, just north of Tel Aviv. It holds approximately 15 auctions a year on a variety of subjects. Tiroche Auction House is notable in that it features international impressionist and modern and contemporary art as well as local Israeli art.

The site lists upcoming sales and, interestingly, the results of previous sales. The lofty pricing gives you an idea of the high reputation of the offerings, which include world-renowned artists. This site is worth viewing just to see some of the paintings on display.

The Jewish Institute for the Arts
http://www.chaim-goldberg.com/jiarts/index.html

This home page is a platform for Chaim Goldberg and his artistic activities. One reviewer categorizes his works in the following manner:

"Jewishness is what most of Mr. Goldberg's work is all about. His subject matter ranges from the daily chores of the Jewish baker or the tailor to the joys of the Jewish market place, the Hasidic dancers or the lively feasts of the shtetl. But he also does not forget the horrors and atrocities the Jews have been victims of. ..."

Goldberg has been painting since his youth in Warsaw, before World War II. His paintings have been exhibited throughout the world and can be found in several major institutions. If you are into Jewish paintings and lithographs, you are likely to have come across this artist. If you take the time to visit his Web site, you can see more of his works and learn about him.

Stamps of Israel
http://www.macom.co.il./stamps/index.html

This incomplete Web site of Israeli stamps tells the story of the beginnings of Israel's philatelic services. It currently only shows stamps for a single year. This could grow into a very interesting site if the listings are made more comprehensive.

The Land of Israel Reflected in Coins and Medals
http://www.coins.co.il/index.html

This site contains scant information on ordering coins from the Israel Government Coins and Medals Corporation. There is little actual material about the coins and medals available from the Israel government at this site (but there is a picture of Uzzi Narkiss, the chairman of the board). I would rather have photos of some of Israel's medals.

Ben Uri Art Gallery
http://www.ort.org/links/benuri/home.htm

The Ben Uri Gallery, located in London's West End, has a collection of more than 700 paintings, drawings, prints, and sculpture by Jewish artists. Reproductions of the entire collection are available on CD, and a fair number of them are here.

This site is one of the few that display a number of images in a well-organized fashion. You can either take a tour, or you can choose images from a number of Jewish holidays and festival categories. Either way, you get a small image with a detailed explanation of the work and the artist and are given the option to download a full-size version of the image. The organizers did a really nice job, one that more art museums ought to emulate.

Room of Israel Artists
http://www.art.net/TheGallery/Avi_Room/Israel_Artists.html

An interesting concept—eleven artists put images of their work on this one page, along with their postal addresses (and sometimes phone numbers and e-mail addresses). I suppose you could call this a mini-cybergallery. There are some interesting pieces of contemporary art here.

Jewish American Virtual Art Gallery
http://www.intercall.com/~harriet/gallery2.htm

This is a virtual art gallery in every sense of the word. This one showcases American Jewish artists and provides a low-cost alternative to renting out real space and high commissions. Here, artists provide their work for a small fee, and interested art aficionados can view at their leisure and make purchases (with no commissions).

I must admit to having been very skeptical about this site, but once I saw it, I became a believer.

There are some beautiful images here, and some of the pieces are not terribly expensive. It deserves a look. I was particularly impressed by the pottery of Jo Hasson. Take a look and decide what you like best.

Yiddish

What is Yiddish? Yiddish is, in essence, a Jewish dialect of German, written with Hebrew characters. The first site listed in this chapter explains:

> "It arose (c. 1100) out of a blend of a number of German dialects in the ghettos of Central Europe, and from there it spread to other parts of the world. Phonetically, Yiddish is closer to Middle High German than is modern German. Its vocabulary is basically German, but it has been enlarged by borrowings from Hebrew, Slavic, Romance languages, and English.... Yiddish is a highly plastic and assimilative language, rich in idioms, and possessing remarkable freshness, pithiness, and pungency."

Before the Holocaust, Yiddish was spoken by more than 11 million people. Today, it is spoken by about 4 million Jews in all parts of the world.

That is a definition or explanation of Yiddish. However, I am reminded of a story. It's about a dowager who commissioned a well-known painter to do a portrait of her. The commission was a handsome one: $25,000. The artist worked diligently. He made the dowager look really good. He removed the wrinkles and the extra chins. He made her jewels look larger and shine more brightly. He took off some 20 years from the dowager's real age. He did a masterful job.

On the day he unveiled the portrait, he expected accolades from the dowager. Instead she scorned his work. "Why?" the artist asked, "You look wonderful." She replied, "How wonderful could I look if my own dog doesn't recognize me." Sure enough, the dog who accompanied the dowager everywhere didn't show any sign of recognizing the figure in the portrait. The artist was crestfallen. But the dowager said, "Don't worry. I know you're a very talented person. Take some time out and come back to me when you have the new portrait and I will reward you with an increased commission."

The artist left the dowager's home with the scorned painting under his arm. He did nothing with it for six months. One day he called the dowager for another appointment. Just before entering her house, he unscrewed the cap of a jar of *schmaltz*. He plastered the schmaltz all over the face of the painting. When he walked into the house the dog immediately began to nip at his heels. It licked at the face of the painting in ecstasy. The dowager was elated. She cheerfully wrote the artist a check for the agreed amount. He walked out happy. The dowager was happy. Even the dog was happy. What did it? The "Schmaltz".

But how do you define schmaltz? Its a Yiddish word for rendered fat that is made from goose or chicken or even from meat. But it's more than that—well, it's schmaltz. It gives off a flavor and a pungency all its own. Yiddish is more than that, too. It defies a real description or definition. It is the sum of the experience of the Jewish people through thousands of years in exile and the real day-to-day life of Jews in Europe for almost a thousand years.

The Yiddish Homepage
http://www.bergen.org/AAST/Projects/Yiddish/English/

This site is a well-written historical introduction to the Yiddish language, and also includes brief material on Yiddish literature, theater, and Yiddish words found in English.

Der Yiddisher TamTam
http://www.col.fr/tamtam/

TamTam, a bimonthly Yiddish newspaper published in Paris, is available here in PDF, which means you need an Acrobat reader to read it. (If you don't have the Acrobat reader already, you can download it from this site for free).

Mendele: Yiddish Literature and Language
http://world.std.com/~yv/mendele-brochurele.html

Mendele is a Yiddish literature and language mailing list. This site offers instructions on how to subscribe, and links to the archives of past discussions. One of the links is a Web site, with searching capabilities (provided your browser is forms-capable). All in all, while there is a great deal of Yiddish material at this site, it is a bit difficult to find your way around. It helps if you know what you're looking for. This is not a particularly user-friendly site. On the other hand, if Yiddish is your passion, and you want to check out messages from other Yiddish-ists, this is the place.

The Virtual Shtetl
http://sunsite.unc.edu/yiddish/shtetl.html

This site is a nice little resource. It includes a small picture dictionary (English-Yiddish-Hebrew-German-Russian), and a rather large number of links to other Yiddish resources; from mailing lists, books, and newspapers to a page describing post-secondary Yiddish courses (from Brandeis to UCLA), to an archive of Jewish cooking recipes.

While this site was originally created to show the vitality of Yiddish as a language, it also reflects the life of the Jewish community in general. There are links to a series of guides to Jewish communities. None are in-depth pieces but they all have some sparkle of interest, and some include maps. You really don't know where you will go with them until you get there. At the Crakow site, for example, you'll find a history of the Yiddish language and a series of Yiddish proverbs.

The *shtetl* was not restricted to Eastern Europe. This site also has links to some other fascinating *shtetls*, namely, Chicago's Maxwell Street, London's East End, and New York's East Side.

One snippet from Chicago's Maxwell Street makes the whole site very special:

Fish Crier
by Carl Sandburg (1916)

"I know a Jew fish crier down on Maxwell Street with a voice like a north wind blowing over corn stubble in January

He dangles herring before prospective customers evincing a joy identical with that of Pavlova dancing

His face is that of a man terribly glad to be selling fish, terribly glad that God made fish, and customers to whom he may call his wares from a pushcart"

The Maxwell Street Market isn't there anymore. But the spirit of the *shtetl* still exists. See a little bit of it for yourself.

Raphael's Yiddish Home Page
http://www.cs.engr.uky.edu/~raphael/yiddish.html

Do you know Yiddish, but have a hard time getting a hold of actual Yiddish publications? This site contains over two dozen Yiddish poems and songs—ranging from *Dona Dona* to a translation of *Waltzing Matilda* (*A tentsl, mayne kale*). It's all in Yiddish, all in graphics, so that you don't need a Yiddish language reader for it.

If you know people who speak or read Yiddish, ask them to read and explain some of these selections to you. You will see a twinkle in their eyes as they do so.

Yiddish poem of the week
http://www.cs.brandeis.edu/~hhelf/stuff/poem.html

The poems don't actually appear every week, but when they do, they are usually worth it. The transliteration of the poem is accompanied by an English translation. Some of Yiddish literature's major figures have appeared on this site.

Years Have Sped By—My Life Story
http://www.ncc.com:80/dvjcc/Yiddish/contents.html

"This is a tale of family life and love... of Chaya Rochel, who strives so mightily not to forsake her beloved Yiddish, where only other languages are spoken... and where she maintains her love and knowledge of the beloved Yiddish classicists, her idols."

This is Chaya Rochel Andres's autobiography. She was born in Suwalki, Poland, just before the turn of the century. She left the old world and her immediate family in her early twenties, spending weeks on steamships, going through Ellis Island, and then spending two more days, on a train, destined for her aunt, uncle, and nine cousins in Dallas. This engrossing story will transport you back in time.

It is in English and in Yiddish (displayed as rather large graphic files, but worth the wait for Yiddish-ists).

Shtetl: A Journey Home
http://www.logtv.com/shtetl/shtetl.html

This is the Web home of the famous film *Shtetl: A Journey Home*.

"Each of us wants to return to the place we came from. A place where the journey to understand who we are begins and ends. In Yiddish this place is called *shtetl*. And when we get there, we hope to meet a righteous man."

The film starts when filmmaker Marian Marzynski accompanies Nathan Kaplan, a 70-year-old Jewish man from Chicago, to Bransk, a small Polish *shtetl* in Eastern Poland.

Unbelievably, the entire script is available here for viewing or downloading. (This is obviously not a Hollywood-produced film!) It is a very powerful film about life in the *shtetl*. LogIn (its producers) did a first class job on this site.

The film itself can be seen on PBS, various screenings around the world (a schedule is here), and it can be purchased or rented for public viewing.

Jewish Short Stories From Eastern Europe and Beyond

http://www.kcrw.org/b/jss.html

When is a book not a book? When it's an audio cassette! You'll find stories by the masters: Sholom Aleichem, I.L. Peretz, Y.L. Agnon, and Isaac Bashevis Singer, which can all be heard on-line via RealAudio. You will not believe the all-star lineup of readers. If you like the stories, the site offers you an opportunity to buy a series of cassettes. This rich literature is a welcome diversion.

The Jeremiah Kaplan Fellowships in Modern Jewish Culture

http://hamp.hampshire.edu/~kaplan/kaplan.html

The home page explains:

> "Hampshire College and the National Yiddish Book Center have created a partnership to provide college students with one-year visiting fellowships that offer a distinctive opportunity and context in which to study Jewish history and culture. The Jeremiah Kaplan Fellowships in Modern Jewish Culture draw on courses offered at Hampshire and the other member institutions in the Five College Consortium: Amherst College, Mount Holyoke, Smith, and the University of Massachusetts at Amherst."

The National Yiddish Book Center itself does not have its own Web site. The story of the Center is really fascinating. It literally saved tens of thousands of Yiddish volumes from the garbage heap. The Center has been instrumental in keeping Yiddish alive. It is to be commended for its efforts.

You'll find other material on Yiddish in several other chapters in this book: Music; History; Books; and Newspapers and Magazines.

PART IV

Jewish
Intellectual
Life

CHAPTER 1 7

Classes and Commentary

The Talmud illuminates Jewish dedication to education thusly:

> "These are the precepts whose fruits a person enjoys in This World but whose principal remains intact for him in the World To Come. They are: the honor due to father and mother, acts of kindness, early attendance at the house of study morning and evening, hospitality to guests, visiting the sick, providing for a bride, escorting the dead, absorption in prayer, bringing peace between man and his fellow—and the study of Torah is equal to them all."

This statement is part of the morning prayer ritual. Looked at in the context of the other precepts mentioned, the importance attached to education in Jewish life becomes obvious.

Jewish education began with Abraham, Isaac and Jacob. But the real concept of teaching, as such, began with Moses receiving the Torah from The Almighty after the Jewish Exodus from Egypt. Moses was confronted with the task of having to explain Judaism and Jewish law to a large number of individuals who had emerged from the captivity of Egypt to their new-found freedom as a Jewish nation—and he is often referred to as *Moshe Rabbeinu*, Moses our teacher.

The basic educational texts of Judaism and its traditions may be divided into two parts—the Written Law and the Oral Law. The Written Law refers to the *Tanach*, or what is referred to in non-Jewish circles as the Old Testament or The Bible. The Tanach itself can be divided into three parts (in fact the word itself is an acronym for those parts): the *Torah*, which consists of the Five Books of Moses; the *Nevi'im* or Prophets; and *Ketuvim*, or later writings. Nevi'im and Ketuvim give great insight into the lives of Jews in biblical times. These writings have been given great attention by scholars. But the basic kernel of Jewish law stems from the Torah. It contains the 613 *mitzvot* (deeds) that are the responsibility of the Jew. They are the basis of all Jewish law and human conduct. The total contents of the Tanach are placed in one intellectual vessel and are collectively referred to as the *Torah Shebiktav* or the Written Law.

Around these writings have evolved what is commonly know as the *Torah Sheba'alpeh* or Oral Law. Why the term Oral Law? Traditional Jews hold that it, too, was given at Mt. Sinai. In any event, the Oral Law's codifiers didn't commit it to writing until much later than the Written Law. Only after the need became overwhelming was the Oral Law committed to writing—both the *Mishnah* (the six orders of the law that was redacted by Judah Ha Nassi), and the commentary on it, referred to as *Gemarah*. These works, collectively, are known as the *Talmud*. Today, the Talmud contains both those writings and a substantial amount of rabbinical commentary. (There is a great picture of a Talmud page at http://www.ucalgary.ca/~elsegal/TalmudPage.html.) The Talmud is written in a form that would appear to today's readers as "stream of consciousness" writings—the concepts are explained and debated, and are mixed in with various legends and stories. An example of this lack of linear structure is that the rules for Hannukah are in the middle of the book on Shabbat. The complexity of the law and the ancillary codes and subsequent addenda gave rise to further commentaries and codifications of the law. The monumental *Shulchan Aruch* and Maimonides's *Mishneh Torah*, both written in the Middle

Ages, were just two attempts to extract the legal part of the Talmud and compile it in an organized manner.

Jewish law simultaneously developed a *responsa* literature. No matter how in-depth any code of law is, there are always new situations that arise that aren't covered, or aren't even contemplated. When these questions arose, local rabbis would try to answer them. The more difficult questions were sent to world-renowned Jewish scholars. These questions and their answers became known as the Responsa literature. *Responsa* literature actually goes way back in Jewish history. The most famous collection of ancient *responsa* were found in the Cairo Geniza (a genizah is a repository of holy documents. These documents are not destroyed or thrown away. They are either buried or placed in a special "repositor". (See the Geniza Research Unit site at: *http://www.cam.ac.uk/Libraries/ Taylor-Schechter/.*)

Education, particularly religious education, experienced an earth-shattering revolution at the end of the 15th century with the invention of the printing press. (It is no coincidence that the first book ever printed was The Bible—and that before the end of the century, the entire Talmud was produced in this manner.) Suddenly, much of this material was available to an audience that was unimaginable just decades before.

We are going through a similar revolution today. Many of these texts are available on CDs, and a growing number of them are appearing on the Web. (After all, anything written before the 1920s is well past its copyright expiration date.) This is particularly important for Jews who do not live near a center of Jewish learning, and particularly exciting for those teachers and institutions that have embraced the new technologies. Cyber-universities can be formed in a one-room office—with reference materials on the Web, and gifted teachers and students from around the world.

Now you can receive lectures from noted scholars, study texts, even find a study partner, all from your computer, on your own schedule. As if this weren't incredible enough, almost all of this is absolutely free.

Of particular note are a few organizations that are at the leading edge of this new educational paradigm: Project Genesis, the Virtual Beit Midrash, the Tanach Study Center, Maqom, and the Interactive Torah Study Forum. No one can know what the future of Jewish education will look like, but I suspect that it will look something like what these organizations are already offering, and that is tremendously exciting.

Judaism 101: An Introduction to Judaism

http://members.aol.com/jewfaq/

This is one of the best set of Jewish introductory and reference materials anywhere. As the author writes, "My goal in creating this web site is to make freely available a wide variety of basic, general information about Judaism, written from a traditional perspective in plain English."

This site carries a wealth of material on just about any aspect of Jewish life. It covers everything from education to marriage to conversion to signs and symbols in Judaism. If this is your first introduction to Judaism and Jewish education, downloading this site is more than worthwhile—it's like a free hyper-linked textbook. You can use it as a starting point in your explorations, or as an index to other links.

But don't let the "Introduction" in the name mislead you. There are some solid reference materials here for Jews of all education and experience—for example, a complete list of the 613 Mitzvot, along with their biblical sources, as well as solid explanations of the holidays, kashrut, and a whole host of other topics. This site should be bookmarked on the browser of anyone reading this book.

As an added bonus, the entire site is downloadable as a Microsoft Word document.

Major Sources For Educational Aids

CAJE, the Coalition for the Advancement of Jewish Education

http://www.caje.org/

CAJE, the largest North American Jewish educators' organization, brings together Jewish educators from across the ideological spectrum. One of its goals is to elevate the status of Jewish education on the Jewish communal agenda.

The site, called the CyberCAJE project, gives you information on CAJE annual and regional conferences and has a listing of education materials that are available from CAJE. The list contains some very solid materials. The project also "provides Jewish educators with online resources including articles, curricula, and links to other Web sites relevant to Jewish educators. In addition, online discussion groups, upcoming events, and news about CAJE and CyberCAJE are available." CAJE members can also order from an extensive databank of curriculum materials.

JESNA, the Jewish Education Service of North America

http://www.jesna.org/

JESNA "was created in 1981 by the Jewish Federation movement to serve as its continental instrument of Jewish educational planning and services. JESNA's mission is to enhance the quality and increase the impact of Jewish education in North America by strengthening the motivation, knowledge, and skills of lay and professional leaders and by encouraging concerted community action to expand and improve Jewish education in all its forms and settings."

This site has a wide range of educational resources, including links to general education pages and solutions to some specific problems of Jewish educators. Some of the highlights include: links to other community Jewish educational agencies; materials and information about special-needs education; lists of schools in the Jewish community day school network; and a list of JESNA publications with lengthy abstracts of each one.

This site is important for those in the field, and even for those who would simply like to put together some adult education activities. Unfortunately, however, it is not well organized, so it may take a bit of time to find what you need. But much of what you need in the field of Jewish education is probably accessible from this site.

Jewish Education on Line

http://www.slip.net/~bjesf/

Jewish Education on Line is a good example of how a local Jewish community, in this case the San Francisco Bay area, can showcase its resources and make them known to their target audience. (It is one of several communities that have done this—many can be reached from links at the JESNA site).

The site also offers a variety of interesting programs, most geared towards educators: These include: a Jewish Web project, book time for families, a Jewish heritage video collection, and so on. More importantly for the community, there are announcements of local conferences and other events. As on the JESNA site, there are pages with many interesting links to other Jewish sites across the Web. And, like the JESNA pages, this site is not particularly well organized. Nevertheless, it is a worthwhile site for Jewish education, and an important site for the San Francisco Bay area.

The Melton Centre For Jewish Education In the Diaspora

http://www2.huji.ac.il/www_melton/top.html

The Centre's activities include M.A. and Ph.D. programs in Jewish education, training programs in formal and informal Jewish education, the development of curricula and other educational materials and research in Jewish education. The Melton Centre provides consultation services to schools and educational workshops throughout the world. Course (and mini-course) descriptions are here, but the pages at this site are *slow*. If you click on "school," you'll find yourself downloading a 225K picture of the school, and a few links to other places where the actual information is.

The Pedagogic Center

http://www.jajz-ed.org.il/

The Pedagogic Center is a part of The Joint Authority for Jewish Zionist Education. The site is not easy to get around in, but there are some real gems hidden in the pages. In the festivals section, there are a tremendous number of links to resources as varied as essays and role-model simulation games. The center will facilitate *twinning*, matching a school, or any group of middle- or high-school group of students with its like in Israel, for correspondence, exchanges of work, and the like.

A particularly nice section is one called "Ethics in Everyday Life," where traditional Jewish sources are applied to real-life everyday situations that children face, e.g., "My mother told me to throw out the papers, when my father got home he angrily asked 'who threw away the papers?'" The answer, of course, is not so nearly as important as the method of examining the issues.

There is a nice search facility to help you find what you might need, as well as a general index.

Ort Educational Resources

http://www.ort.org/edu/edu.htm

This site ought to be called "Educational Links O'Plenty." There are links for teachers and kids, links to the "Web66 schools on line" (which in turn attempts to link to every school in the U.S. that has a Web site), nice illustrated pictorials of holidays, and much more.

One link from this site is to "Navigating the Bible," such an awesome resource that it earned its own separate entry in this chapter. There are on-line educational quizzes, "Ask Dr. Math," information about educational conferences, and the like.

Other Jewish projects are under development and you can learn about them at this site. I would bookmark this site. It's worth remembering.

For children and special needs, there are also some great sites to visit.

Pirchei Shoshanim

http://www.pirchei.co.il/

How do teachers and parents inculcate the essential values of Judaism to our children? In an era of "family values," this question seems even more pertinent. As the creators of this site write, "The demands are great, and resources are limited. There is a growing need for innovative materials that can capture our children's attention in an ever-changing world."

Pirchei Shoshanim produces wonderful pictorial children's books, most of them related to morals and ethics, and six of them are reproduced in full. (Warning: Pictures take a long time to download!). They also produce educational materials such as contests, an international correspondence program for children in schools around the world, (via regular mail or the Internet), membership cards, stickers, T-shirts, certificates, and the like.

Particularly noteworthy is their section on special education. The site has a listing of special-education resources for children with disabilities and a link to *Down Syndrome Magazine*. This is extremely important. Special education in cases of the very religious actually causes a double burden. Separation of church and state in the United States already creates a situation where the public schools are essentially free (we're leaving out the issue of taxes here), while religious schools are not. Add in the extra costs associated with special education, and you see quite a financial burden. Pirchei Shoshanim shows some of the support and programs available for these children.

But that's not all. This site also includes a famous letter from Maimonides to his son (he instructed his son to read it at least once a week), and a letter from the Vilna Gaon to his family. There are subscriptions lists and copies of *Issues in Torah Education*, a special area with Jewish educational computer games available for downloading, and another section specifically for principals.

The site also contains other innovative ideas for use in religiously oriented schools and provides links to Orthodox educational resources.

The following are Internet-based educational institutions.

Project Genesis

http:/www.torah.org

Project Genesis is the best site for serious Jewish education on the Internet—period. It has won more awards than any other in Jewish cyberspace. This is a wonderful example of how the Internet can pull together resources and offer them, free to users worldwide, in a way that couldn't be done face to face.

Project Genesis offers a wide (and growing) range of classes that can appeal to the beginner as well as the advanced Judaica student, with classes on Torah, ethics, *halacha*, and more. A few of the classes are translated into other languages (e.g., Spanish and Russian), and all the classes are entirely free and fully archived.

The site is beautiful, with links directly to classes, a commentary on the current week's portion, and other timely and seasonal events—such as a commentary on Bill Moyers's PBS *Genesis* series. While this is written from an Orthodox perspective (as is most of the educational material found on the 'Net), partisanship takes a back seat to enthusiasm, optimism, and scholasticism.

Virtual Beit Midrash (Yeshivat Har Etzion)

http://www.virtual.co.il/education/yhe/

This site is a truly outstanding Jewish educational resource. It is run by Yeshivat Har Etzion, founded in 1969, which "is the largest Hesder Yeshiva in Israel, combining the study of Torah and army service in a five year program."

There are links to daily and weekly lessons in Torah, but the heart of the site is the Virtual Beit Midrash—which, like Project Genesis, offers in-depth courses at no cost. The idea behind VBM is to give every Jew the opportunity "to learn in a real yeshiva, virtually." Currently there are multiple Torah courses (including one for beginners), Talmud courses, *halacha*/Jewish law courses (including one for beginners), and Jewish philosophy courses. A few of the best lectures from their courses, as well as articles from Yeshiva publications, are at http://www.virtual.co.il/education/yhe/webarch.htm. (The material here is so good, one wonders why the archives don't contain *all* of the previous material).

Also at the site is "Surf a Little Torah," a short *d'var torah* (exercise on a specific topic of the law) that is updated daily; and a section called "three questions" relating to the current week's Torah portion (as well as answers from the previous week).

The depth and breadth of material available from VBM, particularly in their free e-mail classes, is simply exceptional.

The Tanach Study Center
http://www.virtual.co.il/torah/tanach/

This is a brand new site (it began in February, 1997) that promises to rival Project Genesis and the Virtual Beit Midrash in terms of serious, comprehensive, and free Jewish education.

In addition to discussions of the current week's Torah portion, this center has questions for preparation that will help you study the portion and the commentary; questions for the shabbos table, short questions and answers suitable for family discussion; and a section that will discuss disputes among classical commentators' writings on the current week's portion. After all, what's a good discussion without questions and even disagreements?

Promised to be added later are weekly discussion on the *Haftorah* portion (which is not as common as Torah discussion), as well as a weekly talk on a section of "The Prophets", that is, the *Nevi'im* part of the Tanach (even more rare), starting with the book of Joshua.

The archives contain all of these lessons, organized and index in a variety of ways, and promise to contain "all related material, as well as other 'electronic' resources, such as an interactive study site, a FAQ (answers to frequently asked questions), a glossary, bibliography, and 'student center' where one can use the bulletin board to find a virtual (or real) 'chavruta' and/or a volunteer tutor."

Maqom
http://www.compassnet.com/~maqom/

This site is unique in many aspects, not the least of which is that it is a "Cyber-School for Adult Talmud Study" run by a Reform female rabbi, Judith Abrams, a prominent author on Talmud studies. A Talmud passage is posted (or e-mailed) about every two weeks with study questions. Students discuss them and post their thoughts, which are answered by Rabbi Abrams, and everything is sent back out to subscribers. A full archive of past material is available, with very readable commentary.

There is also some nice Talmud background information—including a summary of "rabbinic literature," the different eras, and an excellent summary of the English Talmuds that are available.

You won't become a Talmudic scholar from enrolling with Maqom, but you will learn some passages with unrivaled depth for a beginner-level audience.

Interactive Torah Study Forum

http://www.jcn18.com/forum/study/abrams.htm

According to tradition, a person should study some Torah, some Mishnah, and some Gemarah every day. This site, also under the direction of Rabbi Abrams, attempts to fulfill that precept. Each week, an excerpt of the weekly portion appears, along with a small passage of related Mishnah and Gemarah, and some opening questions.

Readers are invited to post comments, which then are posted at the site itself, along with interspersed reactions to the comments by Rabbi Abrams. This is a truly novel approach to cyber-group learning.

Aish HaTorah's Discovery Seminar

http://www.aish.edu/discovery/

Aish HaTorah, an Israeli institution with U.S. roots and offshoots, attempts to bring into Judaism young men and women who have never participated in traditional Jewish practices or espoused traditional Jewish beliefs. Their blurb says it best:

> "Each year, close to 10,000 people from New York to Nairobi experience the thrill of Discovery. With its crisp, entertaining style and state-of-the-art educational techniques, Discovery packs the wisdom and relevance of Jewish values and ideas into a spectacular and moving demonstration of the case for Judaism."

Indeed, Aish HaTorah has a novel approach—one that works for some and not for others. It offers summer programs, campus experiences, e-mail experiences and more. It tries to talk to young people in their own idiom. Look at this site to consider their methods and see if they appeal to you.

Aish Das Society
http://aishdas.org

The AishDas Society is committed to the advancement of meaningful worship in the Orthodox Jewish community. Their charter opens with "Let us prevent the cold of intellectualism and the apathy of habit from penetrating our relationship with Hashem (God)."

The site carries a great many links to Torah study sites on the Web, as well as other interesting features: a telephone contact for people who want to adopt Jewish children; a site that discusses the redemption of Jews who are held in countries against their will (this includes Israeli MIAs, Russians who are still in jail, and others; and a site for the recitation of *Tehillim* (psalms) for those who are ill. The latter is a well-known tradition among Jews. When someone is ill, people pray for their *refuah*, or return to the state of wellness. This page gives you the opportunity to send in names of sick people and to retrieve names of such individuals so that you can recite *Tehillim* for them.

If you're interested in weekly Torah study, there are many sites you'll want to visit.

The Torahnet Page
http://shamash.org/reform/uahc/torahnet/

The proliferation of weekly Torah studies on the Internet in the past few years has been simply astounding—this page can help point you to them. *The Torahnet Page* includes hundreds of references to weekly *Parsha* pages, to e-mail lists of weekly (and some daily) Torah studies, and links to extensive archives containing gigabytes of commentary. Additionally, you can subscribe to almost all e-mail lists mentioned right from this site. The author also provides a bit of commentary on the commentary. This is an extremely valuable resource, updated frequently, and a must if you want to sample a variety of Torah study options.

All of the Torah study entries below, along with their archives, can be accessed from *The Torahnet Page*.

Torah Tidbits

http://www.cyberscribe.com/tt/

This *aliya*-by-*aliya* weekly summary, published by the NCSY Israel Center, comes with some unique features: ParshaPix (nice graphics suitable for parent-child activities), statistics (the numbers of words and letters the portion contains, as well as the mitzvot). Splashy graphics makes this a fun place to visit and learn.

Torah Outreach Program

http://www.IsraelVisit.co.il/top/

These lengthy *d'vrei torah* are written from a truly traditional, yet modern and open, religious Zionist perspective. They include a synopsis of the entire portion and of the *haftara*, the accompanying prophetic reading, with comments of sages from all ages, including many allusions to current events. This sounds like an eclectic mix, but if you read a few of them on this Web site you'll understand better. These are unlike any other *d'vrei torah* you've ever read, guaranteed.

TorahFax

http://www.netaxis.qc.ca/torahfax/

TorahFax was founded by Rabbi Zalmen Marozov in September, 1992, in Montreal. The purpose of TorahFax is "to give the businessman and professional, with a busy schedule, a chance to learn a little Torah on a daily basis," and it began with daily fax transmissions of Torah study. In April, 1995, TorahFax went on the Internet. (There are no past archives on-line).

Ohr Somayach

http://www.jer1.co.il/orgs/ohr/thisweek.htm

Ohr Somayach produces an immense amount of material each week, and makes it available here, mostly in four formats: Web pages, text files, Microsoft Word, and Adobe Acrobat. Commentaries on the weekly portion are here (in English and Spanish), as well as highlights of the past week's *Daf Yomi*.

The site also has an "Ask the Rabbi" section, where questions range from extra-terrestrial life, to drugs, to reading someone's e-mail on a shared account.

Daf Yomi (page of the day) is a program where thousands of Jews across the world study the Babylonian Talmud (be it in classrooms, independently, or through the Internet), one page per day—on a schedule, so that everyone is studying the same material. (This process takes 7 1/2 years!) Highlights of this study are presented weekly.

Drasha

http://www.torah.org/learning/drasha/

Drasha, the e-mail version of the FaxHomily, takes a different approach to the weekly portion. It takes one aspect of the weekly reading and surrounds it with a story or homily, usually taken from the writings of one of the illustrious scholars of previous generations. If you prefer, you can still sign up to receive the original version (i.e., via fax). Complete archives are also available at this site—yet another offering from Project Genesis.

Chancellor Schorsch's Parashat Hashavuah

http://www.jtsa.edu/pubs/parashah/

This site contains weekly *sedra* (portion of the Five Books of Moses) reviews by Chancellor Ismar Schorsch of the Jewish Theological Seminary, the rabbinical school for the Conservative movement. They are thoughtful and incisive. Dr. Schorsch has accumulated several years of these summaries on this Web site. It is interesting to see what he has to say each time; he frequently refers to current events. This *sedra* review is also available by e-mail subscription.

L-Torah

http://shamash.org/reform/uahc/torahnet/l-torah/

This site attempts to prove the point that Torah study is not just for the Orthodox. L-Torah (the L stands for *liberal*) commentary actually comes from a variety of authors from across the spectrum, although most are on the liberal end. The goal of the list is to move beyond denominational divisions and beyond any dissent about the authorship of the Torah, in order to simply examine the text as is, and to find meaning in it for everyday life. Does it succeed? Check it out.

The Shamash Archived D'vrei Torah

http://shamash.org/tanach/dvar.html

Within the archives of Shamash are probably more gigabytes of Torah commentary than are on any other server, and it's all accessible with a solid search engine. You'll eventually end up with simple text files—but you can easily find literally scores of commentaries on any portion on which you might be doing research.

Jewish Torah Audio
http://www.613.org/

The Web has gone from linear text to hyperlinks and now to audio as well. The organization called "613.org" offers hundreds of hours of commentary, classes, stories, poetry, and even timely speeches, all in RealAudio or downloadable audio format. As you no doubt know, audio files are pretty large, but it's a good bet that the technology for audio files will continue to improve. You can also find instructions for getting the free software to handle Internet audio.

Haftorah
http://www.torah.org/learning/haftorah/

The Haftorah is a portion of the Prophets that is read after the completion of the Torah reading during services. As the site explains:

> "The reading of the Haftorah dates back to the Second Jewish Commonwealth, during the era of the Greek empire. Our enemies recognized the vitality of the Torah and banned us from reading the weekly Torah portion. In response, the Rabbis of those days substituted the reading of a segment from the Prophets, commonly known as the Haftorah. They carefully chose specific sections of the Prophets which correspond to the sedra and intended through this to capture the lessons of the weekly Torah portion. Although the Torah reading has been restored, the Haftorah remains an integral part of Shabbos and Yom Tov experience."

While Torah commentaries (in print and on the Internet) are ubiquitous, commentaries and writings on the Haftorah are relatively rare, adding value to this site.

Like the other classes from Project Genesis, you can receive weekly e-mails or peruse through the complete archives here.

Rabbi Frand OnLine
http://www.torah.org/learning/ravfrand/

Rav Frand teaches a weekly class in Jewish law and ethics. He takes a subject, and uses the portion of the week to feature its relationship to a particular topic. His lectures are so well-known that they have been taped, transcribed, and archived here. As Project Genesis describes, "While the actual class contains an extensive discussion of Halachic issues, these transcripts concern only the hashkafa section- that dealing with philosophical questions." Project Genesis and 613.org have made a few of the tapes available via RealAudio.

There are several sites available if you're interested in additional text study.

A Page of Talmud
http://www.ucalgary.ca/~elsegal/TalmudPage.html

If you have never seen an actual page of Talmud, you must check this site out. On a typical page there may be up to 17 different components of text—Mishnah, Gemarah, *Rashi* (Rabbi Solomon ben Isaac (1040-1105) the most prolific and accepted commentator on the Bible and Talmud.), *Tosafot* comments by 12th-14th Century pupils of Rashi and his descendants), and more. Now, I could spend 1,000 words describing the way these pages look, or you can look at the image on this Web site and get the picture.

The Book of Job
http://www.torah.org/learning/iyov/

The Book of Job is one of the most intriguing, ambiguous, and prominent books of the Ketuvim, the writings part of the Bible. This is a set of classes from Project Genesis, with full archives, of the "major themes within the Book of Job based mainly on the writings of the Malbim (Rabbi Meir Leibush Malbim) with important additions from the Ramban (Nachmanides) and the Biur HaGra (commentary of the Vilna Gaon)." Here is yet another example of the power of the Internet. While Project Genesis is based in Baltimore, the teacher is a dean of a yeshiva in Jerusalem.

Pirkei Avot with a commentary of The Maharal

http://www.torah.org/learning/maharal/

Rabbi Judah Loew Ben Bezalel (1525-1629), better known as the Maharal of Prague, was a gifted scholar and mathematician. His classic work on *Pirkei Avot* ("Ethics of the Fathers") entitled *Derech Chaim* ("The Way of Life") is studied here. The site explains his writings thusly: "We shouldn't mistake *Pirkei Avot* for a rabbinical version of *Poor Richard's Almanac*. This perspective helps understand how and why the Maharal goes below the surface of the text in trying to understand the words of the authors of *Pirkei Avot*."

Gossip

http://www.torah.org/learning/halashon/

Have you ever heard the expression "words can kill?" Judaism takes this extremely seriously. The laws of gossip are based upon two works: *Shmiras Haloshon—Guarding Your Tongue*, and *Chofetz Chaim*, which was such a well known piece of work early in this century that the author of both of them, Rabbi Yisrael Meyer Kagan, is now much better known as "the Chofetz Chaim."

This site examines the laws in detail and teaches us about the moral issues. We all talk about other people. What, exactly, is prohibited? What is acceptable? What are the consequences? Look for yourself.

Shema Yisroel - Hear O Israel

http://www.shemayisrael.co.il/shema.htm

The Shema is incontestably the most important Jewish prayer, and is often referred to as "the watchword of our faith." If a Jew knows only a single prayer, it is most likely the six-word first sentence of this one. Religious Jews say it four times a day, including when they arise in the morning, and just before they go to sleep. The opening sentence of the prayer has accompanied many Jews on their way to the death camps in modern time and to other oppressions in days long past. It has stood as a symbol of the unity of the Jewish people and their acceptance of the divinity and the unity of the Almighty.

At this site, the author analyzes the Shema line by line. Its excellent commentary brings new depth and understanding to the Shema. If you want to learn the deep meaning of a single prayer, or make this most important single prayer more meaningful to you, then read this site.

Pirkei Avot

http://www.pirchei.co.il/pictoral/avos/

Pirkei Avot ("Ethics of our Fathers") is a treatise devoted to ethics. This site is actually a book, *Pirkei Avos in Pictures*, a pictorial guide to the Pirkei Avot with commentary by Rabbi Dovid Goldschmidt. Each of the verses is illustrated, and the message of each illustration is clearly explained. This is a novel approach to the topic. Since this site is mostly large graphic files, be prepared for time-consuming waits.

This book is actually one of nine pictorial books at the parent site (*http://www.pirchei.co.il/pictoral/*); others include *Shmiras Halashon* and *How to Make Shabbos*. As for the utility of this site, it is probably more useful for deciding whether to purchase them than for reading cover to cover. The pictures just take too long to download.

Rambam's Mishne Torah

http://www.torah.org/learning/rambam/

Moses ben Maimon, also known as Maimonides or the Rambam, stands as one of the all-time giants of Jewish thought. His famous *Mishneh Torah*, or review of the Torah, covers the entire breadth of philosophical and legal topics that are the foundation of traditional Judaism. This ambitious class on the *Mishneh Torah*, brought to you by the folks at Project Genesis, is a detailed study of the work. Like everything else on the web, this is a work in progress—but a sizable section of this landmark work is now available on the web along with extensive commentary.

On-line texts are also available. Be sure to look into:

Navigating the Bible
http://bible.ort.org/bible/

This is an incredible resource for anyone interested in studying Torah. The Torah is broken down by book, and then by weekly portion, and finally by *aliyah*. Each verse in the Torah is available in Hebrew, in English, and in transliterated Hebrew. There are commentaries, as well as graphics that show what the verse actually looks like in the Torah (which is written without vowels and other marks), and, incredibly, sound files so you can hear the proper chanting.

ORT (the organization for Rehabilitation Through Training) is an international network on educational institutions has developed a rather nice bar/bat mitzvah program around this site, so that prospective students can learn their Torah and haftorah portion and their blessings in the comfort of their homes. A nice bar/bat mitzvah portion calculator is included, too. Plug in your date of birth, and *presto*—out comes the portion you should be celebrating 12 or 13 years later.

Hypertext Halacha
http://www.torah.org/learning/halacha/

If you're interested in a serious study of Jewish law, this is the place: a work in progress studying the *Shulchan Aruch*, which is probably the most important work in the field of *halacha*, with accompanying commentary from the *Mishnah Berurah*. The editors do a good job translating into English for beginners, but nonetheless the topics are complex and are discussed in detail. It is hard to convey the significance of this project—*halacha* is the Jewish law regarding activities in daily life, and reference materials are complicated, and full of cross-references. To put it all, with commentary, in a hypertext format, is a wonderful gift to observant Jews, and to other Jews who want to study.

Web Shas

http://www.virtual.co.il/torah/webshas/

Name the subject and it can be found in the Talmud. To prove the point, go to Web Shas. The author divides the Talmud into different study categories: personal conduct, societal issues, and intellectual and theological issues. Each of these major categories is then further divided into many other subcategories, and so on. Eventually you will reach a phrase and its source in the Talmud.

This site is a wonderful source of information about a great many religious practices and their sources in the Talmud. However, be prepared to take out your edition of the Talmud to look up the actual text and the context in which it is written. While these pages give you a Talmudic citation, the text itself does not appear. This site is not for everyone—but it is a fantastic source for those in the beginning stages of serious Talmud study. As anyone who has ever learned any Talmud can tell you, it is nearly impossible to quickly find anything in the Talmud unless you know exactly where to look. The laws of Chanukah, for example, are scattered throughout chapters on Pesach, Sukkot, and Shabbat. This is one of the few resources in existence where you could find a key research parameter like that out.

The authors have not completed their dauntless task, but they have made a very important dent in the task of doing so.

Documents of Jewish Belief

http://www.netaxs.com/~expweb/jewish_belief.html

This Web page assembles many of the seminal documents of Judaism and varying views of Jewish belief—from all of the major American Jewish denominations. When the copyright to a document expires (anywhere from 50 to 100 years, depending on varying factors—consult your local lawyer), it becomes part of the public domain. This site takes advantage of that, and is intended "as the first steps in an ambitious effort to provide an archive of Judaica texts" on the Web. Among the historical works are those by Solomon Schecter, one of the founders of the Conservative movement; Mordecai Kaplan, creator of the Reconstructionist movement, some of Reform Judaism's platforms, and *Tanya*, by Schneur Zalman, the founder of Chabad-Lubavitch. This site has a tremendous amount of potential if additional materials are added—currently, just over a dozen documents are actually linked from the page, and the list doesn't appear to have been updated recently.

Maimonides' Thirteen Principles of Faith

http://www.utexas.edu/students/cjso/Chabad/moshiach/
techiya-masim.html

What are the basic principals of Judaism? While there have been many attempts at summarizing them, the best known are the 13 principals enumerated by Maimonides. These principals have gained wide acceptance among the Orthodox, so much so that a recitation of them have found their way into daily morning prayers. Throughout history, though, there has been some controversy over them, particularly the Thirteenth Principle, the belief in resurrection of the dead. This site is actually an excerpt from a book, *The Wolf Shall Lie Down With the Lamb*, which is an in-depth discussion of the Thirteenth Principle.

Mitzvah Mania

http://www.valuu.net/users/mitzva/

According to Jewish tradition, there are 613 commandments, or *mitzvot*, contained in the Torah. And all of them are listed here—divided into 248 positive commandments and 365 negative commandments—along with the biblical source. While this information appears at other sites (most notably the Judaism 101 page), this site is also a nice reference to a few other areas of Jewish practice: for example, there is a list of blessings said over food and such diverse things as the blessing made on seeing a rainbow or a king or on hearing bad news; a list of all the books of the Tanach, or Bible, and a list of the weekly Torah portions. Promised soon will be a "Cyber-Siddur"—a list of all the prayers in the standard Jewish prayer book, along with information, sources, and explanations of them.

Maimonides: The Laws and Basic Principles of the Torah

http://www.fordham.edu/halsall/source/
rambam-yesodei-hatorah.txt

The Rambam also wrote a book called *Ten Basic Principals of Torah*. It's been translated into English, and the entire text, with ten chapters of commentary, appears here. This is another good example of using the Web as a repository of classic works from the past.

The Seven Noahide Laws

http://www.planet.net/peterr/noahide.html

Jewish belief requires certain action on the part of Jews, but what about non-Jews? According to Jewish tradition, there are only seven fundamental commandments, those given to Noah, in order to be a righteous person, and to "have a share in the world to come." These commandments are known as the Seven Noahide Laws. As this site explains: the "Code of Seven Fundamental Laws is so far-reaching that it gives structure and scope to life for all time, guiding mankind to realize his highest potential as a being created in the image of G-d."

Personalities

Scholars and Sages

http://members.aol.com/jewfaq/sages.htm

Brief biographies of a few major figures in Jewish tradition appear in this part of the Judaism 101 page discussed above. They include: Hillel and Shammai, Rabbi Akiba, Judah Ha-Nasi, Rashi, Maimonides, and the Baal Shem Tov. It's a nice little introduction, but we hope this resource will be expanded further.

Mail Jewish Material on Rav Soloveichik

http://shamash.org/mail-jewish/rov.html

Rabbi Joseph B.Soloveichik, or "The Rav," as he was known to thousands of his students, was considered to be one of the leading authorities on Jewish law and was a towering intellectual figure in the Orthodox Jewish world. Indeed, he was the "Rosh Yeshiva" at Yeshiva University for 40 years, and, as such, probably ordained more Orthodox rabbis in America than any other person. His brilliance was accepted by people of all persuasions and from all walks of life. This page contains various information files concerning the life and writings of Rav Soloveichik, put together by members of the list in the weeks following the Rav's death in 1993. Various list members put together summaries of some of the *hespedim* (funeral orations) and *shiurim* (lectures) that were given in his memory at that time. Some of these are masterpieces. All of them attempt to describe an indescribable figure in Jewish life.

Rambam: His Thought and His Times
http://www.jtsa.edu/melton/rambam/

> "A thematic approach for 12 year olds and older to important religious issues discussed by Maimonides and his contemporaries. The themes: the Life and Times of Maimonides; the Concept of Talmud Torah; the Concept of God; the Idea of Messianism; Mitzvot. "

This site is part of the Melton Research Center for Jewish Education. Here you can find the complete introduction to the teachers' edition of *Rambam: His Thought and His Times*. It uses the teaching of Maimonides as a vehicle to explain many of the essential core values of Judaism, along with Jewish history in the Middle Ages, to religious-school students in the 12- to 14-year old range. The material here is excellent and includes a rather nice bibliography.

Rav Shlomo Zalman Auerbach
http://www.yated.com/rsza.htm

How rare it is to be one of the most humble and beloved figures of a generation and to be one of its most brilliant *halachic* authorities. People would line up at such a scholar's door to ask him questions, and he would answer them—from the simplest to the most complex. When Rav Shlomo Zalman Auerbach of Jerusalem died in 1995, more than half a million people lined the streets to pay homage to him (a figure greater than the entire population of Jerusalem). The mourners were from all walks of life, religious and nonreligious alike. The articles on this Web site explain why these admirers came.

Breslov Research Institute
http://www.breslov.org/

Rebbe Nachman was the great-grandson of Rabbi Israel, the Baal Shem Tov—"Master of the Good Name"—founder of the Chasidic movement. During his short lifetime (he passed away in 1810, at age 38, after being ill with tuberculosis for several years), he became an outstanding *Tzaddik*, Torah sage, mystic, teacher, Chasidic master and storyteller. During his lifetime, he attracted a devoted following of Chasidim who looked to him as their prime source of spiritual guidance in the quest for God. Rebbe Nachman's influence remains potent. His teachings spread by word of mouth, and with the printing of his writings, he became established as one of the leading Jewish teachers of all time. Some of his works are currently used in college courses throughout the U.S.

While the Breslov Chasidim have not had a leader since 1810, this site makes it apparent that Breslov still has many adherents. While certainly not a mainstream movement with large numbers of followers, it is more than just an interesting oddity. This site tells you about the Breslov Chasidim, and their beliefs, writings and activities. A number of Rebbe Nachman's teachings are on-line here, as well as a thorough catalog of his writings, writings about him, and works which follow his philosophy.

More educational sites are:

Snunit Educational Information System

http://ietn.snunit.k12.il/

This is not a Jewish educational site in the conventional sense. This site is for teachers of English as a second language (ESL). Israel, after all, is an immigrant nation, and English is often used as a second language. Not only does Israel have close ties with many English-speaking nations, but much of Israel's technology business is conducted in English, as it is around the world.

There are links here to timely topics, relevant news items, and the Israeli Ministry of Education—all in a well-organized and attractive layout, although it has a lot of graphics on the home page, and Americans may find that getting them all from a server in Israel highlights why some call it the World Wide Wait.

This site is particularly valuable for American, Canadian and other English-language schools hosting immigrants from the Soviet Union, Iran and other countries of dispersion. There are links to newsletters, Israeli government publications, other teachers' resources, and other directories of links. In fact, the more you explore, the more it seems you will eventually find a link to every Israeli site in existence. One particularly noteworthy link is to the "Hebrew on the Internet" page (*http://www1.snunit.k12.il/heb.html*), which explains how to get Hebrew to show up on your computer. This is an incredibly useful site.

Kolel: A Centre for Liberal Jewish Learning

http://www.cherniak.on.ca/kolel/

A liberal Jewish yeshiva? The new Kolel Centre, based in Toronto, offers everything "from introductory 'Basic Judaism' to advanced Talmud from a modern, progressive Jewish perspective." Read all about it (and wish you lived nearby) on this Web site. While you can register for classes on-line, you can't actually take any courses electronically— although Torah commentary does appear at the site (and seems to be written by an all-star cast). There are also order forms for other materials and tapes of classes, and coming soon, an "ask the rabbi" section.

Bat Kol: A Feminist House of Study

http://home.sprynet.com/sprynet/batkol/

Located in Jerusalem, Bat Kol asks: "Why is this study program in Israel different from all other study programs in Israel?" It answers that it is "the first Jewish feminist house of study in Israel. While Israel is full of Jewish study programs, only Bat Kol explores Judaism from a feminist perspective." This is a new site, sure to grow—particularly after its initial study session, scheduled for the Summer of 1997.

Jewish Identity

http://www.ort.org/anjy/hadracha/identity/jew-id.htm

Here, you'll find an essay "about Jewish identity and how to maintain our Jewishness when we live in a non-Jewish society." From the B'nai Akiva movement of the Religious Zionist movement in Great Britain, this page discusses assimilation and what should be done about it, in part through a *d'var torah*. There is a section called "The Last Jew," which is particularly poignant. Here is the first paragraph:

> "My name, my name is not important. Who am I? I am the last British Jew. The year is 2010, the place is the Natural History museum in London. I am in a glass-fronted cage, on exhibit. People pass my way, staring and pointing , sometimes laughing at me, the freak on show. On the walls are hung the remnants of the Jewish culture; a Talit, a Sefer Torah, a Siddur, Tefillin etc., and on a little metal table nailed to the floor is a Menorah. Each day as I sit here I wonder how the hundreds of thousands of Jews who lived in Britain could have vanished away. "

You'll have to read the rest of it for yourself.

Plaguescape

http://www.plaguescape.com/

If you know the story of the Jews' exodus from Egypt, you're aware that it was preceded by the Ten Plagues. There are many interpretations of these plagues. The introduction to this site states that:

> "Causes and interpretations of the ten plagues of Egypt have fascinated theologians, historians, Egyptologists, musical composers, scientists, and physicians for centuries. More recently, modern scientific disciplines —epidemiology (the study of the occurrence of disease in human populations), epizootiology (the study of epidemic disease in animals), entomology (the study of insects), microbiology (the study of microbes) and toxicology (the study of the effects of poisons)—have attempted to explain exact causes for one or more of these plagues. In recent years, re-interpretations of ancient texts as well as new information about environmental factors and disease causation, have allowed unique interpretations of this series of early public health catastrophes.

Yet, despite centuries of speculation and study, fundamental questions remain."

A novel explanation appears at this Web site. Interestingly enough, the interpretations bear lessons for us today (about biohazards, for example). While the site looks at the plagues from a scientific point of view and tries to identify them, they assert that their "explanation doesn't preclude the role of God," but rather shows how God used "nature's forces to create physical and environmental catastrophes." It's really quite interesting and educational.

Institute of Traditional Judaism
http://www.utj.org/business/home/metivta/

The Institute is the rabbinical school for the Union for Traditional Judaism. As befits the newest branch of Judaism in the U.S., this site is small—but contains the essential information, such as the programs offered (both a *Semicha* program for ordination, and continuing education classes), entrance requirements, and tuition.

Judaism Reading List: Periodicals (Pt. XII)
http://shamash.org/lists/scj-faq/HTML/rl/per-index.html

This is a section of the massive monthly reading list posted to the "soc.culture.jewish" newsgroup. The bad news is that the list is a bit out of date and needs some refurbishing. The good news is that this is probably the largest list of Jewish periodicals anywhere on the Web, and an excellent starting place if you want to see what's out there.

University-level Jewish education is also available. Several sites are listed, including:

Book Exchange
http://www.pirchei.co.il/torah-umesorah/books.htm

Torah Umesorah, The National Association of Jewish Day Schools, embarked on a school textbook exchange. If you have textbooks that are no longer needed by your school, you can list them with the exchange. Likewise, if you need books for your school, you might look up the exchange and see what it has for you. The books are free. All you have to pay for is shipping.

Higher Education

In Israel and around the world, Jewish scholars have a plethora of choices for pursuing specialized education in both religious and secular subjects. Many of these academic institutions are represented on the Web, where you can see course listings, program specializations, lists of faculty, and resource archives. The design for these noncommercial sites is generally more functional than attractive, but if you are interested in advanced studies, the sampling of primarily Israeli educational sites in this chapter will give you an idea of the vast options available.

Jewish/Israel Academia & Education
http://ucsu.colorado.edu/~jsu/academic.html#schools

This Web page, part of the copious University of Colorado site, lists and links many educational sites in Israel, the United States, and Canada. Many of them are university Web sites, others are in the K–12 educational category, and some are student organizations and less formally accredited courses. While this page is nothing but lists and links, it is as strong a directory site to Jewish academia as you will find anywhere.

Among the linked sites are both obscure and prominent institutions for Jewish academia, including: the Jewish Study Center of Washington; the Columbia University Center for Israel & Jewish Studies; the Near and Middle East Department of the University of London; Massada College in Adelaide, Australia Tisom (the Tel Aviv

International School Of Management); Israeli Aerospace Medicine Web sites; the Israeli Schools on the Internet 1996 Official Unofficial List; the Twinning Project (a meeting point for Jewish schools); the National Jewish Law Students Association; the Canadian Jewish Law Students Association; North American Jewish Data Bank (contains population and survey data); MOSAD-ONET (information on funding opportunities and research grants in Israel); and IOUDAIOS Review (an on-line journal devoted to the study of early Judaism).

Hebrew University in Jerusalem
http://www1.huji.ac.il/

> The Hebrew University predates the establishment of the State of Israel by almost a quarter of a century. The idea for the institution itself goes back to the 19th Century. It has grown from a small institution in a desert country to a world calibre university. But in this long journey it has never forgotten that it is the symbol of Jewish nationhood. This remarkable enterprise was the spawning ground of every other Israeli institution of higher learning and its Jewish National Library is the repository of the printed legacy of our people.

The Hebrew University server and sites are truly remarkable resources. They probably deserve their own book. But I will merely lead you to the home page of the Hebrew University and let you wander about from there. It is a testimony to the creativity of a young nation and its talented teachers and scholars, students and friends.

The Alexander Silberman Institute of Life Sciences
http://www.ls.huji.ac.il/

This is a fairly conventional university Web site. If you are considering a career in the life sciences, or are looking for resources in this vein, then you might find this site for the life sciences department of Hebrew University worthwhile. There are several fields of science classes listed on this site.

Bar-Ilan University
http://www.biu.ac.il/

Bar-Ilan University is the third largest university in Israel, with 19,500 students in its unique program combining Torah and secular studies. Another 2,500 students are enrolled in specialized study programs toward diplomas, academic preparatory programs, and other enrichment studies. The academic staff consists of approximately 1,300 faculty members.

It hosts the Bar-Ilan University Press, which has published more than 350 books in a variety of areas, the Responsa Project (which we detail in Chapter 17), and the Institute for Advanced Torah Studies, which combines academic studies with intensive Torah studies.

The site lists the various units within the university and the study opportunities that are available there for both Israeli and foreign students.

There are also additional Bar-Ilan University Web sites accessible from this one.

Ben-Gurion University of the Negev
http://www.bgu.ac.il/

The Ben-Gurion University of the Negev is located in Beer-Sheva, the primary city of the Negev Desert. It offers a wide range of scientific studies, including the Institute for Desert Research, and also has courses in the humanities. It has a cooperative program with Boston University for a master's degree in Science and Management. On the Web site you can read about these course offerings, university organizations, summer programs, and cooperative arrangements Ben-Gurion has with other schools overseas.

Bezalel Academy of Arts & Design
http://www.bezalel.ac.il/

This academy was founded in the early 1930s. Its first faculty and members were drawn from Europeans fleeing the rise of Nazism. The fascinating tale of the founding of this institution can be found on the Web site. The history was originally written for *ARIEL* magazine and was translated for use on this site. The school has a variety of departments covering virtually all artistic fields.

The growth of the school is reflected in the very modern specialty of animation, as well as the quality of the more traditional arts which made up its earlier focus. This academy is now offering a master's degree in fine arts in conjunction with the Hebrew University of Jerusalem.

This is a well-organized and attractive Web site, and of particular interest are representative works from each department.

The Interdisciplinary Center for the Study of Business Law and Technology
http://www.idc.ac.il/

The Interdisciplinary Center for the Study of Business Law and Technology (IDC) is a pioneering effort to establish Israel's first private university. The Center is run by a group of professors and staff members who are attempting to build a premier school that is both a non profit organization and a self-sufficient entity.

The IDC Web site is utilitarian, but it does detail all the programs being offered by this unique Israeli academic institution.

It presently has three divisions: The Computer and Media Sciences School; the Radzyner School of Law; and the Business School.

The Jordan Valley College
http://www.yarden.ac.il/

The Jordan Valley College is an adult educational and training institute for cities as well for rural settlements in the northeastern region of Israel. It has some very interesting units attached to it, chiefly in astronomy.

These include an academic extension of Bar–Ilan University, a Science Education Center that is home to Israel's

Sea of Galilee Astrophysical Observatory, and an Internet Astronomy School, which you can check out here. The observatory houses Israel's most modern optical telescope, and the only Radio Telescope in the country. The site also has a variety of links to other astronomy-oriented Web sites.

Shenkar College
http://www.shenkar.ac.il/

Shenkar College is a unique institution serving Israel's textile industry. Shenkar is the sole degree-giving institution in textile and fashion studies in Israel, and is one of only a handful of colleges worldwide to integrate all the principal textile disciplines.

The college acts as a research and development center for the textile industry, and provides training, testing, technological innovations and new management techniques.

The Technion
http://www.technion.ac.il/

The Technion is one of Israel's pre-eminent institutions, and one of the finest science institutions in the world. It has been called "the Israeli MIT." A time line of the institution's growth, including several historic photographs, can be found on this site. The rather sleek and efficient design of the site reflects the advanced technological bent of the institution. A number of departments have their own nodes on the Web, accessible through the central Technion site.

A look at these departmental nodes will give you an idea of how sophisticated the faculties of this institution really are, and a better understanding of Israel's technological strength.

Tel Aviv University
http://www.tau.ac.il/

Located in Israel's financial and industrial core, Tel Aviv University is a major center of teaching and research, with nine faculties or schools, 106 departments, and over 75 research institutes.

This is an extremely large school, with a similar breadth of courses to that of the biggest United States universities. The vast archives, course offerings, and contacts offered on the network of Tel Aviv University Web sites connected through this core site convey this quite well.

Other Tel Aviv University-affiliated units also have areas on this Web site, including the Computation Center, Ramot (the University Authority for Applied Research and Industrial Development Ltd.), Lamda Community Site, and the Research Authority. You can also see images of Tel Aviv University's buildings and visit the Tel Aviv University Gopher.

Touro College

http://touro.ac.il/

Since 1986, Touro College, an American school, has offered accredited courses at its branch campus in Jerusalem. It opened the International School of Management in Jerusalem in 1995. The school offers bachelor's degrees in the following disciplines: economics, finance, accounting, and management. The Web site shows the courses, enrollment procedures, and cooperative programs offered by Touro's Israeli branch.

University of Haifa

http://www.haifa.ac.il/

The University of Haifa is one of Israel's younger universities, and is a very active educational institution. Its site is incomplete at the time of this writing. Hopefully, more about the university will be on-line by the time this book goes to press.

At the moment, you can get a quick look at the specialties of this school, as well as extension courses.

The Academic College of Yezreel

http://www.yvc.ac.il/

This Web site describes the courses and idea behind this new, publicly funded, liberal arts college, which provides bachelor's degrees only. This type of program is new to Israel, though it is not uncommon in the United States. The need to accommodate thousands of new students, most of whom are seeking a first degree only, led to the decision by the Israeli government to establish a string of small regional colleges instead of an additional, large research university.

The Weizmann Institute of Science

http://wissgi.weizmann.ac.il/

The Weizmann Institute is one of Israel's most prestigious educational and research institutions in the applied sciences. It maintains a variety of sites on the Web, listing the faculty, courses, and a bit of archival material on the Institute's departments: bioinformatics, biological computing, computing, mathematics, science, physics faculty, and the Plasma Laboratory.

Hebrew College

http://shamash.org/hc/

This Web site provides everything you always wanted to know about one of the nation's oldest schools dedicated to Jewish education. Boston's Hebrew College was founded in 1921, and serves over 2,000 students today, offering undergraduate and graduate degrees. The course catalog is on-line here, as is information on on-line classes. Yes, this entire chapter is full of on-line classes, but the ones at Hebrew College are different—they cost money, and Continuing Education Units are awarded.

Touro Law Center - Jewish Law Institute

http://www.tourolaw.edu/Institutes/AboutJLI.html

"One of the goals of the Institute is to make the Jewish legal tradition an active force in legal scholarship." Many of the same methods that are taught in law school can be applied to Jewish law, or *halachic*, discussions. Articles on subjects ranging from O.J. Simpson to lotteries to the status of civil marriage and divorce on Jewish law appear in the Jewish Law report. A few of the issues are on-line here. If you have a taste for legal-type discussions, you will find this pretty interesting.

The Robert A. and Sandra S. Borns Jewish Studies Program at Indiana University

http://www.indiana.edu/~jsp/

The Jewish Studies Program at Indiana University is one of the oldest and largest programs of its kind. This site describes its undergraduate and graduate programs, and has a full listing of the school's courses.

The Oxford Centre for Hebrew and Jewish Studies

http://associnst.ox.ac.uk/~ochjs/

> "The Centre, established in 1972, is under the aegis of Oxford University but is financially independent and has its own Board of Governors. The Centre is an advanced research and teaching institute which aims to promote international scholarship in the field of Hebrew and Jewish Studies."

This Web site offers information about the Judaic programs that are offered, as well as information about Oxford's libraries and its Judaica collections. But if you look through its list of Fellows and current visitors at the Centre, you'll really be impressed. The list also tells you the topics of the current visitors' research while they are at the Centre. The topics are diverse and fascinating.

If you're interested in studying or obtaining a degree in Judaic Studies from Oxford, you'll find the required information at this site.

The Rothberg School of The Hebrew University

http://www2.huji.ac.il/www_sfos/top.html

The Rothberg School for Overseas Students, located on Mount Scopus, is responsible for organizing study programs for students from abroad. The School, which annually serves some 3,000 students, offers courses in English, Spanish, French, Russian and Hebrew. There are various programs—including year and semester study programs, graduate degrees, and seminars. If you're contemplating any kind of academic study in Israel, you should check this Web site out.

Books

The first book in Judaism is known as the "Five Books of Moses," commonly referred to as the Bible. Actually, it was not a book as we know them today. Rather, it was a scroll. The earliest Jewish writings took the form of scrolls written on animal skins and in various forms of papyrus. The Torahs used in today's synagogues are still written in scroll form. The last book to keep the scroll format is the Megillat Esther that is used on Purim.

The next type of book that was used was the *codex*, or folded pages. By the fifth century C.E., Jewish books were also in this format. However, it was not until the 15th century that Jewish books were printed in a conventional format. The earliest known printers were Gershom Soncino and Daniel Bromberg. Since that time, Jewish books have been printed in great quantity. Many priceless volumes were lost during the Holocaust. Others have found their way into museum and private collections. In the United States, Jewish book publishing has been in existence since the late 19th century. At the end of World War II, the Jewish publishing business in this country became larger, due to the development of new technologies—primarily offset printing, computer typesetting, and now desktop publishing. While most of the Jewish publishing firms have died out, their place has been taken by general publishing houses. There have been some notable exceptions. Probably the greatest Jewish publishing success story of this generation has been the genesis of Artscroll Publications. Bloch Publishing has disappeared from the scene, as has the once-proud Hebrew Publishing

Company. (Someone has taken over the imprimatur but it is no longer a factor in the Jewish book business.)

Today such publishers as: The Jewish Publication Society, KTAV, Jason Aronson, Jonathan David, Feldheim, Shocken, the publishing houses of the various denominations, major publishing houses such as Random House, Doubleday, Putnam, Harper-Collins and a host of university presses and small publishing houses also print books of Jewish interest.

The two best sources for Judaica on the Net—if you know what you are looking for—are 1-800-Judaism and Amazon.com, both of which are listed in this chapter. Amazon.com lists more than a million volumes. However, a number of the small publishers listed here are probably not included in the Amazon.com directory. With Judaica, you are probably better off asking Jewish booksellers for information because they are more aware of the market than is the general bookseller.

Artscroll Publications

http://www.artscroll.com

Artscroll, one of the most successful and influential Jewish publishing houses in the world, started out printing bar mitzvah and wedding invitations. With typesetting equipment going unused during slack seasons, the owners decided to try publishing. The first Artscroll publication was *Megillat Esther*, the story of Purim. Artscroll has come a long way since then. Now part of Mesorah Publications, Ltd., it has made a significant contribution to Jewish scholarship with prayer books, sacred texts, commentaries and other works that are widely used throughout the Orthodox world. Artscroll publications lean to the right, reflecting the traditional Orthodox/Lithuanian Yeshiva perspective of its editors and publishers.

The Artscroll Web site takes advantage of graphic capabilities on-line to sell its wares. Ten current titles can be viewed in an ingenious format that may someday make bookstores obsolete. Click once in the "Current Titles" section to bring up a color image of your selection, along with a short but informative description of the volume. If you like what you see and you want to open the book, click again. You can actually read a page inside the book! This is particularly helpful if you are considering, for example, an edition of Talmud, perhaps with a translation. Is the page appealing? How modern or traditional is the translation? Does the English text follow the traditional layout? Is it easy to connect an English section to its Hebrew counterpart and vice versa? Once you are finished, you can easily return to the Artscroll home page or even to the previous page, just by clicking the appropriate button. Or pull up information for ordering the selection.

Most of Artscroll's extensive offerings, however, do not follow this format. They are part of an alphabetical listing, which is comprehensive but not very browser-friendly. Each entry includes title, author, price and ordering code.

The Association of Jewish Book Publishers
http://www.avotaynu.com/ajbp.html

The Association of Jewish Book Publishers, founded in 1962 to promote the sale and use of Jewish books through educational programs and activities, offers a forum for publishers, authors, individuals and institutions concerned with Jewish books to discuss their mutual interests.

The site lists its members alphabetically, with general descriptive information, a contact person, address, phone number, fax number, order phone number, e-mail address and URL, with a Web link, where available. Forty-one publishers are included, from prominent presses such as Jason Aronson and the Jewish Publication Society to lesser-known or highly specialized presses, such as Avotaynu, "the largest publisher of information and products of interest to persons researching their Jewish family history." Though far from a comprehensive guide, the list offers useful and accessible information about a variety of Jewish presses in an easy-to-digest style.

Blue Flower Press

http:/libertynet.org/~flower

Without offering any background information about the press, this Web site takes the viewer right into Blue Flower's latest projects—and the journey provides a satisfying view of what this press is all about. One project, *Face to Face, Encounters Between Jews and Blacks,* is a photo-text work by photographer Laurence Salzmann, available as a book and as an exhibit. This work pairs Philadelphia Jews and Blacks, offering their comments on how their special relationships affect them personally and shape the worlds in which they live. Four other projects are also on-line, including *The Last Jews of Radauti,* which tells the story of a pre-World War II Romanian community through photographs and video.

The Web site explores the capabilities of the Internet—each entry is a mini-exhibit that you can romp through at your own pace, viewing photos, text, and surprise! There's an aural component to the experience, if your computer is up to it.

The press is clearly quite small, specializing in intellectual, artistic endeavors with Jewish themes that involve more than just the print medium. Come to this site for the combined pleasures of browsing in a specialty bookstore and wandering through a small exhibit.

Cambridge University Press

http://www.cup.org/Titles/religious.html#Judaic

This prestigious press, affiliated with the University of Cambridge, has branches in the United States and Austria. Founded in 1534, it has consistently published intellectual works by distinguished authors in a wide variety of fields, from literature to astrophysics.

The general CUP Web site offers some background and history of the press, but focuses on current projects and titles. Once at the "Judaic" division of the section called "Titles," you will find a list including only the basics: author and title. Because there are no descriptions offered, the site is useful mainly to get a sense of the breadth of Cambridge University Press publications in a particular area of Judaica, or to check whether the press publishes a particular author, book or series.

Feldheim Publishing Company
http://www.shemayisrael.co.il/feldheim/index.htm

The Feldheim home page is colorful and promising, but this is an under-developed Web site. The publishing house itself is a wonderful source of quality traditional Jewish materials.

The Freeman Center
http://freeman.io.com/books.htm

The Freeman Center for Strategic Studies in Houston, Texas "attempts to aid Israel in her quest to survive in a hostile world," and "commissions extensive research into the military and strategic issues related to the Arab-Israeli conflict and disseminates pertinent information to the Jewish community worldwide."

The Freeman Center site is well-designed, complete with graphics for each section, inviting the viewer to explore the Freeman Center and get a sense of its mission. It even includes a short, timed message from the Freeman Center that flashes a variety of tough questions regarding Israel and her borders onto a blackened screen, and finishes with a request for support. This is a very effective, if unabashedly political, far-right Web site. Surf over to this site regardless of your politics for a great show of current technology.

The site includes a book department, which offers books published by the Freeman Center and selected titles by other publishers at a member discount. There are also in-house analysis papers available. Of the 21 volumes listed at the time this viewer cruised the site, most reflected the extreme right-wing bias of the Center, though a few slightly more mainstream selections were also available.

Hebrew Books and Manuscripts in the Leiden University Library

http://www.leidenuniv.nl/pun/ubhtm/ubor/heb-syr.htm

Part of the Web site of Leiden University in the Netherlands, this page is devoted to the Hebrew holdings of the Leiden University library, and reflects the academic thrust of a university site.

It offers an excellent, if brief, history of the library's interest in and acquisition of Hebrew books. The collection is notable for its size and for the age of its manuscripts, which date to the 17th century. It contains such treasures as the manuscript for the first printed edition of *Talmud Yerushalmi*. Unfortunately, the Web site includes only four titles from the library's holdings and no graphic images.

Broder's Ancient Judaica

http://members.aol.com/bookssss/judaica.html

The owners of Broder's Rare and Used Books have been collecting volumes for years. At their site, still being designed, you can go directly to the section on Judaica, or you can look through a wide variety of categories including everything from "Americana" to "Children's Vintage" to "Women's Studies."

Under "Judaic Studies" you can find books on art, politics, Bible stories, religious rituals, Kabbalah and more. Graphics are sprinkled sparingly around this site, and they help break up its basic list format. For example, click a graphic image of a handshake and an order form pops up.

When skimming the descriptive information about a particular volume—title, author, publisher, date of publication, pages and price—look for the short summary of the book's content and the description of the book's condition. These can be quite helpful. Sometimes, there's a special tidbit such as "Signed by Author" or a word or two of praise. Titles range from well-known authors and works to relatively obscure ones.

Henry Hollander, Bookseller

http://www.hollanderbooks.com/

Henry Hollander, Bookseller, located in San Francisco, is an antiquarian and scholarly bookstore specializing in Judaica. It carries a wide selection of out-of-print and hard-to-find books and ephemera on Jewish history, Jewish literature, theology, the Holocaust, art, music, theater, humor, mysticism, cooking and children's Judaica. There are books in English, Hebrew, Yiddish and German, and you will also find specialty books on Africa.

This site carries the warmth of the person behind the Web site, a person willing to conduct a special request book search for you at the touch of a button, eager to share his own favorite Judaica sites and happy to offer a link to his children's home pages. The opening graphic, a yeshiva *bocher* zipping off with books in hand, gives the site some extra personality.

A click of a button offers directions to the shop in San Francisco; a click of another downloads a catalogue of titles available. The catalogue is a list of offerings in typewriter font that is not very user-friendly, particularly compared with the bright beginning of the site. There are moments when the site does deliver: My favorite click brings up a beautiful page of art from *A Song of David, A Limited Edition Facsimile of the Moss Haggadah* offered with *A Song of David, Commentary to the Facsimile* by David Moss.

The site promises a clip art library of Jewish images and an easier method for searching the catalogues, both coming soon.

Jewish American Literature

http://omni.cc.purdue.edu/~royald/jewish.htm

A larger-than-life headline announces this site as "Jewish American Literature." A rather idiosyncratic list maintained by Derek Royal at Purdue University, it includes material that may interest both the common reader and the academic. As you scroll down from the heading, past the counter telling you how many people have visited the site, you will find a terrific collage of black and white photos of famous modern authors, including

Grace Paley, Woody Allen, Cynthia Ozick, E.L. Doctorow, Joseph Heller, E.M. Broner, even the mouse from Art Spiegelman's Maus. Underneath the collage, click an author's name to bring up a guide to his or her works. The guide is divided into primary works (fiction, nonfiction and interviews) and critical works (books, articles and parts of books). Each author's page also includes his or her photo from the collage.

A link to Derek Royal's home page gives a sense of the personality behind the page, but not more than that. This is a fine resource, but without knowing more about Mr. Royal, the viewer should not assume that the list is either trustworthy or comprehensive. It is fun, though, and offers a taste of how easily individuals with a special interest, career or hobby, can share information they have accumulated.

Jewish Short Stories from Eastern Europe and Beyond

http://www.kcrw.org/b/jss.html

When is a book not a book? When it's an audio cassette! The National Yiddish Book Center and the California radio station KCRW-Santa Monica are distributing a 13-part series from National Public Radio featuring stories by modern Jewish writers, read by leading actors. Although this Web site, part of the KCRW-Santa Monica site, is basically an ad for the series, it's great fun—all of the stories can be heard on-line. And of course, if you like the stories, you can buy the cassettes.

Authors include Isaac Bashevis Singer, Cynthia Ozick, Isaac Babel, Grace Paley, I.L. Peretz and Philip Roth. Actors include Walter Matthau, Lauren Bacall, Alan Alda, Elliot Gould, Claire Bloom, Jeff Goldblum, Carol Kane and others. It's a welcome diversion.

J. Levine and Sons

http://www.levine-judaica.com/

At the J. Levine and Sons home page, there's a photo of the original East Side storefront in full color. The door to the store appears to be open, inviting the viewer inside the shop. This "department store of Jewish books and Judaica" located in midtown Manhattan has a well-earned reputation as one of the best. In business in New York since 1905, the owners claim the company was actually founded in Lithuania five generations ago, and simply moved to New York with its owners.

At the site, you can begin shopping by pulling up a buying guide and opening it to the table of contents. If you want to browse further, though, you will have to purchase the guide. An order form is provided. The owners promise a display of its wares on-line soon.

Kar-Ben Copies

http://www.karben.com/

The brightly-colored illustration of a boy and girl in an old-fashioned kitchen making latkes, with a raccoon, goose, and squirrel keeping them company, tells the viewer that this publisher focuses on Jewish books for children and young families. With eight to ten new titles each year, the company builds its Web site around themes: books for toddlers, fall holiday services, fall holidays, Hanukkah, Tu B'Shevat, activity books, Purim, Passover, Bible, Israel, Shabbat, Jewish life, concept books, Jewish calendars, and my very own Jewish library.

Under each subject, the viewer will find basic information—author, illustrator, price, etc.—in an easy-to-read format. Each listing also includes either a description of the book written at the book's reading level, or an excerpt, giving the child a glimpse. A special section devoted to books on upcoming holidays makes quick work of gifts and even includes a color image of the book cover with each listing, a nice touch that the owners might consider offering with every title.

For the aspiring children's book author or illustrator, the site includes a section inviting submissions of manuscripts and art, with instructions on how to do so and what to expect in terms of feedback and remuneration.

The Adventures of Mendy and the Golem
http://www.nauticom.net/users/judaica/Mendy/Mendy.html

This site promises the only kosher comic strip in town. Everybody knows about Superman, Captain Marvel, and Batman and Robin. Now Jewish children can have their own comic hero. All they have to do is download "The Adventures of Mendy and the Golem" from this site.

The only problem with the comic strip, which has a pretty hip blacked-out screen for an opening page, with groovy ghost-writing and bright yellow and red accents, is that my computer couldn't download the actual comics. The site warned that it might take a while. I was patient. But after nearly ten minutes, I gave up. And my computer fell into a hopeless loop and I had to reboot it. Also frustrating at this site is the inability to access the comic strip directly. I had to start at the URL for "A Jewish Global Village" and work my way to Mendy.

Try using the URL above, but ending with "judaica," and leaving off everything after that.

Judaism Reading List: Periodicals
http://www.cis.ohio-state.edu/hypertext/faq/usenet/judaism/
reading-lists/periodicals/faq.html

Judaism Reading List: Traditional Literature and Practice
http://www.cis.ohio-state.edu/hypertext/faq/usenet/judaism/
reading-lists/traditional/faq.html

Part of the same parent list, these two sites together offer a glimpse of a much larger listing of Jewish material. Under the Web sites of Ohio State University Computer and Information Science, the lists offer no satisfying explanation of purpose, owners, or connection to Ohio State.

The first of these two sites is a listing of Jewish periodicals in very small typewriter font. Though the list is pretty up-to-date and contains numerous periodicals on a wide variety of topics, from general interest magazines to organizational publications to intellectual journals, it is neither comprehensive nor easy to read. The site is simply not user-friendly, and does not acknowledge or incorporate any graphic capability of the World Wide Web.

The second of these sights is more focused, part of a larger list on Traditional Judaism, but suffers from some of the same problems as the first. It offers the following explanation for itself:

> This list provides a collection of sources on 'traditional' practice. While no book can substitute for a formal course of instruction guided by one's Rabbi, these books are useful as reference material for the knowledgeable, and as an introduction for the not-yet-knowledgeable about Judaism.

As a reading list for Traditional Judaism's perspective on liturgy, philosophy, ethics, responsa, prayer, traditional practice, the household, life and death and the holidays, it is useful. With better fonts and a better structure than the first, it is more user-friendly. Taken as a whole, however, this remains a very perplexing site.

Sefer—The Israeli Book Club—The Best of Israeli Books (in Hebrew)
http://www.netvision.net.il/~ancient/

If you sign on and join the club while on the Web, you will receive a comprehensive listing of books published in Israel, updated monthly, at your e-mail address. The owners will also search for any book that is not on the list. This site is not exactly on the cutting edge of technology, and the owners offer little background information. They do, however, send what they promise. As soon as you leave the Web, check your e-mail and you'll find your first list. A little awkward, but better than no site at all.

The Shock of Withdrawal...The State of Israel from the Land of Israel

http://www.shef.ac.uk/students/md/md911783/tsow.html#tsow18

Elyakim Ha'etzni, an Israeli attorney and founding member of the Council of Jewish Communities in Judea, Samaria and Gaza, wrote a booklet in 1986 presenting his case against withdrawal from any part of the Land of Israel. The Committee to Abolish the Autonomy Plan, a right-wing group which describes itself as "a forum for self-expression and action to ensure Jewish survival," has published the booklet on-line at this Web site.

Following Mr. Ha'etzni's treatise is an appeal to support the organization, with the following warning: "The risks described in this booklet are by no means theoretical. In fact, certain segments of Israel's National Unity Government are now working round the clock to ensure their practical realization. These dangers threaten you directly and are liable to determine the future of Israel and your family." The booklet does not reflect the current political regime in Israel, but the owners contend that it has been updated and remains relevant.

Targum Press

http://www.targum.com

This ten-year-old press located in Southfield, Michigan made its mark with the publication of *Halichas Bas Yisrael: A Women's Guide to Jewish Observance* by Rabbi Yitzchak Yaakov Fuchs, translated by Rabbi Moshe Dombey. Targum is an Orthodox publishing house, and its wares reflect this orientation. The press is committed to bringing out high-quality books that provoke thought and comment, and its materials are short on puffery and long on substance. They range in topic from Jewish law to business ethics to the laws of inheritance to *halacha,* or the legal structure in Jewish thought. Targum also claims to be the first Orthodox publisher to give women a forum for expressing literary talents and the first to produce a series for preteens, teens and young readers.

The Web site makes good use of graphics, and follows a user-friendly format for providing basic information about available titles. Although the site promotes Targum's bookazine, *Horizons*, it is not yet offered on-line. Highlights of selected books are promised, which will be a wonderful addition to the site.

Jason Aronson Publishers
http://www.aronson.com

The elegance of Jason Aronson's home page reflects its position as one of the premiere Judaica publishing houses today. With a dual interest in Judaica and psychotherapy, a very strange combination; it offers a comprehensive guide to both and has over 1,000 titles in print. This press has published some exceptionally interesting material that crosses the entire spectrum of Judaica, adding quite a bit of pizzazz to the Jewish book market over the last decade.

The Web site is the best of the lot. It is well-designed, visually interesting and easy to use. The home page includes the cover of a newly published book, and the site is divided into sections including new books, best sellers, interviews with authors and ordering information. Each option is available at every page of the site, part of what makes it so user-friendly.

Every title gets special treatment. There is always a color image of the book cover, a large title and author line and a brief review of the book. Most entries offer the option of viewing the table of contents; some feature my favorite option: an interview with the author. The interview option is creative and informative, and it takes advantage of Web technology. Every interview begins with a short biography and includes a photo of the author. Each interview also includes every title by that author available through Jason

Aronson, and if you like, you can click directly into the interview section and a list of authors will pop up.

Want to search for a particular book or a particular subject? The search feature at this site is the best I have seen. Use the query option to write in your own search, or choose from one of the 45 narrowly tailored subjects already offered. Because these topics are so focused, searching is a manageable endeavor. For example, among the areas of interest, you will find "Death and Bereavement," "Drama," "Maimonides," "The Temple," "Steinsaltz, Adin" and "Folklore and Storytelling." Clicking into any subject brings up a group of titles. Each title follows the format described above.

If you'd like to order, the site suggests that you visit your local bookstore, but also offers a variety of international locations as well as a telephone number.

It's a must-see, especially if you're thinking of selling books on-line. You can even join a Jewish book-of-the-month club! I did.

Newspapers and Magazines

The Jewish press has been in existence in America since 1823, when *The Jew* was first published. While it only lasted two years, since then, approximately 2,500 dailies, weeklies, monthlies, quarterlies, bulletins and annual reports have appeared in English, German, Hebrew, Yiddish, and several other languages.

The Jewish press has served many functions. First, it sought to give its readership a feeling of community, which, in America, was often made difficult by the large distances between Jewish settlements and the isolation felt by Jews living in a new country. Reading Jewish newspapers help the newcomers gain a sense of community and reduce their sense of isolation. The papers served as a meeting place. It brought news of the "outside world." It spoke about communities and events that were both far away and yet connected to them.

It also had a second purpose. It helped them learn about their surroundings, the politics of America, the economy, and the customs and mores of a nation. Immigrants could read all about it in their Jewish newspapers, using familiar idioms and their own languages.

There were some early English-language Jewish newspapers in the United States, and a few in Hebrew. By the mid-1850s, several German papers appeared as well, a reflection of the heavy German-Jewish immigration of that period. But the massive flood of Eastern European immigrants at the turn of the 20th century changed the American landscape, including its press. No paper personified the immigrant experience as well as the *Jewish Daily Forward*. Abraham Cahan's paper promoted social justice, and spoke intimately to its readers. The "Bintel Brief" (the original Yiddish Ann Landers) was a part of the *Forward*, and it highlighted the problems of the immigrants: husbands who didn't want to work, wives who cheated, children who didn't understand the plight of their parents.

This and other early newspapers were a critical factor in helping the new immigrants participate in the American dream. They told the stories of local synagogues and Hadassah chapters, the *Landsmanschaften* (organizations whose members come from the same geographical location in Europe; the members knew each others families and friends and had similar histories and outlooks on the world) and births, marriages and deaths of community members. At the height of their popularity toward the end of the First World War, more than 500,000 copies of Yiddish newspapers were sold each day in the United States!

The immigrants' children became Americanized. The Yiddish papers read by their parents disappeared, their place taken by English-language community newspapers that sprang up in every part of the United States and Canada. They brought the big city news to the small towns and gave these small-town denizens an identity—a Jewish identity of their own. Wherever Jews lived, there was a Jewish newspaper, sometimes even two. Few, if any, Jewish publishers ever became millionaires from their efforts, but they served a vital communal purpose. They made the Jews in their small communities feel cohesive, a part of a larger entity.

Today, approximately 100 of these publications still exist. Some are consolidations of several newspapers. Many are no longer privately held, but are owned by the Jewish federations that sponsor and subsidize them. Some have grown into major publications. Others are just waiting for a new generation to take over the cause.

But there is also a spark of hope—the Internet. It allows communities to share their communal spirit in the new electronic media. There are many talented people out there who feel Jewish and want to make a contribution to a

Jewish future. As I have watched the Internet grow and have seen the proliferation of Jewish sites, I have been struck by the genuine thirst for Jewishness that pervades every nook and cranny of this country.

Undoubtedly, Jewish media will take part in this change. It is already doing so. *The Jewish Bulletin* of Northern California was the first American English-language Jewish paper to be published in its entirety (minus its advertising) on the World Wide Web, and other papers have followed. For the most part, the electronic versions of the papers are not duplicates of the print version. They are only partial copies of the papers. But this will change. As America embraces on-line media, so will Jewish media move toward the Internet.

Jewish Bulletin of Northern California
http://www.jewish.com/jb/

The Jewish Bulletin is a case of innovative use of media to aid a community in marketing itself to its members. This San Francisco-area newspaper was founded in 1946 as a successor to the *Emanuel,* which had served Bay-Area Jews for 50 years before being merged into the *Bulletin. The Jewish Bulletin* has taken a small newspaper that never had a major impact and made it a major player in Jewish life in California.

The *Bulletin's* editorial coverage includes local, national and international news, as well as analyses of trends in the community that affect Jews. It has gathered all the information relevant to Jews living in the Bay Area and made it available on-line. In fact, the entire publication is on-line and well-organized, from news items to calendars of events to classified and personal ads. There is also a facility to search back issues, an unexpected find for a local paper such as this.

Like many community Jewish papers, the *Bulletin* prints an annual "Guide to the Community" issue—which includes synagogue listings, social services, kosher restaurant listings, and the like. This supplement is also available on the Web site.

This is an incredibly valuable resource to the Northern California Jewish community—other communities would be well-served to have something like it.

Jewish Exponent

http://www.libertynet.org/~exponent/

The *Jewish Exponent* has long been viewed as one of the finest Jewish publications in the United States, and is now making its electronic presence felt. The complete *Guide to Jewish Philadelphia* is here, as well as some 30 links to other Philadelphia-based Web sites. At this time, however, only a few articles from just a few issues are available on-line. That makes this site a valuable resource for Jews in Philadelphia, but not for others reading the publication itself.

Jewish Family & Life

http://www.JewishFamily.com/

How does one raise a Jewish family in the 90s? How can one adopt family values in a Jewish manner? These are precisely the questions that *Jewish Family & Life* tries to answer. It is "a source of user-friendly, family-oriented information and entertainment for a new generation." This is the first Jewish publication to become totally a "Webzine." Yes, you can still subscribe to get a magazine in the mail, and join an e-mail list, but the Web site has it all, and is frequently updated.

Titles indicate that they indeed attempt to deal with the realities of raising a family today—with such subjects as Jewish opportunities in Girl Scouting, choosing colleges, and the like. Additionally, many archival articles are easily accessible, such as the holiday page. Better archives might help, but it's hard to complain when you can get so much information here for free. This Webzine has great potential.

The Jewish Post of New York

http://www.jewishpost.com/

The *Jewish Post* has been around for a while. At one time there were editions of the *Post* in a number of American cities. The on-line version is quite new, and is being published bimonthly. The stories are well-written and in-depth, but there aren't a whole lot of them yet, so the publication does not have much breadth to it. But there is a bright spot and it really shines!

The *Post* has come out with a series of sites on Jewish holidays that are excellent. Their Jewish Holidays and Festivals on the Net is a very informative piece of work. I think that the *Post* has found an important formula here. By taking a single issue or area of interest and maximizing it, they have accomplished a great deal. New York is a very big city. Covering it in a single site would be a major undertaking requiring a great deal of time, effort and money. Hopefully, the *Post* will take other aspects of Jewish life and devote the same attention and detail to these topics as they have to the holiday ones.

JTA On-line Edition

http://www.jcn18.com/jta/

If you read a Jewish paper, you've probably heard of the JTA. "The Jewish Telegraphic Agency is an international news service providing news, analytical stories and features to some 100 Jewish newspapers around the world. Its dispatches are available daily by mail, fax or e-mail." At least that's what it says at the Web site. When we visited, we found that it had been "under construction" since April 1996. There's nothing here yet. We hope the situation will change, as access to the incredible volume of information the JTA produces would be a very worthy goal for this Web site. However, you can find its materials on the Jerusalem One site and on AOL.

Forward

http://www.forward.com/

The *Forward*, founded in 1897, established a preeminent place in Jewish journalism in America and is still held in high regard by American Jews. Under founding editor Abraham Cahan, "The *Forward* fought for social justice, helped generations of immigrant Jews enter American life, broke some of the most significant news stories of this century, and was one of the earliest opponents of Communism. At one point this Yiddish newspaper reached a daily circulation of 250,000."

It was published in the largest building on New York's East Side—a testament to the contributions it made to social justice and bringing the strange world of America to generations of immigrants who didn't speak English.

Today the Forward building is owned by a Chinese group. You have to look to see the name "Forward" carved in the building's facade. Like the East Side, the *Forward* has also changed. It's no longer published on a daily basis, nor is it published in Yiddish. Now the *Forward* is published in English, and has added a Russian edition. Its weekly edition is slim, but it still carries the bylines of some of American Jewry's most creative writers. Isaac Bashevis Singer was no stranger to the *Forward*. Nor was Elie Wiesel or Saul Bellow, Chaim Potok or Philip Roth. Art Spiegelman's *Maus* was serialized in the Forward before it won the Pulitzer Prize.

The on-line version of the paper has a number of articles from its most recent edition, and archives that go back a year. There are also interesting highlights from 90, 75, and 50 years ago. This Web site is worth a look—even if just to remember how the *Forward* once was.

B'nai B'rith International Jewish Monthly Online
http://www.bnaibrith.org/ijm/

This publication of B'nai B'rith is one of the oldest and best Jewish periodicals in the English-speaking world, and now has an on-line edition. In a recent issued highlighted on its site, the IJM discussed a timely issue: whether former Soviet Jews, deprived of Jewish culture and religion, will find faith in America." Read the answer at this Web site.

A very exciting possibility is the IJM's promise to have tables of contents from all their back issues on-line. As the publication was founded in 1886, this will be an incredible boon to researchers. They should be complimented for their efforts.

The Jerusalem Post
http://www.jpost.co.il/

http://www.jpost.com/

The Jerusalem Post is Israel's foremost English-language newspaper, and has been so since 1925. The Internet edition of the *Post* appears daily. You can read about major Israeli news stories, often before you see them in the American papers, and the coverage is much more in-depth than anything you can get in the U.S. It is amazing, too, to see how many facts are missing or overlooked in American reporting of Israeli news.

You'll also find some in-depth stories on a wide variety of subjects at this Web site. The *Post* doesn't try to propagandize for Israel. It shows good points and sore points. It delivers the type of information that you'd expect from a major American paper; that is, not only features, columns, business and editorials, but sports and real estate too.

By now you must get the idea that I'm some sort of an Internet junkie. Well that's not quite the case. But I do admit to reading *The Jerusalem Post* on-line every morning. Sometimes it makes my day. Sometimes it breaks it. But no American newspaper ever makes me feel that I'm really a part of what's happening in Israel the way the *Post* does. Additionally, the issues are indexed going back to July 1, 1996, with an easy textual search engine.

A CD-ROM version of earlier editions of *The Jerusalem Post* is also available. If you need English-language information about Israel's past, then it's quite useful.

By the way, there's one other nice feature—the *Post's* Internet edition appears at two Web sites, which might be just the cure for when those transworld downloads take too long!

Jerusalem Report

http://www.virtual.co.il/news/news/j_report/

If you have one international Jewish publication to read, let it be *The Jerusalem Report*. This excellent bi-monthly news magazine has a number of outstanding features, as well as a few annoying ones. The Web site has not yet matched the overall excellence of the print publication, but is worth a look to get a snapshot of what this publication offers.

The *Report's* "Reporter/14 days" feature delivers an excellent summary of Jewish events that have occurred during the past fortnight. It has a host of excellent columnists. Almost anyone can find something of interest, and there is always the political cartoon "Dry Bones."

The Jerusalem Report doesn't consider anything sacrosanct. Very often religion is the target, particularly of columnist Ze'ev Chafets. Then flip the page and you'll read a summary and explanation of the week's Torah reading. A magazine is entitled to have diverse viewpoints, and *The Jerusalem Report* is no exception. All in all, *The Jerusalem Report* is presented and packaged in an attractive manner and makes you chuckle a bit, too. Unfortunately, while tables of contents going back to early 1996 are available on this Web site, only a few of the actual archival articles appear on-line.

LINK

http://link.co.il/

This monthly Israeli business magazine is a very sophisti-cated piece of work. Several of its features, such as "New Products In Israel," give a whole new dimension to the meaning of Israeli business and technological ingenuity. Within the pages of this magazine, there's a feeling of the vitality and depth of Israel's technological development, and why Israel can play such a crucial role in the develop-ment of the economies of the entire Middle East region.

Their Web site allows searches for issues going back to 1994. There are also Web links to, and directories of, gov-ernment agencies, embassies, nongovernment institutions, and professional associations in Israel.

London Jewish Chronicle

http://www.jchron.co.uk/

The London Jewish Chronicle is one of the finest English-language papers in the world. It just went onto the Web a short time ago. It's offerings include news on England, other members of the British Commonwealth, Israel, and the world.

The online Chronicle tells you what's going on in vari-ous Jewish communities around England, the latest travel information—including some good travel hints, college and campus information, and even interesting information on food and recipes.

The Chronicle has been in business since 1842. This site is a testament to its efforts.

New Moon Magazine (UK)

http://www.newmoon.co.uk/

I can't describe this bimonthly any better than this blurb from their site does. *New Moon* "was launched five years ago as the only publication in the U.K. serving the 18-35 Jewish community. Modeled on London's *Time Out* magazine, *New Moon* features listings of Jewish events around the U.K., irreverent and witty comment on Jewish issues, and in-depth investigations into Jewish political and social affairs. Its personal columns have blossomed into the largest Jewish dating service in the U.K."

The Web site gives you just a taste of the magazine, as only a few articles appear here. If you fall in this target audience, or sophomoric humor is your cup of tea, you might want to check it out.

The Jewish Quarterly
http://www.ort.org/communit/jq/start.htm

The Jewish Quarterly, a nonprofit publication by the Jewish Literary Trust, is published in London, and describes itself as "one of the foremost Jewish literary and cultural journals available in the English language." It is well-known for its literary awards, which receive considerable coverage.

The Web site does not yet reflect the depth of the print journal. When this book was written, most of the content was a press release describing their latest award-winners, and the tables of contents of their issues for the last few years.

Tikkun Magazine
http://www.panix.com/~tikkun/

While this magazine recently started its second decade of publication, *Tikkun* (taken from the Jewish injunction to engage in *tikkun olam*, "to repair the world") and its editor, Michael Lerner, were thrust into the public spotlight several years ago when Hillary Clinton spoke of reading *Tikkun*, and her interest in Lerner's version of "the politics of meaning."

Tikkun is part of The Foundation for Ethics and Meaning, described as "a progressive educational and research institution that seeks to counter the growing social, economic and political power of conservative thought in both major parties, and counter the impact of the Religious Right and others who seek to impose a patriarchal family, a narrow form of patriotism, homophobia, a 1950s lifestyle or a distorted notion of biblical and spiritual values."

Quite a mouthful. *Tikkun* and Lerner are major intellectual forces on the American left, and offer some fundamental rethinking about how society ought to work. They are not shy about taking on any issue, nor about criticizing others' ideas and conduct, regardless of the target's political slant.

Timeliness is a weakness of *Tikkun*'s Web site: as of this writing, the most recent issue featured on-line is December, 1995. Furthermore, not all the articles, nor all the text of those articles, appear at the site. That's too bad, and we hope the situation will change soon.

Jewish News Media List
http://www.libertynet.org/~anderson/jprintnewsmedia.html

This is a site full of not just links, but addresses, phone numbers, e-mail addresses, and Web sites of nearly 300 publications devoted to Jewish news. The listings of U.S. media is particularly impressive.

A. Engler's Jewish News Links
http://www.libertynet.org/~anderson/newslist.html

This site has Web links to some 50 Jewish publications, with occasional short descriptions of them. Between this site and the one above, you have the most comprehensive Internet-related list of Jewish news media available anywhere.

News

With all the news about Israel that appears in the daily press and on radio and television, it's easy to forget that Israel is a very small country—about the size of (and with a population less than) New Jersey. And yet, with the high demand for news from Israel, several services have sprung up recently that offer a great deal of information. Some of the news sources that are available are a bit limited, but the field as a whole is expanding rapidly. You'll get a variety of news on each site we refer to in this chapter. In order to get the full story, you might want to select two or three of these sites and compare.

The sites you select will depend upon your specific interests. Ideal starting points are the *Jerusalem Post* and *The JCN Daily News* pages. If your politics are to the left or right, you might consider news sources from those perspectives.

Israel Line

http://www.math.technion.ac.il/israeline/

Israel Line is the daily summary of Israeli Press, edited by the Israeli Consulate General in New York. This site also maintains an archive of news since November, 1994, searchable by date, subject, and other methods. In fact, it may have the best search engine of all sites reviewed in this chapter. This is an invaluable site—where else can you find for free, on the 'Net, what some particular cabinet minister said two years ago? Information about free e-mail subscriptions appears here—get the news delivered to your mailbox, five days per week.

MidEast Dispatch
http://www.borealis.com/sns/

Shomron News Service
http://www.snsnews.co.il/

These two news services are both descendants of the old Shomron News Service, which was established in March, 1994 in response to demands from the Diaspora for news from Israel (particularly news about the peace process.) *Shomron* is Hebrew for Samaria, which is now a geographic term used by those Jews who believe that Judah and Samaria (which are also called the West Bank) should eternally be part of Israel. The SNS had a right-wing tilt. In late 1996, however, the business office and chief writer decided to part ways—the business office believed that the chief writers were a bit too far to the right. There were also disputes about the appropriateness of editorials.

Today there are two services. The old SNS subscribers were switched over to the MidEast Dispatch and kept the old URL. The chief writer kept the SNS name, started over with new subscribers, and created a new Web site.

If it sounds a bit confusing—it is. To add to the mix: while the new SNS is fairly small, its new, award-winning Web site is excellent, and includes such features as a week-in-review section, and other Israeli news-related links. The MidEast Dispatch, on the other hand, while larger, does not have a particularly compelling Web presence as of this writing, although it is sure to grow.

We can say about both of them that with a free e-mail subscription, you get in-depth coverage 24 hours a day, with e-mail bulletins at a rate of one to three per day; and you hear about breaking news as it happens. Both of these are tremendous services.

Ariga: The Business of Peace

http://www.ariga.com/

Ariga takes the business of peace very seriously. It is a Web site committed to the peace process and to making available a great deal of information in support of their aims. There are links to Peace Now, B'Tselem (the leading human-rights organization in Israel), a Middle East Peace FAQ, and the full text of the Oslo "interim" agreement. While this site leans decidedly to the left, the pieces here are not mere propaganda—they are thoughtful essays by respected Israeli opinion-makers.

Kol Israel

http://www.artificia.com/html/

Kol Israel provides "audio daily news from Israel in real streaming mode along with other useful data and resources from Israel and around the world. You will be able to chat and debate about Israeli issues and even get video news and other surprises."

In addition to the news, this Web site maintains links to a wide range of other Israeli Web sites. It gives you an idea of the breadth and depth of Israel's involvement on the Internet. This is worth bookmarking.

Arutz 7

http://www.arutz7.jer1.co.il/

There's no question where this news service stands. Arutz 7 was established in 1988 "to combat the 'negative thinking' and 'post-Zionist' attitudes so prevalent in Israel's liberal-left media." They claim to be Israel's only independent national radio station, and, in way, that is true—they do not have a broadcast license, and so they operate from a ship off the Israeli coast.

There is a lot of information here, including back issues of opinion pieces, archives, and audio files of the current day's news. Another interesting feature is a survey of what the Arab press is saying about Israel and Mid-East politics.

I log onto three programs every morning: CNN Interactive, The Jerusalem Post and Arutz 7. You'd be surprised at the diversity of opinion these sites present.

Globes Arena
http://www.globes.co.il/

This is an on-line edition of *Globes: Israel's Business Newspaper.*

The difference between this Web site and any other in this chapter is immediately apparent when you log in. This is a serious site, with serious news, and it's obvious that some serious resources went into developing it. If you want an electronic version of an Israeli *Wall Street Journal*, this is it. It's published five days a week, and has all the business news of Israel you could ever want. It has links to the stock market, the latest price indices, and even access to Standard and Poor's analysis of Israeli companies. The top nonbusiness stories of the day are also here.

In addition to information on conventions and exhibits in Israel and a host of other interesting features, this site has extensive archives and a solid search engine. If you are contemplating doing business with Israeli ramifications, this site is an absolute must.

Israel Ministry of Foreign Affairs
http://www.israel-mfa.gov.il/

The official word on everything Israeli—from ancient history to private sector wage information to geography and climate—is here.

There are links to Israel Line (see above), as well as other selections from the Israeli Press, and a section called "The Back Page," which includes sports, weather, and stock markets. There are extensive background materials about current major events—including, for example, the full text of the Hebron agreement, with all associated protocols, and 'notes for the record.' It's outstanding.

There are also Web links to some of the other major news media in Israel, and subscription forms for a variety of Israel Ministry e-mail publications.

News In Hebrew

http://www6.snunit.k12.il/hebrew_news/

The daily news in Hebrew is available from Snunit, and is posted on this Web site. You can read and download it if you have Hebrew fonts on your Web browser.
JCN Daily News Pagehttp://www.jcn18.com/news/

This is a very mainstream source for stories of interest to Jews around the globe. While you may be able to find most of these stories elsewhere, here they are all grouped together—a listing of headlines and direct links to the *New York Times*, CNN, Reuters, *Times of London*, and more, where the full stories appear. This is an excellent resource, and also contains links to other Israeli and American news media. This site should rate a bookmark on your Web browser.

News from Arab perspectives can be found on the following sites:

Arabia On-Line - News

http://www.arabia.com/news/

Much like JCN's news service (above), this is a compendium of news from a variety of sources, though in this case they are sources throughout Arabic media. The latest headlines and editorials are here, as well as links directly to a whole slew of on-line Arabic newspapers in English: including the *Jordan Times, Egyptian Gazette,* and the *Palestine Times.* This excellent Web site is part of Arabia On-Line, easily one of the slickest-looking sites in this chapter.

The Palestine National Authority Web site:

http://www.palnet.com/

This site contains an information guide on the Palestinian economy, with information on trade and business opportunities, a governmental and business directory, and a list of laws and regulations for doing business in Palestine. The 'live' news content of the site is minimal, but this is a useful site for background information.

This is a fledgling site, much like its sponsoring entity. We'll have to wait and see what develops on it.

USA Today

http://www.usatoday.com/weather/basemaps/weut1.htm

This Web page will give you the weather for Tel Aviv and Jerusalem.

The Jerusalem Post

http://www.jpost.co.il/com/Weather/

This page has weather coverage for all of Israel's major cities.

Israeli LOTTO and TOTTO

http://www.artificia.com/html/lotototo.htm

If you want to see what the winning numbers are for the Israeli lotteries, you can sign up for a membership at this site and get the results on-line.

For other news sources on Israel, read Chapter 20 for newspaper and magazine Web sites, including top-notch ones like the Jerusalem Post Internet Edition and the Jerusalem Report.

PART V

Current Issues in Judaism

Jewish Medical Ethics

Jewish law and morality concerning medicine and faith is a fascinating area to study. Some of the core tenets and questions are explained by J. David Bleich in the following excerpt from his book Contemporary Halakhic Matters, Volume 1.

"In Jewish law and moral teaching the value of human life is supreme and takes precedence over virtually all other considerations. This attitude is most eloquently summed up in a talmudic passage regarding the creation of Adam: Therefore only a single human being was created in the world, to teach that if any person has caused a single soul of Israel to perish; and if any human being saves a single soul of Israel, Scripture regards him as if he had saved an entire world (Sanhedrin 37a)....

"The obligation to save the life of an endangered person is derived the Talmud from the verse Neither shall you stand idly by the blood of your neighbor (Leviticus 19:16)....

"The application of this principle to medical intervention for the purposes of preserving life is not without theological and philosophical difficulties.... The patient in seeking medical attention, may be seen as betraying a lack of faith, in failing to put his trust in God... This view is rejected by Rabbinic Judaism...

"Maimonides established an obligation requiring the physician to render professional services in life threatening situations. Every individual, insofar as he is able, is obligated to restore the health of a fellow man no less than he is obligated to restore his property."

Medical bioethics has become an increasingly important focus of religious decision-making. The advances of medicine in this century and the changes in medical practice have raised serious problems for the ethical values of Judaism. This chapter presents a number of on-line discussions about problems that have arisen. They are mostly text-driven pages, with few of the bells and whistles other topics have called for. These Web forums are just the tip of the iceberg. The vast majority of material in this field is not on the Internet. For this reason we have appended a short bibliography of relevant documents at the end of this chapter. Each of them has merit in its own right.

The Institute for Jewish Medical Ethics
http://www.hia.com/hi

With the advent of modern medicine, the choices left to the physician and medical professionals are often quite difficult. There are many questions that require spiritual guidance as well as medical knowledge. The Institute for Jewish Medical Ethics Web site deals with these problems.

You can get an idea of the breadth of issues involved just by reading the topics of their 1996 conference, which include: *halachic* considerations and alternatives to just about every medical issue there is.

Another site worth checking out for an overview of the wide range of Jewish medical ethics is the Ethics/Bioethics site at *http://ncgr.org/elsi/elsi.tc4b.html*. This is a reading list that includes a number of articles on the Jewish point of view regarding Bioethics. The articles are not as current as one might like, but they are a good foundation on which to build.

Tay Sachs Disease
http://ncgr.org/elsi/elsi.tc10f.html

This site has a very large list of articles that delve into the study of Tay Sachs disease, a hereditary illness that Jews are more likely to be born with than are non-Jews.

There are many issues unique to a disease that can be detected before birth, and this Web site will give you a good idea of what these issues are and how to find out more information about them. Topics of the featured articles include screening for Tay-Sachs disease, how a matchmaking scheme solves the Tay Sachs problem, and Tay-Sachs and the abortion controversy.

This site does not contain the actual articles referenced, but it will tell you where to go to find them.

Pain Relief and the Risk Of Suicide: A Jewish Perspective
http://www.sfhs.edu/critint/v5_n2/mackler.htm

This Web page has the text of a paper that deals with the serious illness of a patient, the use of medicine to relieve pain and the possibility of suicide by the patient. In light of the ongoing controversy over Dr. Jack Kevorkian and his role in relieving pain by assisting suicide among terminally ill patients, this paper, excerpted below, is of great interest.

> "Jewish ethics values healing and the preservation of life as important goods and as activities mandated by God. The case presented, involving a 29 year old male with AIDS who requests large doses of analgesics and sedatives, may involve some degree of tension between these values: actions taken to relieve pain, supported by a mandate to heal, might contribute to a patient's death by suicide, ending life and violating a traditional Jewish norm. Upon closer examination, it appears that thoughtful provision of pain relief and supportive care has the potential both to relieve the patient's suffering and to lessen the likelihood that he would feel compelled to end his life."

The following two articles are from the Jewish Bulletin Online (*http://www.jewish.com*) site:

Assisted-Suicide Case Opens Debate on Jewish Stance
http://www.jewish.com/bk950721/usstance.htm

This Web page contains various interpretations of Judaism's attitude toward assisted suicide. The article was prompted by a New York resident who helped his terminally ill wife end her life. It offers opinions from Orthodox, Conservative and Reform representatives.

Experts Debate the Ethical Dilemmas of Managed Care

http://www.jewish.com/bk960301/sfameman.htm

The difference between a recession and a depression is described as follows: A recession is when your neighbor is out of work. A depression is when you yourself are out of work. The same analogy can be used for saving money on health care and the underlying reasons for what has come to be known as managed care. On this Web page, the author raises the question of dealing with managed care from a Jewish point of view. He highlights several viewpoints, from rabbis, doctors, and medical ethicists, addressing this concern.

Nursing Ethics in Israel: Dilemmas in Neonate Intensive Care

http://www.biol.tsukuba.ac.jp/~macer/EEIN41E.html

The Eubios Ethics Institute Newsletter from January, 1994 has this article:

> "With the help of advanced technology, medical advances, modern midwifery, new approaches to neonatal care, and with the impetus of the belief in the right to live—the boundaries of life have expanded far beyond what we once could of (sic) dreamt of. These factors have lead to the sharpening of the question: where and when may we decide to limit our active intervention with the course of nature? And who has the right to make such decisions?"

The question begs an answer. This article attempts to provide one.

Duty and Healing: Foundations of a Jewish Bioethic

http://www.mcgill.ca/CTRG/bfreed/

This on-line book by Dr. Benjamin Freedman uses traditional Jewish sources to explore some of the more common ethical issues encountered in hospitals today. It is the first book in the field of bioethics to be published in this format. The electronic publication of this volume allows for the dissemination of ideas to as large an audience as possible.

"20 to 30 million people worldwide have access to the Internet, including almost every university in the world," Dr. Freedman says. By contrast, an academic volume of this nature would sell a maximum of 2,000 copies and in all likelihood would not be reprinted.

Another aspect of Internet publishing that appeals to Freedman is the opportunity for communication between the author and readers. He intends to use the feedback he receives via e-mail as a basis for clarifying and revising the text as needed.

This Web site is an invaluable and novel presentation of many critical issues in Jewish medical ethics.

Briefs: Information Centre for Jewish Law (Halacha) and Bioethics

http://www.biol.tsukuba.ac.jp/~macer/EJ52K.html

"The Institute for Settlement Rabbis, Yeshivat Nir, Kiryat Arba, Israel, is establishing an International Information Centre for Jewish Law (Halacha) on biomedical ethics. We wish to serve the international bioethics community by providing information and answering specific bioethical questions from the standpoint of Jewish Law."

People with questions about an Orthodox perspective on biomedical ethics will enjoy this site and the personal feedback it promises. Questions can be submitted by mail or fax in Hebrew, English, French, German or Spanish.

UAHC Committee on Bio-Ethics
http://server.huc.edu/rjbackup/uahc/bioethic.html

> "This subcommittee of the UAHC Committee on Older Adults is charged with the development of programs to be used within congregations that reflect the dynamic challenges of medical technology and how Jewish tradition in general and Reform Judaism in particular may respond. In addition, the committee has undertaken the study of several contemporary issues and helped create positions for the Movement. Under way now is the discussion dealing with assisted suicide and comfort care at the end of life."

Each year, the committee publishes a study/program guide that is used within congregational programs, all related to the practical ramifications of the current discussion.

Ethics of Cardiac Surgery
http://yu1.yu.edu/riets/torah/medethic/medical1.htm

This Web site contains the transcript of a particularly incisive seminar held at Jews' College, London, on the ethics of heart surgery, which is a more complicated and engrossing subject than one might think.

The answers are not as black-and-white as they would seem on the surface. For an understanding of the issues involved, this on-line reference is a must-read.

The Ethics of Organ Donations
http://www.med.umich.edu/trans/transweb/donation_folder/rab bi_tendler.html

This page contains a short paper presenting a Jewish view on organ donation, and how confusion about the *halachic* rulings on this critical subject is hampering the effort to find donors and save lives, as the author explains in this excerpt.

> "Organ donation by Jews; 10 die each day for want of an organ. Unfortunately, even amongst the irreligious, religious fervor comes out when confronting death. Ignorance of the actual halacha (religious law) is the greatest enemy of organ donation."

Symposium on Ethical Dilemmas Regarding HIV Patients and Care-Givers

http://law.touro.edu/institutes/jewishlaw/april95/part1.html

This fascinating symposium from the Touro Law Center which can be read in full on the Web site, is a discussion of problems brought on by the spread of, and stigma attached to, the HIV epidemic. Many of these problems affect care-givers every day of the week, as this excerpt explains:

> " Unfortunately the AIDS disease has spread tremendously over the last two decades and has reached epidemic proportions. This creates not only serious medical problems but also social problems and ethical dilemmas. "

> "Doctors and care-givers of HIV patients sometimes face a dilemma when they realize that their patient's disease may have a devastating effect on the lives of other people if not informed on time. The question is, should they warn the other people of the patient's disease or not. "

Bibliography on Jewish Medical Ethics

Rosner, Fred and Moshe D. Tendler, *Practical Medical Halachah*, 3rd ed., Ktav Publishing House, 1990, ISBN: 0881253367.

Bleich, J. David, *Contemporary Halakhic Problems*, vol. 4 Ktav Publishing House, 1995, ISBN: 0881254746.

Bleich, J. David, *Contemporary Halakhic Problems, Library of Jewish Law and Ethics*, vol. 16, Ktav Publishing House, 1989, ISBN: 0881253251.

Rosner, Fred, *Medicine and Jewish Law*, vol. 2, Jason Aronson, 1993, ISBN: 0876685742.

Maier, L, *Jewish Values in Bioethics*, Human Sciences Press, 1986, ISBN: 0898852994.

Meier, Levi, ed. *Jewish Values in Health and Medicine*, University Press of America, 1991, ISBN: 0819181730.

Sinclair, Daniel B., *Tradition and the Biological Revolution: The Application of Jewish Law and the Treatment of the Critically Ill*, Edinburgh University Press,1989, ISBN: 0852246366

DIVORCE AND DOMESTIC ABUSE

When a man takes a wife, and marries her, and it comes to pass that she finds no favor in his eyes, because he has found some unseemly thing in her, then let him write her a bill of divorce, and give it in her hand, and send her out of his house. And she departs out of his house, and may go and become another man's wife. (Deuteronomy 24:1-2)

These verses teach us that a woman is divorced from her husband and permitted to remarry by means of a "bill of divorce" which the husband gives her. The document is called a *get* in rabbinic terminology. (For the actual text of the *get* see the first site listed in this chapter. To understand the contents of the document, you may want to read *Introduction to The Mishna, Gittin* by Pinhas Kehati, Dept. of Torah Education and Culture, Jerusalem, 1994.)

As you will see on the Jewish Outnet Web site listing, the bill of divorcement is as essential in Jewish law as the actual *ketubah,* or wedding contract, if not more so. Orthodox or Conservative rabbis will simply not perform a wedding of a couple whose previous marriages have ended in divorce without proof of the delivery of a *get.* Anyone attempting to get married in Israel will have to have proof of the divorce as well.

Judaism does not require an overwhelming reason for divorce. It recognizes that sometimes people simply can't get along. It attaches no stigma to a divorce, other than prohibiting the woman from marrying a *Kohen,* or member of the priestly class. Rabbinic Judaism has gone to great lengths to protect the woman from an unjust divorce and from making certain that she is provided for financially. The Talmud and Codes are replete with examples of the genuine concern of the rabbinate with the status of the woman in the divorce. However, Jewish law commands the man to give the *get* to the woman, and not vice-versa.

It occasionally happens that a woman refuses to receive a *get*. If this happens, and she refuses to appear in court and is not swayed by disapproval from the community, a "permission from 100 rabbis" may be granted to allow a man to take a new wife. But if a husband does not agree to a divorce, no rabbinic recourse is currently possible for women. This is referred to as the *agunah* problem—*agunah* literally means "chained."

When Jews lived in a close-knit society this did not present a great problem. The rabbinate could apply strictures on the husband until he agreed to a divorce. In Israel, where marriage and divorce are solely in the hands of the rabbinate, there have been instances where licenses have been revoked, and occasionally even imprisonment, until husbands finally agreed to grant a divorce. A rabbi in England imposed a *nidui* on a recalcitrant husband—an order that no observant Jew come within six yards of him. In the United States, many Orthodox communities are able to solve these problems through rabbinic pressure on the husbands, but because the rabbinate does not have the civil power to compel a husband to give his wife a divorce, it can be a tragic situation when husbands are willing to turn their back on the Orthodox community. A woman sometimes lives out her entire life unable to remarry because the husband would not give her a *get*.

Various attempts have been made to overcome this problem. The Conservative movement developed what is commonly called "The Conservative Addendum to the *Ketubah*," (also referred to as the Lieberman Clause after its author, Professor Saul Lieberman), which seeks to protect the woman by mean of what is essentially a prenuptial agreement. The amendment is one of the documents listed in the first Web site in this chapter.

In 1980, the Reconstructionist movement created an egalitarian *get*, which can be issued by a wife whose husband refuses to grant her a *get*. This is an entirely new development in Jewish law, and certainly solves the problem—at least as far as Reconstructionists go—but creates more problems than it solves from the point of view of those Jewish movements who do not recognize such a divorce.

In the Orthodox world, the Rabbinical Council of America (probably the largest association of Orthodox rabbis with about 1,000 members) endorsed a prenuptial agreement for rabbis to urge marrying couples to sign. However, only about half of the RCA's rabbis do so.

At times, there have been attempts to deal with the problem via state civil law. A recent law in New York, for example, directs the court, when dividing property in a divorce, to take into consideration either party's actions in creating barriers to remarriage. This can make for further complications even when a *get* is given, because some Jewish authorities feel that nonreligious coercion can invalidate a *get*.

Clearly, no solutions have yet been universally accepted by the rabbinate. The major reason for this is the hesitancy of the rabbinate to make changes in the law, no matter how tempting such changes often are perceived to be. *Halacha* (Jewish law) evolves over long periods of time. There is tremendous pressure not to yield to the needs of the moment lest the very fabric of the law itself be torn. One great figure in 20th century Judaism put it this way:

> The *Halacha* has its own orbit, moves at its own certain, definite speed, has its own pattern of responding to a challenge, its own criteria and principles... but *chidush* (nuance) is certainly the very essence of *Halacha*....there are great *chidushim* (nuances). But the *chidushim* are within the system, not from the outside. You cannot psychologize *halacha*, historicize *halacha*, or rationalize halacha, because this is something foreign, something extraneous... instead of complaining against the inflexibility of *halacha*, let us explore its endless spaces.

It will undoubtedly take bold and persistent action by respected members of the rabbinate with the approval of their peers to effect such changes.

In the meantime, we bring you a series of Web sites that explain the current difficulties in real terms.

The Jewish Domestic Abuse and *Agunah* Problem Web Page

http://users.aol.com/Agunah/

> This page is dedicated to: (1) the plight of Jewish individuals plagued by Domestic Abuse (e.g., physical abuse, psychological abuse); and (2) the plight of the *agunah* in Jewish culture. An *agunah* is: a woman who is prevented from remarrying [in Jewish religious law], either because of the disappearance of her husband, absent proof of his death, or because of his refusal to grant her a *get* ["bill of divorcement," or religious divorce] (usually from the last reason).

This is an incredible site—it has just about everything you ever wanted to know about the *agunah* problem. Most importantly, there is current information to help those who may be in a difficult situation—a listing of resources for victims of Jewish domestic abuse (shelters, legal services, hotlines, contact persons); a listing of Agunot-related agencies (from the International Coalition for Agunah Rights to Get-Free); and a full set of Jewish legal family documents and descriptions of Jewish family law. This last page includes the full text of a *ketubah*, (the marriage contract), a *get*, the Conservative movement's addendum to the *get*, the Reconstructionist egalitarian *get*, and some good reference *Responsa* on the problems of wife abuse. *Reponsa* are answers by talmudic scholars to queries.

The Article section is probably the best place to visit to find the latest developments in this area. Here, you can read about the RCA's endorsement of the prenuptial agreement, and the new use of *nidui* by a rabbi in England.

Mark Cwik's bibliography of books and articles on the subject has got to be the longest such list anywhere on the Internet. He will even help you obtain reprints. And, finally, this site has a nice collection of links to other Web sites addressing Jewish abuse—these links include not only domestic abuse, but alcohol and drug abuse problems.

The Jewish Outnet
http://www.ziva.com/joc/

This Internet publication of the Jewish Outreach Congregation raises another important issue in relation to Jewish divorce—that many Jews don't realize that they need a *get* in addition to their civil divorce. Sadly, many are first made aware of the need for a *get* only when they attempt to remarry. When they are asked to provide proof of their Jewish divorce they are taken aback. This situation is further complicated if they can't find their ex-spouse. Estimates are that of over 800,000 American Jews who have been divorced, less than 12% have gone through the Jewish divorce procedure. Furthermore, if these people remarry and have children, those children and their descendants may be unable to marry observant Jews. Should the descendants choose to become observant Jews themselves, this could be particularly problematic. In an effort to avoid these potential problems, the Jewish Outreach Congregation provide free *gitten* (the plural of *get*) for non-Orthodox marriages. If you have a question as to your status, check here. This is also useful for a good overview of the problem, as well as other thoughtful materials about marriage problems in general.

Intervention by Non-Jewish Courts in Jewish Divorces
http://law.touro.edu/institutes/jewishlaw/aug94/part1.html

This article, in *The Jewish Law Report,* a publication of the Institute of Jewish Law at Touro Law School, is a thorough examination of the complicated *halachic* issues involved when state courts intervene in Jewish divorces. The issue is a complicated one. On one hand, Jewish law itself says that "the law of the land is the law"—for most cases. On the other hand, a *get* must be given under free will and without coercion—in most cases—while "indirect" compulsion has its own considerations. Having a non-Jewish court intervene thus makes for quite a complicated mix of issues, without even mentioning the potential breach of church-state separation.

This article, by Dr. Chaim Povarsky, sorts it all out—to the extent that is possible, and makes for good reading for those who can handle law review articles.

Jewish Divorce Law Binds Women

http://www.startext.net/raw/1:RELIGION72/
1:RELIGION72121695.html

This Associated Press article appeared in the *Fort Worth Star-Telegram*. It cites specific cases, and gives an overview of the *agunah* problem, and potential solutions. This Web page is a good place to see the problem with some real faces.

Domestic Violence in the Jewish Community

http://lifestylesmag.com/jew-family/

This Web site has excellent resources for those who might be involved in a serious domestic problem, including the breakup of a marriage. Included here are articles such as "Safety Tips for Leaving a Violent Partner," "How to Help Battered Women," telephone numbers of hot lines, and the entire final chapter of Rabbi Shlomo Riskin's recent book, *Women and Jewish Divorce: The Rebellious Wife, The Agunah, and the Right of Women to Initiate Divorce in Jewish Law. A Halakhic Solution.*

K'ddushei K'tana (Marriage of a Minor)
http://yu1.yu.edu/riets/torah/halacha/bleich1.htm

> The Jewish community has been shocked by reports of a father who has inflicted potentially grievous harm upon his minor daughter as a means of extorting concessions from his estranged wife. The husband alleges that he has exercised the authority vested in a father by biblical law in contracting a marriage on behalf of his daughter. In doing so, he has deprived her of capacity to enter into any future marriage so long as the first marriage is not dissolved by death or divorce.

This aberration of Jewish law received attention in the national press in 1995-1996. For this reason we have included it in this section. The author of this article is Rabbi J. David Bleich, a well-respected authority in Jewish law and a professor of law at the Cardoza Law School of Yeshiva University. Rabbi Bleich strongly condemns what happened, terms it a failure of society, and calls for strong community-wide action in this matter.

Feminism

Writing about Jewish feminism is no easy task; what I say will be open to interpretation, since I am looking at the issues from a male point of view.

Judaism does not minimize the role of the woman in Jewish life. Jewish law grants the woman rights and obligations and expends considerable effort in guaranteeing her honored place in society. But traditional Judaism does claim that there are differences between men and women and expresses these differences in the rights and obligations of the woman. To some, this is understood to mean the denigration of the role of women, and to others, it symbolizes the special place that a woman has in Jewish life. The answer probably lies somewhere within these two perceptions.

While Judaism may show the woman more respect than do some other societies, there is no getting away from the fact that women are treated differently than men. In the modern fight for equal rights, this is very much a problem. Rather than trying to address the problem by presenting my own opinions, I have attempted to bring you those of others, especially women. There is not a great amount of material on this subject on the Internet, but as more information comes along, we will be able to pass it on to you. Though Jewish feminism has but a small presence on the Web, the subject is being actively pursued. We suggest that you look through the bibliographies on this site. They will lead you a variety of additional, non-Internet sources.

We would also like to point out that in our chapter on divorce we have attempted to highlight the problems faced by women in Judaism. We have paid special attention to the difficulties arising with *Agunot* (Agunot is a state of marital limbo which is discussed further in Chapter 23.) and hope that this difficult problem will find resolution soon.

Kol Isha—The Voice of Women

http://www.dircon.co.uk/ujs/kolisha.html

The home page asks: "There are many misconceptions surrounding the curious concept of 'Jewish feminism'. Is it the ultimate contradiction? Are the two things irreconcilable? Is it an impossible paradox for there to be a Jewish feminist?" And of course, they provide an answer: "The Kol Isha campaign says that far from being a threat to Judaism, the women's campaign can be an injection to revitalize Judaism."

This site has links to a variety of feminist resources. It also has links to a few articles, including, for example, "Is Judaism Sexist?" It would be nice to see some of this treated more deeply, however.

Jewish Feminist Resources

http://world.std.com/~alevin/jewishfeminist.html

A simple straightforward page of some two dozen links to Jewish Feminist information—such as articles on women of the Torah, gender-sensitive prayer books, Jewish feminist publications, education and prayer groups, women's conferences and several newsletters. It is not particularly lengthy, but then the whole concept of Jewish feminism did not exist except in the minds of a very small number of adherents until the past decade or two.

Bridges: A Journal for Jewish Feminists and Our Friends
http://weber.u.washington.edu/~iowen/bridges/

The home page says it all: "Bridges illuminates a variety of landscapes: for activists, Jews, feminists, lesbians, it is both bread and roses. In these pages, contemporary Jewish feminist culture and politics come alive in all their tumultuous diversity." At the site are some past articles, a community bulletin board, and links to other sites.

Other interesting Web pages about related topics include:

The Role of Women
http://members.aol.com/jewfaq/women.htm

This is from the Judaism 101 site, which is written from a more traditional point of view. The section is an interesting synopsis, and starts with:

> The role of women in traditional Judaism has been grossly misrepresented and misunderstood. The position of women is not nearly as lowly as many modern people think; in fact, the position of women in Jewish law that dates back to the biblical period is in many ways better than the position of women under American civil law as recently as a century ago. Most of the important feminist leaders of the 20th century (Gloria Steinem, for example) are Jewish women, and some commentators have suggested that this is no coincidence: the respect accorded to women in Jewish tradition was a part of their ethnic culture.

Women and Judaism—Reading List
http://shamash.org/lists/scj-faq/HTML/rl/gen-women.html

In this section, you'll find a wide variety of material, from the strongly feminist perspectives of Reform Judaism to the more traditional perspectives of Orthodoxy, with a few more general books relating to feminism and women within in a religious context in general.

Bat Kol: A Feminist House of Study

http://home.sprynet.com/sprynet/batkol/

This resource is detailed in the Education chapter; it is a sign of the growing influence of women in both teaching and studying Jewish law, which has traditionally been reserved for men.

Finding What You Want on the Internet and World Wide Web

Using the Internet poses a variety of choices and problems to the novice user and even to the experienced surfer. There is no single solution.

For the real novice user we would suggest using America Online. This commercial on-line service has a wonderful Judaica selection. It accesses a lot of data and presents it in an intelligent and entertaining fashion. You may very well want to start there.

However, if you feel a bit braver or more experienced, you have the choice of using any of the Internet service providers (ISPs) that abound on the Internet. Your local paper will have listings of them. You will also have your choice of *browsers*—those friendly interfaces between you and the on-line world. We have used Netscape Navigator extensively and have been quite happy with it. It's really a toss up between Microsoft Explorer or Netscape Navigator. Both are easy to use and have essentially the same tools.

Next, you have the problem of finding the sites in which you are interested. Once you have done your first few searches, you will get the hang of looking around on the Web, but the going—at least in the beginning—might be tough. There are a few major Jewish indexes on the Web that you should be aware of if you want to find more on-line Judaica than this book describes.

Maven—The Virtual Know-It-All
http://www.maven.co.il

This index is updated regularly. But you have to understand that the methodology of inclusion on the index is based upon a mechanical search with just minimal human intervention. What that means is that it can find you a lot of resources, but it doesn't discern the good from the bad, so a lot of the sites listed are less than satisfying. However, of the Jewish indexes that are available, it is my favorite.

Judaism and Jewish Resources
http://shamash.org/trb/judaism.html

This is the other major Jewish index that I have found most useful. In addition to sites on the Internet, this index also provides you with a host of useful information about various Jewish Web servers, how to read Hebrew on the Net, downloading audio files and tools, and hundreds of other useful pieces of information.

The Ultimate Jewish/Israel Link Launcher by Steve Ruttenberg
http://ucsu.colorado.edu/~jsu/launcher.html

This is a set of links—lots of links! It contains more than 4,000 links to Jewish Web sites. I have downloaded its file onto my hard disk and keep it handily by my side.

Hillel Rokowsky's Bookmarks
http://www.geocities.com/SiliconValley/5375/
bookmarkupload.htm

This list of bookmarks (a list of Web addresses you can save and jump to easily once your browser memorizes their locations) contains a host of links to Jewish sites that will be of interest to you. It's not in the same league as the other sites previously mentioned in terms of sheer size, but it has some general links that they don't have.

Shamash—The Jewish Internet Consortium
http://shamash.org/

This on-line group hosts the Web presences of a large number of Jewish organizations and educational institutions. This site and Virtual Jerusalem, at *http://www.jer1.co.il/* provide a great many links to sites that you simply must go to, including many Israeli ones. Virtual Jerusalem is presented in a beautiful graphic fashion and is a pleasure to look at. Navigating it is another matter. But it has come a long way.

Search Engines

Finally, there will come a time that you will want to "look for yourself" and not be dependent on others. To do this, you have your choice of Internet search engines. Some of the best are:

> Yahoo: http://www.yahoo.com
>
> Webcrawler: http://www.webcrawler.com
>
> Alta Vista: http://altavista.digital.com

Yahoo is the premier "directory-style" search engine. It's structured much like a Yellow Pages—choose a subject heading in Yahoo, then subheadings under them, then use the entries listed to find the Web site you need. If you search Yahoo and don't find what you want you can go to the bottom of its home page and use Web Crawler, Alta Vista, or any of the other word-driven search engines on-line. These search engines ask you for key words and then give you lists of Web sites containing those words.

There is a knack to performing an effective search. That is a matter of experience. You might also want to invest in *Web Search Strategies* by Bryan Pfaffenberger (MIS:Press, 1996), a comprehensive and easy-to-read guide to searching the Web. Just because you don't find what you are looking for with one type of search tool does not mean that it isn't on the Net. You have to persevere. You can acquire information from many different sources. You may also acquire *the same* information from several different sources. Why? Because there is no strict structure to the Internet.

The Internet is a free-spirited operation. Its membership ranks are open to everyone. At the time of this writing there is no censorship on the Internet. There has been some movement in the U.S. Congress to regulate the Internet. But many people are afraid that this will infringe on the concept of freedom of expression that is a fundamental principle of the Constitution of the United States. The first attempt to abridge this freedom, the Communications Decency Act of 1996, was ruled unconstitutional by the courts.

What's a Web Address?

What do I mean by addresses on the Internet?

A typical address might read *Harvey@withit.ucsb.edu*. *Harvey* is the user identification (generally, a person's name or pseudonym). The rest of the address—everything after the @ symbol—is the domain. In this case the domain is *withit.ucsb.edu*. The domain is very informative; it tells you with whom the user is affiliated (in this case, *ucsb*, which stands for the University of California at Santa Barbara).

There are seven basic domain types. They are described in Table A.1.

Table A.1 Domain Types

Type	Description
.com	Commercial or business site (e.g., Wells Fargo Bank)
.edu	Educational institution (e.g., Columbia University)
.gov	Governmental agency (e.g., The House of Representatives)
.int	International organization (e.g., United Nations)
.mil	Military organization (e.g., U.S. Navy)
.net	Networking organization (i.e., network provider
.org	Nonprofit institutions (e.g., AIPAC)

Additionally, addresses can have country codes. You will note certain addresses in this book include:

.il for Israel

.uk for England

.ca for Canada

Most of the addresses in this book are from the United States and Israel. There are some Canadian, British and French addresses as well. However, you will note other addresses on the Web from a variety of other nations. That's why they call it the World Wide Web. It means that people from almost every conceivable part of the world are hooked up to the Web and the number of connections in countries throughout the world is growing exponentially. You never know who you are going to meet on the Web.

NOTE You can get lost surfing the Internet. It is addictive. Don't just surf the Internet! Focus your activities. Make up your mind that you are looking for something specific and try to get there. If you see something interesting along your travels, make a note of it but don't get diverted. Otherwise, you will spend countless hours on the Internet and will end up wondering what you did with your time.

Every address on the Web is unique. Until just a few years ago, the Web was a maze. You had to know the exact address of the site you were looking for. If you didn't, it was almost impossible to find the addressee. As the Web grew, some ways of looking for these far-flung addresses developed.

Two major developments were software that enable one to search large libraries of individual were maintained by universities and other large institutions with heavy computing power and browsers—software that removed the uneducated user from the mysteries of the Internet by creating a GUI (graphical user interface) that uses pictures and symbols. The addressing system did not change, it just became easier to use.

By using the previously mentioned browsers, one can search the Web, retrieve materials many different locations, and view them without going through all sorts of machinations and computer gobbledygook.

We urge the user to learn a little about the Internet before really going into this book or attempting to gain access to the sites mentioned in this book. You can become extremely frustrated just surfing the Internet. You need the knowledge of just a few basic tools before you begin. Your library and/or bookstore carries a multitude of titles on the Internet and each of the commercial services like America Online, CompuServe, and the Microsoft Network. I'm a fan of a book called *The Complete Idiot's Guide to the Internet* which is well-written and makes the Internet easily understandable.

Additionally, you might want to look at some general computer magazines to learn how people are using the Internet for fun and profit. One magazine which we recommend to you is *Netguide*. This monthly publication has the latest listings on the Internet and highlights some of the more interesting sights.

Unless you have a very fast connection to the Internet, you will sometimes be put off by the time it takes for the information to come across the wire. Remember, much of the information you are acquiring is coming from very distant points in countries around the globe and from many servers in the United States.

NOTE

Think of it this way—you can't acquire this information more quickly in any other fashion! So have a little patience. Keep a book handy! You probably won't need it too often. But it may help you get rid of some of your frustrations.

I N D E X

A

Abayudaya, 7
abortion issues, 345
Abraham ibn Daud of Toledo, Spain, 6
Abrams, Bonnie, 242
Abrams, Rabbi, 278
abuse, domestic, 354
The Academic College of Yezreel, 305
academic institutions, 299
Acrobat reader software, 260
ADL online, 137
The Adolph and Rose Levis Jewish
    Community Center, 62
adult education, 56, 61, 62, 277, 302
    See also education
The Adventures of Mendy and the
    Golem, 318
Africa, 13, 39, 46, 140, 239, 315
African Jews, 136
Agam, Yaakov, 250
agunah, 352, 354, 356
Agunot, 360
Ahavas Yisroel (love of fellow Jews), 93
AIDS information, 349
AIPAC's CyberCenter for Pro-Israel
    Activism,   134
Aish Das Society, 279
Aish HaTorah, 193, 250, 267, 268,
    270, 275–283, 286, 287, 290,
    292–296, 301, 309, 330, 351, 360
    Discovery classes, 186
Aish HaTorah's Discovery Seminar, 278
AJGS. See Association of Jewish
    Genealogical Societies
AJHS. See American Jewish Historical
    Society
Akiba (also spelled Akiva), Rabbi, 127,
    174, 175, 291
Akko Festival, 245
Albert Einstein School of Medicine,
    81–82

Albert L. Schultz Palo Alto Jewish
    Community Center, 66
alcohol abuse, 143, 192, 355
Alda, Alan, 316
The Aleph Institute, 134
The Alexander Silberman Institute of
    Life Sciences, 300
aliya, 280
aliyah, 287
Allen, Woody, 316
Alliance Israelite, 7
All of Us. See Kulanu
almost, 233
The (almost) Complete Guide to WWW
    in Israel, 19
Alta Vista, 365
Amazon Bookstore, 310
amcha, 248
America-Asian Kashrus Services, 193,
    201
American Association of Museums, 215
American Conservative movement, 52
The American-Israel Public Affairs
    Committee (AIPAC), 134
American Jewish Committee, 135
American Jewish Historical Society, 17
The American Jewish Historical Society,
    4
American Jewish Joint Distribution
    Committee, Inc, 136
American Judaism, xxix, 4, 5
    community issues, 51
    denominations of, 75–78
    in Israel, 140
    religious requirements, 52
American Museum of Natural History,
    194
The American Physicians Fellowship for
    Medicine in Israel, 137
Americans for a Safe Israel, 32
America OnLine (AOL), xxxi, 61, 327,
    363, 368

EASY ACCESS

Live links to all the Web sites mentioned in this book can be accessed at the following page from the MIS:Press Web site:

http://www.mispress.com/judaism

Add this address to the 'favorite addresses/bookmarks' section of your Web browser, then use these links to jump to any sites that sound enticing.

At our site, the author and publisher invite readers to make suggestions about future editions of *Judaism on the Web*. The Internet is ever-changing and expanding, and your suggestions will help us make later editions even more comprehensive.